MUSIC, NATIONAL IDENTITY
AND THE POLITICS OF LOCATION

Vanessa Knights 1969–2007

In the final stages of the preparation of this book, Vanessa Knights, my co-editor, close friend and colleague passed away. She had been struggling with an auto-immune disease for some ten years and it had weakened her heart. She had a massive heart attack on Monday 5th March, 2007 and slipped into a coma from which she never recovered. She died on Saturday 10th March with her husband David and family by her side.

Vanessa leaves an extraordinary legacy.

I worked with her on a number of projects, including the biennial festival of musics from Spanish- and Portuguese-speaking origin, *¡VAMOS!*, our annual co-sponsored symposia at Newcastle on popular musics and the Conference of Popular Musics of the Hispanic and Lusophone Worlds in Newcastle in 2006. This book is also one of the outcomes of a project that she and I worked on together, a conference on Popular Musics and National Identities held at Newcastle in 2000.

Her work dealt with Spanish-speaking cultures on both the Iberian peninsula (especially her work on Spanish feminisms) and especially in Latin America. She published on the bolero, nationalism, diaspora, science fiction and was working before she died on a collection of essays on music in the TV series *Buffy the Vampire Slayer* with my colleague Paul Attinello. She also published on feminism and women's movements in contemporary Spain and Latin America and Contemporary Spanish and Spanish American narrative.

She was well known and respected in her field. She was vice-president of Women in Spanish, Portuguese and Latin American Studies in 2003–2004 and was a member of numerous scholarly organizations including the Association for Contemporary Iberian Studies, the Association of Hispanists of Great Britain and Ireland, the International Association for the Study of Popular Music, the Society for Caribbean Studies and the Society for Latin American Studies.

In the pursuit of her love for traditional and popular musics from Latin America, she travelled to Brazil, Puerto Rico, Cuba, Colombia, Mexico, Chile, Uruguay, and Venezuela where she made friends and dazzled everyone with her extraordinary energy, wit, charm and intellect. She leaves behind bereaved friends all over the world.

I feel extremely privileged to have worked with her and to have been able to count her amongst my friends, I will miss her terribly.

This book is dedicated to her.

Ian Biddle, March 2007

Music, National Identity and the Politics of Location

Between the Global and the Local

Edited by
IAN BIDDLE
and
VANESSA KNIGHTS

ASHGATE

Published by
Ashgate Publishing Limited
Gower House
Croft Road
Aldershot
Hampshire GU11 3HR
England

Ashgate Publishing Company
Suite 420
101 Cherry Street
Burlington, VT 05401-4405
USA

Ashgate website: http://www.ashgate.com

British Library Cataloguing in Publication Data
Music, national identity and the politics of location :
   between the global and the local. – (Ashgate popular and
   folk music series)
   1. Popular music – History and criticism 2. National music –
   History and criticism 3. Nationalism in music 4. Popular
   music – Social aspects
   I. Biddle, Ian II. Knights, Vanessa
   306.4'8423

Library of Congress Cataloging-in-Publication Data
Music, national identity, and the politics of location : between the global and the local
   / edited by Ian Biddle and Vanessa Knights.
      p. cm.— (Ashgate popular and folk music series)
      ISBN 0-7546-4055-8 (alk. paper)
   1. Popular music—Social aspects. 2. Popular music—Political aspects. 3. Popular
culture. 4. Music and globalization. I. Biddle, Ian D. II. Knights, Vanessa. III.
Series.

   ML3918.P67M85 2006
   781.63'1599—dc22

                                                                           2006005310
ISBN 978-0-7546-4055-4

Printed and bound in Great Britain by MPG Books Ltd, Bodmin, Cornwall

Contents

List of Figures

List of Contributors

Ian Biddle is Senior Lecturer and Head of the International Centre for Music Studies, Newcastle University and Director of the Centre for Excellence in Teaching and Learning (Music and Inclusivity). He has published widely on music, gender, identity and politics and is author of the forthcoming *Listening to Men: Musical Thought, Masculinity and the Austro-German Tradition in the Long Nineteenth Century*. He has also written on German music and national identity, music theory and music and psychoanalysis, and flamenco vocalities, and has given papers at conferences in Montreal, Philadelphia, Oxford, Marseilles and Rio. He is also co-convener of the popular music research network at Newcastle, co-founder of the new Newcastle-based journal *Radical Musicology* and one of the co-organizers of the biennial ¡VAMOS! Festival of Latin and Luscophone cultures.

Brian George currently works as an adviser on modern foreign languages and international understanding with schools in south Wales. He was previously lecturer in French and Education at Westminster College, Oxford, and prior to that taught French at secondary school. He has published articles and book chapters on contemporary French theatre and popular music, with a particular interest in work from southern France which engages with Occitan language and culture. He also writes fiction and poetry, and his first collection of short stories, *Walking the Labyrinth*, was published by Stonebridge Publications in 2004.

Stan Hawkins is Professor of Musicology at the University of Oslo, Norway. He is author of *Settling the Pop Score: Pop Texts and Identity Politics* (2002) and has published numerous articles on British, Scandinavian and North American artists and groups. He is co-editor of *Music, Space, and Place* (2004) and has contributed chapters to *Sexing the Groove* (1997), *Reading Pop* (2000), *Analyzing Popular Music* (2003), *Normalitet* (2006) and *Queering the Popular Pitch* (2006). Hawkins is Editor-in-Chief for *Popular Musicology Online* and editor of the Norwegian musicological journal *Studia Musicologica Norvegica*, and is a key researcher in the inter-faculty project at the University of Oslo, CULCOM, Cultural Complexity in the New Norway (2004–2009).

Robert Hudson is Reader in Contemporary European History and Cultural Politics at the University of Derby, where he chairs the Identity, Conflict and Representation Research Group. A graduate of the School of Slavonic and East European Studies, University of London, he held a Yugoslav government scholarship as a Post-Graduate Fellow at the University of Sarajevo. He taught previously at Exeter College of Art and Design and the University of Rennes II – Haute Bretagne. He is also a faculty member of the European Doctoral Enhancement Programme (EDEN) in Peace and Conflict Studies, which is organized by Humanitarian Net, a thematic network funded by the European Union. He visited Yugoslavia and its successor states frequently in the 1990s and has written widely on the cultural politics of the region. He co-edited *Politics of Identity: Migrants and Minorities in Multicultural States* (2000) and is currently editing a book entitled *Yugoslavia: Death and Transformation*.

Vanessa Knights was appointed Lecturer in Hispanic Studies in the School of Modern Languages at Newcastle University in 1995 and promoted to Senior Lecturer in 2005. She published widely on romantic Latin American music, the mass media and modernity, and Hispanic queer icons, and, when she died on 10 March 2007, she was working on AIDS and popular music, and Nuyorican music and poetry. She was also co-editing with Paul Attinello (also Newcastle University) a collection of essays on music and sound in the cult TV show *Buffy the Vampire Slayer*, forthcoming from Ashgate in 2008, and a volume on the bolero in Latin American literature. She was also specialist editor on the board of the journal *Popular Music*, on the advisory board of *Music, Sound and the Moving Image* and on the editorial collective of *Radical Musicology*. She was co-convenor of the popular music research network at Newcastle and one of the co-organizers of the biennial *¡VAMOS!* Festival of Latin and Lusophone cultures. She will be dearly missed by her colleagues and friends.

Richard Middleton is Emeritus Professor of Music at Newcastle University. A leading figure in Popular Music Studies, he is the author of *Pop Music and the Blues* (1972), *Studying Popular Music* (1990) and *Voicing the Popular: The Subjects of Popular Music* (2006), editor of *Reading Pop* (2000) and co-editor of *The Cultural Study of Music: A Critical Introduction* (2003). He was a founding editor of the journal *Popular Music* and has also authored several entries in the *Encyclopedia of Popular Musics of the World* and the *Revised New Grove*.

David Murphy is Senior Lecturer in French at the University of Stirling. He has published widely on sub-Saharan African literature and cinema in French, and has a particular research interest in modern Senegalese culture. He has also worked extensively on the relationship between Francophone studies and postcolonial theory. He is the author of *Sembene: Imagining Alternatives in Film and Fiction* (2000) and co-editor of two collections of essays: with Aedín Ní Loingsigh, *Thresholds of Otherness/Autrement mêmes: Identity and Alterity in French-Language Literatures* (2002); with Charles Forsdick, *Francophone Postcolonial Studies: A Critical Introduction* (2003). He is currently preparing a co-authored book (with Patrick Williams) entitled *Postcolonial African Cinema: Ten Directors* (forthcoming 2007).

Parvati Nair is Reader in Hispanic Cultural Studies at Queen Mary, University of London. She is the author of *Configuring Community: Theories, Narratives and Practices of Community Identities in Contemporary Spain* (2004) and *Rumbo al norte: inmigración y movimientos culturales entre el Magreb y España* (2006). She is also co-editor *of Gender and Spanish Cinema* (2004). Her research focuses on representations of ethnicity and migration in music, film and photography. She is currently writing a book on the photography of Sebastião Salgado.

Regina Nascimento is a research assistant in the Department of International Relations of the Polytechnic School of the University of São Paulo. Having completed a Masters dissertation on minority writers in Lusophone Africa for the University of Sao Paulo, she is currently finishing a doctoral thesis for the University of Sheffield on neo-realism in contemporary Brazilian, African and Portuguese fiction.

John O'Flynn is a music lecturer at the University of Limerick, Ireland, where he also directs a taught Masters in Music Education. His research interests include the sociology of music, Irish popular music and music education theory and practice. He has contributed to international publications in the areas of national identity and music, popular music and intercultural music education, and has presented papers and keynote addresses at conferences in Ireland, the UK, Greece, Italy, Australia and China. In 2004 he convened the biennial conference of the UK and Ireland branch of the International Society for the Study of Popular Music, at the University of Limerick. He is currently preparing a book on the theme of music and identity in Ireland, due to be published by Ashgate in 2007/2008.

Helena Simonett received her doctoral degree in ethnomusicology at the University of California, Los Angeles, and is currently teaching at Vanderbilt University, Nashville. She has conducted extensive research on Mexican popular music and its transnational diffusion. Her publications include *Banda: Mexican Musical Life across Borders* (2001) and *En Sinaloa nací: Historia de la música de banda* (2004), as well as numerous journal and encyclopaedia articles. She has taught at the University of Zurich, Switzerland, and has presented papers and lectures throughout the United States, Canada, Latin America, Europe and Australia. Her new field project and interest centre on the role of religious ceremonies and music in defying the ongoing 'mestizoization' of the Indian way of life – that is, the national incorporation of the indigenous into modern Mexico.

Joanne N. Smith is Lecturer in Chinese and a member of the Popular Music Research Group at Newcastle University. Her research interests include the formation and transformation of ethnic, national and hybrid identities among the Uyghur of north-west China, representations of these identities in popular music and popular culture, and the influence of social group differences on competing nationalisms in Uyghur popular music. Dr Smith organized a multidisciplinary panel 'Representations of Uyghur National Identity in Popular Culture and Everyday Discourse' for the Association for Asian Studies Annual Meeting held in New York in March 2003 and was co-organizer of an international conference 'Situating the Uyghurs between China and Central Asia,' held in London in November 2004. She is co-editing a selection of papers arising from that conference for a volume in the Ashgate series Anthropology and Cultural History in Asia and the Indo-Pacific.

Robin Warner is Honorary Research Fellow in the Department of Hispanic Studies of the University of Sheffield from which he recently retired as Senior Lecturer and Director of Portuguese Studies. He is the author of *Powers of Utterance: A Discourse Approach to Lorca, Machado and Valle-Inclán* (2003) and has co-edited and contributed a chapter to *The 'I' of the Beholder: Advertising and Identity in Europe* (2000). He has published articles on a diverse range of Spanish and Portuguese linguistic and socio-cultural topics, including studies of Portuguese electoral discourse and of parallel language versions of popular song. His research interests include discourse studies approaches to humour and Brazilian popular song. From 1996 to 1999 he was Chair of the Association for Contemporary Iberian Studies.

General Editor's Preface

The upheaval that occurred in musicology during the last two decades of the twentieth century has created a new urgency for the study of popular music alongside the development of new critical and theoretical models. A relativistic outlook has replaced the universal perspective of modernism (the international ambitions of the 12-note style); the grand narrative of the evolution and dissolution of tonality has been challenged, and emphasis has shifted to cultural context, reception and subject position. Together, these have conspired to eat away at the status of canonical composers and categories of high and low in music. A need has arisen, also, to recognize and address the emergence of crossovers, mixed and new genres, to engage in debates concerning the vexed problem of what constitutes authenticity in music and to offer a critique of musical practice as the product of free, individual expression.

Popular musicology is now a vital and exciting area of scholarship, and the *Ashgate Popular and Folk Music Series* aims to present the best research in the field. Authors will be concerned with locating musical practices, values and meanings in cultural context, and may draw upon methodologies and theories developed in cultural studies, semiotics, poststructuralism, psychology and sociology. The series will focus on popular musics of the twentieth and twenty-first centuries. It is designed to embrace the world's popular musics from Acid Jazz to Zydeco, whether high tech or low tech, commercial or non-commercial, contemporary or traditional.

Professor Derek B. Scott
Chair of Music
University of Leeds

Acknowledgements

The editors would like to acknowledge the assistance of the following colleagues and friends in the preparation of this manuscript: Cristóbal Díaz Ayala, David Hesmondhalgh, Bennett Hogg, David Looseley, Heidi May, Richard Middleton, Errol Montes, Goffredo Plastino, José Antonio Robles, Mark Sabine, David Treece and Richard Young.

Thanks are also due to Hugh Dauncey and Colin Riordan, the co-organizers of the conference from which this volume emerged: 'Popular Music and National Identities' held at Newcastle University in November 2000.

Introduction
National Popular Musics:
Betwixt and Beyond the
Local and Global

Ian Biddle and Vanessa Knights

Secreting the Nation-state

At the close of the twentieth century and the beginning of the twenty-first, interest in the dynamic interaction of what recent scholarship has termed the local and the global, its interventions into the production, dissemination and reception of popular culture, has developed its own kind of topicality. One consequence of this new topicality has been that conceptualizations of the national (of nationalisms, nation-states, national mythologizing narratives and other manifestations of national or nationalist ideologies) have been somewhat sidelined or second-leagued in a world increasingly dominated by the processes of globalization, deterritorialization, transmigration and forms of cultural hybridity.[1] However, despite the premature announcements of its demise, the nation, we suggest, remains a crucial but ambivalent category for understanding how cultural texts and practices function in the construction of personal and collective identities. *Music, National Identity and the Politics of Location* brings together a number of authors working on world popular musics, many of whom attended the conference 'Popular Music and National Identities', held at Newcastle University in 2000. Scholars from all over the world gathered in Newcastle upon Tyne to hear some 50 papers which examined a wide range of popular world musics in their social, political and musical contexts, and, most importantly, sought to find some way of theorizing the dynamics of the national, nationalisms and nation-states as one of the critical frames that popular music has articulated and has been articulated by.

It was our view then, and we have had little reason to change it since, that it is possible to discern an almost obsessive focus in recent cultural studies (and popular music studies in particular) on the binarism (or perhaps a better term might be 'syllogism') *local/global* such that cultural geographies that are differently scaled have been occluded or even interdicted. Martin Stokes characterizes this predicament elegantly when he notes that world musics seem to be stuck in the grip of global processes that, almost by implication, exclude the national:

The world music phenomenon tells a simple but resonant story. Suffused with a gentle millennial mysticism as the twentieth century drew to a close, it suggested something quite new was afoot. A world in which ideas, cultures, and senses of identity were woven snugly and securely into place by the nation-state was unravelling. (2003: 297)

In their study of recent tendencies in popular music and popular music studies, furthermore, David Hesmondhalgh and Keith Negus also identify the increasing interest in, on the one hand, the inter- or transnational and, on the other, the minutiae of the local as a qualitative shift of emphasis away from 'the nation as the prime focus for understanding the relationship of popular music to places' (2002: 8). Clearly, then, something new does indeed seem to be 'afoot', but the terms of this new paradigm, its efficacy and the extent to which it is to be welcomed are still unclear.

What seems particularly problematic in this new disposition is the place of the local. The local seems to have been consistently figured in the last decade or so as a kind of supplement to globalization, as the lesser term of the asymmetrical binarism global/local. In their desire to enable the subaltern of the local to speak, scholars have sought to clear space for it and to disengage it from both state-sponsored cultural policy and the mythologizing narratives of nationalist ideologies. This book, far from seeking to retrench this national(ist) dimension, is an attempt to reintroduce the national dimension in a productive and critical manner as the missing middle term of the local/global syllogism in order to reconsider how nation-states and social units like them might operate as, as it were, a 'mediator' of the two outer terms.[2]

In recent popular music studies, then, engagements of music and its situation abound – 'cartographies' of music which examine imaginative geography and how the sense of physical space is given meaning (Connell and Gibson, 2003), studies of place, of the constitution of music practices around localized communities and their intervention in those communities (Frith, 1989; Cohen, 1991; Guilbault, 1993; Pacini Hernández, 1993; Bennett, 2000; Craig and King, 2002; Hesmondhalgh and Negus, 2002), of music as participating in the formation of identities across distributed networks (Kassabian, 1999 and 2004), of music as a site for both personal and collective identification (Manuel, 1998; Hawkins, 2002; Waxer, 2002; Young, 2002), of music as anchoring those identifications 'back into' specific places, towns and territories (Street, 1993, 1995; Stokes, 1994; Negus, 1996; Cohen, 1998) and of music as located in (and/or locating) scenes (Finnegan, 1989; Cohen, 1991, 1994; Straw, 1991; Shank, 1994; Leyshon, Matless and Revill, 1998; Román-Velázquez, 1999).[3] This abundance of studies seeking to connect musical practice to place and place-identification is a symptom of a wider tendency in recent scholarship to foreground micro-communities and their 'local' engagements (whether 'real' or virtual) of cultural resources. We believe this tendency can be understood as an *idealization* of place (of situating in the broadest sense) in the face of the slipping of musics away from their site(s) of creation or production which, for some at least, has come to feel like a debilitating rupture or dissipation of music from 'the human'.

This idealization, moreover, although methodologically extraordinarily productive, has nonetheless tended towards a reactive and thus, perhaps, one-sided attempt at a compensatory re-humanization (in the sense of an attempt to rediscover modalities of 'human' agency) of musical practice in the face of the anonymizing consequences of the intensified globalization of capital and capital flows. In its extreme form, this results in a romanticization of the local as inherently 'subversive', 'oppositional' and 'authentic', and an inverse figuration of the global as always already artificial and inauthentic. In short, the idealization of music's self-situating can be understood as a symptom of a broader tendency in recent scholarship on music understandably to seek to find ways of managing the complexity of the contemporary situation, of coming to terms with the operations of late capitalism by seeking to reground the inter-subjective dimension of cultural practice. This nostalgia for the human in the face of a brutalizing anonymization of culture is one of the driving (and invisible) epistemes of the new paradigm. At this level, the national (in all its varied imaginations) can sometimes seem too cumbersome, too amorphous, wrongly scaled or even hostile to these putatively 'local' 'human' practices. Therefore, the nation-state figures in this episteme as a problem, as something to be overcome, denied, forgotten, secreted.

Late Capitalism and the Global

It is, then, to use a troubled synonym of global capital, late capitalism, as understood by the so-called 'liberal' scholarship (in its broadest sense), which frames this emphasis on and desire for the local/human. The sense of this local/human as under some kind of attack, or at least as under some kind of malevolent pressure from the homogenizing impulse of globalization, is palpable in recent music scholarship and it is an anxiety which many of the contributors to this book share. Nonetheless, the lack of anything approaching a consensus amongst liberal academics as to the extent and ethical desirability of globalization leaves room here for thinking about the missing middle term of the opening syllogism, the nation-state (or units like it at the 'middle-ground' level), as a useful challenge to what we refer to above as the idealization of place. The globalization of capital, the expansion of multi- and transnational corporations and bodies, the rise of 'flexible accumulation' (Harvey, 1990: 135), the secretion of capital flow and the demise of 'simple' networks of supply and demand, all seem to be working towards an erosion of the occidental metaphysics of place, location, *home*. In this sense, late capitalism, so the story might go, has made us all nomads and has effected a vertiginous expansion and multiplication of technologies that accelerate flows of information, goods and people, resulting in the compression of time and, crucially for our purposes here, the reduction of distance and the shrinking of spaces. This state of affairs is unique to this historical moment and represents a challenge to the liberal academy, one which radically problematizes the notion that cultural practice can be neatly located within a simple and mutually constitutive network of producers and consumers. The ever more 'rationalized' global infrastructure of music distribution has tended to make itself felt in at least two epistemologically incompatible ways. It seems that determining the extent to which a 'choice' between these two positions is possible at all has become extremely difficult. On the one hand, it has felt as if the radical decentring of political authority has not led to a breakdown in the fabric of the social order as some have predicted, but to a largely positive and productive reconfiguration of power – its 'localization' – and an extension of what we might term a micro-politics of *choice*, an ever widening availability of new materials and different goods from afar: the rise of world music as a marketing category in the West is often understood in this light as a widening distribution of and omnidirectional encounter with different cultural forms; the rapid availability of information from abroad; the cheapness of air travel and the consequent feeling of the globe's radical navigability; a sense of omnidirectional exchange, dialogue and 'distributedness' to use a term recently coined by Anahid Kassabian (2004). On the other hand, this process towards radical distributedness in 'the West' has also made itself felt, paradoxically, as an impoverishment of our conception of *place*: what globalization as we are describing it here might be said to have effected is a dissolution of the Western metaphysics of belonging, the disintegration of citizens from larger social units, a consequent atomization of those citizens, an emphasis on the very (micro-)local to the detriment of an exercising of effective political power against larger political forces, and, as we have already seen, the emergence of a conception of the local–global dynamic in which the middle ground of experience, that sense often invoked in leftist critiques of globalization of a shared social responsibility, is radically curtailed in favour of the outer terms of the syllogism.

In this context, the West (for want of a better word) has tended to view globalization as *ambiguously* productive – a process of 'democratization', 'liberalization' and, perhaps most controversially, a process of *harmonization*, but one which has also brought about a consequent fragmentation of the network of channels along which effective human political agency can flow. Harmonization, perhaps one of the most theorized and politically contentious elements of the process of globalization, is a term that attempts to capture the tendency implicit in these processes to rationalize the flow of global capital such that markets 'converge', or, put another way, to bypass local and middle-level interests (notably the smaller nation-state) in favour of a more economically malleable and politically diffuse infrastructure. Despite its quasi-utopian overtones, harmonization has yet to lead to a situation in which global markets might be said to 'share' wealth. On the contrary, the mechanisms whereby the so-called 'developing world' has been held in a state of (for the West) productive poverty have been intensified and rationalized in order to maintain the flow of capital into the so-called 'developed' world. Indeed, harmonization as a global process might be said to have had unwelcome consequences for both 'developing' and 'developed' worlds, evidenced in particular in a destabilization of labour supplies, the intervention by multinational institutions in local labour laws in favour of global market-led systems and a debilitating fluidity in job markets and a pointed dehumanization of labour.

Looking for a Middle Ground

It seems that the now famous figuration by Benedict Anderson of the nation as something like an 'imagined community' (1991) has come to serve as testament to the intensification of the epistemological tension between political thought centred on the nation-state as a given and inalienable political unit and thought that has sought to refute the imagining of nations as mythic or nostalgic.[4] Indeed, even as the former enters its 'late' stage, the latter is forced to confront its inability to account for the continued formidable and infinitely malleable potential of nationalist ideologies. In whichever of these two orientations the nation state finds itself articulated, it is always with some disquiet and we frequently encounter a structural rift in thought about the nation state that is located around the concept of 'place' articulated through at least two polarized models, often operating simultaneously, for thinking about contemporary cultural practices. On the one hand, there is a recourse to a 'new traditionalism', a tendency to cite and situate identities as based in a certain kind of 'rootedness' in ethnicity, race, linguistic communities, the local and so on – in other words, what Friedman has termed authenticity as an 'existential phenomenon' (1994: 238) or what Nederveen Pieterse (1995: 61) has termed a territorial, inward-looking sense of place. On the other hand, there is a tendency to celebrate a plurality of globalized cultures, a tendency often identified with so-called postmodern thought in which boundaries and borders become ever more blurred and ever more permeable – what Nederveen Pieterse (1995: 61) has termed a translocal, outward-looking sense of place. Within popular music studies, this distinction can be traced in the discourses associated with 'authentic' world music grounded in the recourse to tradition and roots, and the 'postmodern authenticity' constituted in the syncretic hybridization of the fusion of world beat (see Keil and Feld, 1994: 265–6). The contributors to this book have not sought to understand 'new traditionalism' and globalizing postmodernity as exclusive, but, rather, to see them as outlining the extremities of an extended spectrum of approaches to place, identity and cultural distribution in global networks. This desire to move beyond the impasse of the global/local binarism draws on the work of cultural theorists such as Roland Robertson, who, of course, adapted the term 'glocal' in 1995 from Japanese capitalist business terminology to represent the tendency, as he saw it, for world cultures to operate through the interpenetration of local and global networks.[5] Similarly, in the same year, Jan Nederveen Pieterse re-used the term 'interculturalism', seeking to articulate the kinds of new dialogues that, for him, seem to have emerged between the diverse cultural logics that attend different cultural territories.[6] Both thinkers seemed, then, to be trying to sketch out the structure of a way of understanding cultural practice as played out in two interconnected spheres, each of which casts the other in sharp relief. Other thinkers who have sought to move beyond the either/or polarities of the global and the local, or the universal and the particular, to restate the binarism in Hegelian terms include Nestor García Canclini (1990, 1999), Stuart Hall (1990, 1996), George Lipsitz (1990, 1994), Renato Ortiz (1994), Jesús Martin-Barbero (1998) and Arjun Appadurai (2000), all of whom have critiqued the categorization of contemporary cultural processes as either homogenizing or heterogenizing. In their work, they elucidate the processes of mediation, reconversion and reappropriation of global products by local consumers, and the use of global systems of distribution in the dissemination of local products.[7] As Murphy indicates in Chapter 2 of this volume, his study of Afropop, the resources of dominant culture may be appropriated by the subaltern as strategies to make inroads into global markets. Scholars of the world music phenomenon such as Garofalo (1993), Guilbault (1993, 2001) and Mitchell (1996) have critiqued the centre/periphery model, noting the emergence of multiple centres and polylateral markets, as examples of the fracturing of the West's hegemony. Many contemporary accounts draw on Appadurai's notion of a complex, overlapping, disjunctive order of current global flows in which a perspectival set of landscapes are proposed as the building blocks of 'imagined worlds' (1990: 296).

Globalizing scholarships are in constant danger, as they seek to critique, of entrenching the global as inalienable, putting 'in place' a new metaphysics of distributedness. Global forces, as represented in this scholarship, can be appropriated only precariously, and prising open and forging new and precarious inroads into global networks is always difficult when the human/local is left to carry this burden alone, without mediation. Most crucial for our purposes here, this process works more readily at the level of something approximating a middle ground. In their late capitalist formation, nation-states and nation states represent a blind spot, or, as Žižek would formulate it, a certain invisible site of mediation between local communities and global networks. We do not wish to suggest, of course, that nations and/or nation-states represent the only site of this mediation, but, rather, that they represent one of the many clear and extant examples of the kinds of mediation that we might expect to find in the contemporary globalized and globalizing situation. Our point in this volume has been to suggest that, however much we might like to fall into the seductive notion that we can theorize the nation-state out of the picture, it nonetheless operates as one of those middle-ground social units that can make some claim to intervene in the flow of global capital through protectionist measures, both 'hard' (such as the imposition of import quotas) and 'cultural' (such as the imposition of language-defined play-list quotas).[8] What has changed, of course, is that the monopoly which nation-states used to enjoy in that mediation is no longer in place – nation-states compete with other middle-ground units for that role (one might think here of loose associations of regions within and across national boundaries, linguistic territories, larger trading territories and other non- or transnational units). The ramifications of this work for the enrichment of popular music studies have been profound and far-reaching.

Re-imagining the Nation as a Political Mediator

According to Lipsitz (1994) and Simon Frith (1996), popular music is perhaps *the* cultural product that has crossed (and continues to cross) boundaries and frontiers the most frequently, just as it has demarcated and consolidated local cultural spaces. One way to tell the story of the rise of popular music in the so-called developed world, then, is as the slow journey towards a rationalized and rationalizing global infrastructure where, as David Hesmondhalgh (2000, 2002) has shown, transnational corporations and distribution networks are the order of the day. This infrastructure is at once concerned to address itself to a maximum number of addressees *within* its 'own' territory and, at the same time, concerned also to export that process of address maximization to territories 'outside' the West, until such a time (projecting itself into an infinitely occidental future) as the distinction between being 'inside' and being 'outside' that infrastructure will become ever more difficult to recognize. However, Stokes sounds a well-founded note of caution:

> The material forces that both enable and constrain the movement of music and musicians about the globe are not always easy to comprehend. To a great extent, we hear what large and powerful corporations enable us to hear, though … the grasp of these corporations on music making worldwide is by no means total. (2003: 297)

The cultural imperialism thesis, which posits the 'greying out' of local styles (see, for example, Lomax, 1968), has been comprehensively contested by scholars such as Frith (1991), Garofalo (1993), Feld (1994), Shuker (1994), Mitchell (1996), Guilbault (1997) and Hesmondhalgh (2002).[9] While the dangers of cultural imperialism should not be ignored, they are perhaps overstated in apocalyptic theories about processes of 'McDonaldization', 'Coca-Colonization' (Nederveen Pieterse, 1995: 45) and 'Westoxication' (Featherstone, 1990a: 11) in which cultural differences have been supposedly obliterated.[10] Globalization cannot be unproblematically equated with homogenization.[11] Nonetheless, the 'feeling' or suspicion of a recent quickening of the 'progress' towards homogenization in the last decade has brought for many a number of anxieties about the limits of our individual and collective autonomy within the emerging global 'systems'. This has found particular expression in a radical questioning of the pragmatic productivity of democracy, a deep problematization of political representation and an overwhelming sense of the loss of what might be termed a critical politics of citizenship. In our young century, moreover, these anxieties, in the aftermath of 9/11, the subsequent attacks in Madrid and London, the ongoing violence in

Iraq and Afghanistan and the so-called 'war' on 'global terror', are such that the urgency of committing to an engaged and critical mode of scholarship makes itself felt with an intensity almost unlike any we have encountered before (Žižek, 2004).

The contributors to this volume, then, have sought to write from a number of different perspectives, always alive to pressing ethical concerns of thinking cultures in a highly charged political frame. The pressing nature of this undertaking, it seems to us, is evidenced in particular in some of the ways in which popular musics have shown themselves able to adapt to radically differentiated political situations without fundamentally recasting themselves internally: indeed, one might argue that, above all other cultural forms, popular world musics have been at the forefront of mass political mobilization (the recent Live 8 concerts would seem to suggest as much) and, as Philip Bohlman (1993) has eloquently demonstrated, the study of that music is always already a politically charged undertaking. What becomes palpably clear, though, is that seeking to articulate the national in that undertaking is *always already* fraught with danger: contemporary popular music scholarship as imagined in Northern Europe and North America – born of the intellectual traditions of British cultural studies (grounded in particular in various forms of Marxist practice) and US liberal scholarship (grounded in the various attempts from the 1960s onwards to address the burgeoning needs of identity politics) – is incompatible with thinking about middle-ground territories such as nation-states as sites of affiliation or identification.[12] This danger, then, is epistemological in that those intellectual paradigms have traditionally sought to combat identification with the national by enacting processes of demystification and, in a very important sense, they have always been internationalizing paradigms.

Indeed, one might say that, with some notable exceptions (such as Stokes, 1994 and Bohlman, 2002), popular music studies in the Anglo-American tradition is dominated still by two ideological orientations, neither of which has dealt terribly constructively with nationalism or the conceptualization of the nation-state. The first, essentially Marxist in orientation, has tended to view the nation-state as an antiquated bourgeois construction and scholars touched by this tradition have found it difficult to track the ideological fluidity of nationalist sentiments and their implication in popular music practices (Lomax, 1968; Maróthy, 1974; Porter, 1993; Krims, 2000). The second, essentially a liberal tradition, has tended to view the nation-state as a sovereign but pragmatic unit and scholars of this tradition seek (admittedly often with a critical edge) to reduce national sentiment in popular music to an array of beguiling and seductive differences, available for consumption in the global market (Wiggins, 1996; Letts, 2000). A third, largely 'conservative' tradition, but also drawing on conservationist and green ideologies, seeks to wrest 'national' (and 'regional') musical traditions from the march of a perceived global erosion of difference (Ricros, 1993; Matović, 1995).

As we have seen, except in the third (now minority) approach, theorizations of national identity and nationalist practice have often been eclipsed by, on the one hand, the ethnographic tendency to study musical practices in the local context and, on the other, by theorizations of globalization and so-called 'late' capitalism which seem to all but obliterate the operational efficacy of national units. The reasons for this interdiction are, of course, extremely complex. Only outside the Anglo-American scholarly hegemony (Ferreira de Castro, 1997; Steingress, 1997; Erlmann, 1999; Otero Garabis, 2000) and in a handful of some recent studies within the Anglo-American tradition touched by other traditions (Mitchell, 1994; Askew, 1997; Shabazz, 1999; Radano and Bohlman, 2000; Wade, 2000) have scholars sought to engage constructively with the kinds of cultural practice which characterize nationalist allegiances, the imagining of nation states and national mythologizing narratives.

In seeking to articulate the 'national' dimension in music, scholars are met with an extraordinary set of complex problems. The folk revival in Bosnia and Hercegovina in the late 1960s, for example, saw the emergence of the so-called *novokomponovana narodna muzika* (lit. 'newly composed folk music') which synthesized urban and rural forms and constructed a newly national form quite unlike anything that had come from Bosnia's rural indigenous musical traditions.[13] Similar developments in 1970s Bulgaria led to the growing popularity of the hybrid *svatbarska muzika* ('wedding music') that drew on a huge range of popular and folk styles from Macedonia, Hungary, Serbia and Romania yet is nonetheless articulated by Bulgarians as authentically 'Bulgarian'. How are both idioms to be linked with national identity if they so quickly transform their own musical traditions? What are the political and ideological processes at work that facilitate these kinds of rapid appropriation to nationalist ends of non-indigenous musics? Of course, national ideologies, the imagining of nation-states and nation states, are themselves in a state of constant flux and renegotiation which makes the relationship between 'purely musical' characteristics and national sentiment extraordinarily slippery. Clearly, then, the role of national identity and nationalist ideologies in the formation and articulation of a musical practice is open-ended and since popular music has long been associated with political dissent, the nation-state has consistently demonstrated itself determined to seek out and procure for itself a stake in the management of the possible deployments of 'its' popular musics.[14] Conversely, popular musics have been used 'from the ground up' as a site for populist and popular critiques of the 'mismatch' which often occurs between political state and idealized nation. The rise in popularity of arabesk in Turkey in the 1950s, for example, banned from public broadcast, shows how non-indigenous (in this case Arabic) musics can be appropriated to counter-hegemonic yet nationalist ends (Stokes, 1992). There have been many clear instances of popular music's engagement of the national–political dimension and, indeed, one might say that this has been one of its most powerful functions in most of the globe outside the small Anglo-American territories.

Borders and Boundaries

As we have seen, one of the ways in which globalization has been theorized is as a dissolution of national and other culturally policed borders of what we are here terming 'middle-ground' territories. This putative 'dissolution' of borders (or, perhaps better, their 'destabilization') has been implicated in a number of complex and ambivalent dynamics: that 'dissolution' has been held up as both symptom and cause of the globalization of commodities, the globalization of criminality ('terror' as a new global metaphor), the weakening of national governments' fiscal (and, by implication, political) agency, political disengagement and disenchantment and of the rise of what might be termed *compensatory* nationalisms. This last dynamic is one of the issues explored in this volume, and the contributors have been at pains to examine these 'late' nationalisms as part of a complex array of shifting epistemological figurations of nations and nation-states, including long-distance nationalisms. A number of chapters in this volume engage with recent theorizing of more fluid concepts of the nation such as ethno-nations, transnations, cultural and/or imagined nations (what the Germans have long termed the *Kulturnation*). In Chapter 5 George analyses the adoption of rap by linguistically marginalized communities, which challenges the xenophobic tendencies in the French nationalism of Le Pen et al. to construct a more inclusive imagined nation. As Appadurai (2000: 4) notes, in his study of the cultural dimensions of globalization, diasporas challenge easy boundaries of the local, regional and national. Similarly Nair and Simonett, in Chapters 3 and 4 respectively, focus on transnational or diasporic musical genres in immigrant communities. Simonett discusses the development of technobanda outside the geographically delimited national territory of Mexico as an expression of a translocal collective consciousness based on a shared cultural heritage in which the nation figures as a trope of identity. For Nair, raï also opens a space for the articulation of displaced identities in immigrant communities from North Africa, especially Morocco, in Spain.

It was suggested above that, despite the more critical work of many 'globalizing' critics such as Appadurai and Roberston, the syllogism *global/local* operates as a powerful topos which seeks to ground a new metaphysics of distributedness, or which operates as what Jacques Lacan has called a 'Master-Signifier' (1997). This new syllogism, recognizable, as we have seen, as a historically contingent intensification of the Hegelian dialectic of the universal/particular, has held both liberal and Marxist scholars alike in the grip of an inescapable epistemological bind: we have already shown how, in their more explicitly theorized articulations of place, globalizing ideologies have tended to foreground the local as precisely that place at which the global can be resisted and, simultaneously, as precisely that place at which it is thrown into relief. The putative 'disappearance' of the nation (or at least its attenuated visibility) in this epistemological bind can only be addressed by recourse to a systematic and protracted theorization of that middle ground at which, amongst other social units, the nation-state is located. The critical Hegelian term (one we have only been intimating up to now) of the *vanishing mediator* ([1807] 1980) might serve here as a useful way of understanding the putative disappearance of the nation-state in recent globalizing scholarship. Hegel's notion of the vanishing mediator can be understood as an attempt to articulate a mediating level between two outer levels which, having done its work, vanishes, leaving little or no trace of itself. It is also a term famously employed by Slavoj Žižek (1989, 1991, 1992) (although he takes it from Fredric Jameson, 1988) in his account of late capitalism and feudalism as 'mediated' by Protestantism and in his discussion of liberal democracy as grounded on the vanishing mediator of the Left:

> To find proper names for this New is the task ahead for Left thought. In fulfilling this task, the Left has no need to renounce its past: how symptomatic is today's forgetfulness about the fact that the Left was the 'vanishing mediator' which gained most of the rights and freedoms today appropriated by liberal democracy, starting with the common right to vote; how symptomatic is the forgetfulness about the fact that the very language by means of which even the mass media perceive Stalinism ('Big Brother,' 'Ministry of Truth,' and so on) was the product of a leftist criticism of the Communist experience. (1991: 243)

The rearticulation of this concept by Žižek is centred around a need *to make visible again* that which seems to be vanishing; it serves here as a useful model for understanding the ways in which a set of new cultural conditions can hide the operating territory of its inception: it is useful therefore to think about this tendency as part of the mechanism by which the local/global dynamic has sought to obfuscate the fact that the 'birth' of that syllogism can be traced specifically to nationalist ideologies. One consequence of this argument would be to recognize that the political solidarity of citizens of nation-states to each other through anonymous identification is also that *very same process* whereby global identifications are made. Warner and Nascimento in Chapter 7 of this volume make a similar argument for social solidarity in Habermasian terms in the work of Brazilian singer-songwriter Antônio Nóbrega.

Thus, we should not be surprised to find that new forms of nationalism continue to emerge and the force of the nation as a cultural trope continues to adapt to new political and material conditions. It is this very dynamic, the agency of new forms of nationhood and the continued operative force of 'older' imaginations of nation, that this book seeks to examine in some detail and to elaborate as a useful critical counterpoint to much recent work on globalization that misses this middle dimension. For example, Robert Hudson in Chapter 8 of this book examines the role of the cult of folk traditions and folklore in the configuration of the 'new nation' of Serbia as an intensification of a territorial–national discourse based on 'primordial loyalties' (Friedman, 1994: 86). The role played in that process by popular music is a crucial part of Robert Hudson's argument and centres in particular on the specific cultural work that folk songs can do in the highly charged Serbian context in the early 1990s. By way of counterpoint, Joanne Smith investigates in Chapter 6 'new folk' musics of the Uyghurs in China as a form of resistance to a state trying to impose cultural hegemony by force. In a sense, this 'regionalism', as some might term it, can be figured as a kind of nationalism, centred around a sense not of the local as figured in recent scholarship on globalization, but on the national as an imagined community, to utilize again Benedict Anderson's term. In Chapter 1, furthermore, John O'Flynn demonstrates how the nation-state, far from redundant, has continued to serve as a crucial territory for the operation of global capital and its interests. He analyses the construction of 'Irishness' in popular music as part of a set of fluid discourses that relate in complex ways to the local/global syllogism and which overlap globalizing ideologies in quite complex and self-contradictory ways. Stan Hawkins in Chapter 9 also examines the dynamic relation between the three levels – the local, the national and the global – in the negotiation of constructs of national identity in the auto-parodic dance music of the Norwegian group, Those Norwegians.

Re-encountering the National

If the national can be said to occupy the position of Žižek's vanishing mediator, the re-encountering or uncovering of that mediator in the global/local syllogism ought to open up new critical trajectories for popular music studies. The large and complex history of the encounter between popular music, nations and nationalisms reveals an extraordinary tension between the centralized cultural policies of nation-states and the 'local' or more distributed practices of popular musicians (both professional and amateur). In particular, the re-territorialization of local heterogeneous musics to nationalist ends has often signalled the death or near-fatal displacement of regional identities. In this regard, the case of flamenco is interesting, especially since it was clearly the victim of a long and focused campaign during the Franco regime to appropriate it as a national trope in constructing a homogenous and specifically Spanish national popular culture (there are also striking parallels to be drawn in other post-war dictatorial regimes, not least, in Portugal, the Salazar regime's appropriation of fado as a *canção nacional* [national song]). Since the transition to democracy and the emergence of the *autonomías* (administrative areas of the country each of which has a degree of local autonomy), flamenco has embarked on a process that might be termed, somewhat clumsily, 're-Andalusianization'. But this is not simply an articulation of the local/global dynamic in which the repressed 'local' has returned with a vengeance. On the contrary, this process of Andalusianization is modelled on those *very same* nationalist discourses which founded national ideologies in the first place – the notion of a 'discovery' of an anonymous alignment to an ideal territory, an idealization that works through some founding political trauma (in this case the enforced professionalization and homogenization of flamenco in the *peñas* [commercial flamenco clubs] of Franco's Madrid).

The complexity of flamenco's engagement with ideas of territory and globalization can be demonstrated in the emergence, during the transition to democracy, of the popularity of what might be termed the 'second wave' of flamenco recordings which just preceded the transition, exemplified in particular by the work of Camerón de la Isla in the late 1960s and, perhaps, the work in the 1970s of artists like Lole and Manuel. These artists deliberately departed from the strictures of traditional flamenco performing styles, choosing instead to look to mix flamenco styles with the musics from the United States and Northern Europe. During the transition to democracy, it was this version of flamenco that survived de-Francoization, and the new generation of *flamencos jóvenes* [young flamenco artists] responded to the challenges laid down by the second wave with new and hybridized forms and with a certain self-conscious return to tradition (again we note the coincidence here of two mutually incommensurate epistemological positions, held together in the same instance).

This process has continued apace. In 1996, for example, Enrique Morente, with the Spanish alternative rock band Lagartija Nick, produced the extraordinary album *Omega*. The first (and title) track of the album lasts some ten minutes and combines words by Spanish author Federico García Lorca ('Omega, poema para muertos' ['Omega, poem for the dead'] from the 1936 collection *Poemas sueltos*), Morente's fabulous voice and the full resources of the band. It seems to conjure up a liminal 'interspace' between a historicized imagination of flamenco and the rock sensibility, which no doubt many contemporary commentators would articulate 'simply' as an example of musical hybridity. According to the liberal–global hypothesis, this mythic interspace could be viewed as a utopian space in which regional, national and other ideological affiliations are levelled out. However, we must also inflect the notion of hybridity in order to be able to recognize the power relations at work in this mixing of styles here: in any encounter of musical types, there are never simply even-handed or playful encounters free from the operations of ideology.[15] On the contrary, what is at work here, it seems to us, is the complex and contested encounter of a music seeking to re-regionalize itself with a more generalizing (perhaps, even globalizing) musical style.

In this encounter, danger is always apparent: the first five minutes of the track consist of a long, sustained, tonic pedal from the bass guitar over which Morente produces elaborate flamenco melismas, almost as if the flamenco idiom here were unable to get purchase on the alien materials from rock and is only gesturing at the tonal centre of the track, somehow ghostly and emptied of its material specificity (the use of reverb here adds to this effect). After this opening gesture, the texture thins out and we are left with the crude confrontation of the spectre of flamenco and the 'bones' of rock in the unmediated slow beating of a drum. This stripped-down duality of drum and voice is eventually overturned by Morente's almost shamanic invocation of 'lost' voices from the flamenco tradition: Antonio Chacón, Manuel Torres and la niña de los peines (Pastora Pavón). These samples are layered over each other until they seem to be clamouring for release, crowding the soundstage to the point of saturation. This extraordinary moment (about 6'50" into the track) might be understood to consist of a traumatic territorialization, an attempt at an erasure of the rock sensibility and a rooting of flamenco space within a national space through the recurrence of the sonic phantasms of its history. As with many so-called hybrid musics, the power relations at work are uneven. The rock idiom emerges here in the end as a violent *Durchbruch*, literally 'breakthrough' in Freudian terms, that obliterates Morente's attempts to clear a sonic space for himself but which is nonetheless touched by the flamenco tradition in its use of *palmas* (the characteristic clapping that accompanies certain forms of flamenco). These materials can never guarantee a cohesive or singular reading, but they do suggest something of the complexity of thinking about musical materials and their relationship to the sonic projection of territory: viewed in this manner, the encounter between rock and flamenco here is as the encounter between a certain post-war notion of regionalism and of the global as always ready to absorb and redistribute the regional.

Yet within this encounter, we note, in the end, how extraordinarily *located* the flamenco idiom is here: its absolute commitment to its own history, its fulsome and non-parodic self-sampling and its clear and focused refutation of assimilation. This sense of its own 'territory' is not best located at the level of the *local* since it is a rather generalized invocation of the heady gestures of flamenco's *cante jondo* [deep song], not specific to any *palo* [flamenco subgenre]. This rootedness, rather, may be understood in terms which map best onto the structural logic of the middle ground of the national, invoking, as we suggested above, that *very same* ideological ground on which nation-states and nationalisms are situated. The music invokes identification at the most general level, not as a regional 'flamenco de Jerez' or 'flamenco de las minas' or 'alegrías de Cádiz', but as flamenco, a citing, a gesturing towards, a sketching of a fluid national musical space and all its possibilities.

It is clear, then, that popular musics can productively open out the national not simply as the space in which nationalist ideology locates itself, but also as a 'territory' that has symbolic force beyond its parochial–political needs. This territory is fluid, open-ended and productively unstable in its encounter with 'real' nation-states and, also, with 'real' national and nationalist aspirations. It has, furthermore, demonstrated itself to be consistently resistant to its shorthanding by globalizing scholarship as 'simply' uncritical, mythic, atavistic. The contributors to this volume bring together a variety of methodological approaches including cultural studies, new musicology, ethnomusicology and critical anthropology, and their work demonstrates the complexity of the national as a liminal or interstitial space in which the local and the global are mutually imbricated.

Notes

1   A notable exception within post-structuralist scholarship is Homi Bhabha's 'Narrating the Nation' (1990: 1–7) which addresses the nation as a powerful but ambivalent

historical idea which has not been superseded definitively by the processes of late capitalism or internationalism. For an overview of the literature on the development of nations and nationalisms from sociology and cultural anthropology, see the chapters by Hudson and Smith in this volume.

2 As we shall see shortly, reconsidering the national in this way is tantamount to rethinking capitalism itself in terms of its internal contradictions since, as Slavoj Žižek (1989) has suggested, global capitalism is founded on a vanishing epistemological ground that is at odds with the core epistemological assumptions of its contemporary 'late' operation.

3 There is, of course, an extensive literature on world musics which, by definition, is connected to place. See the chapters by Murphy and Simonett in this volume. See also Born and Hesmondhalgh (2000), Feld (2000), Bohlman (2002) and Barañano et al. (2003).

4 See O'Flynn's chapter in this volume on the distinction between nation-states and nation states.

5 Robertson (1990) draws also on Hannerz's earlier rehearsal of the debate in terms of the local and the 'cosmopolitan'. See also Robertson (1992).

6 Within popular music studies, Mark Slobin (1993) has used the term specifically to characterize the interplay between global generality and local specificity.

7 For an example of this process see Regev (1997).

8 See Holton (1998), Kennedy and Danks (2001) and Hesmondhalgh (2002) on the persistence of the nation-state as a forum for cultural industry activity.

9 This draws on the earlier literature on this debate in world music studies including Wallis and Malm (1984), Laing (1986) and Goodwin and Gore (1990).

10 See Tomlinson (1991) for a general overview of the cultural imperialism debate.

11 See Gebesmair and Smudits (2001) for an analysis of the transnational music industry, in particular the essay by Malm on fields of tension or discordant trends including homogenization and diversification.

12 This reflects the anxiety in the liberal academy about the convergence of nationalism and racial/ethnic mythology as justification for particularly brutal ways of consolidating the nation. It is in this anxiety that the discourses of 'Balkanization' and 'Jihad world' are born.

13 See the chapter by Hudson in this volume.

14 See Cloonan (1999) on popular music and the nation state. Some of the ways in which the state intervenes in popular music practice include censorship, broadcasting regulation and sponsorship (festivals, grants, tax breaks and subsidies).

15 There is an extensive literature of hybridity and power relations in popular music. See Gilroy (1993), Sharma, Hutnyk and Sharma (1996), Taylor (1997) and Hutnyk (2000).

Discography

Morente, Enrique and Lagartija Nick, *Omega – Cantando a Federico García Lorca* (El Europeo Música, Madrid, Spain, EEM 001, 1996).

PART I
POSITIONS

Chapter 1

National Identity and Music in Transition: Issues of Authenticity in a Global Setting

John O'Flynn

In this chapter I argue that, far from being a redundant category, national identity continues to have significance in both the production and the consumption of music. However, since the construction of national identities is inevitably situated within global and local historical contexts, it follows that the interface between national identity and music is constantly in a state of flux. Critically, I set out to show how relationships of national identity and music are maintained through transitional processes of authentication.

The overall position adopted here is premised on a number of observations and assumptions. Firstly, I question whether the onset of a 'local–international dichotomy' in contemporary music production and consumption has necessarily effected a 'national bypass' (Malm and Wallis, 1992: 237). Here, I concur with a general critique of popular music studies that tends to focus on the 'local' and the 'global' while ascribing little significance to the 'national' (Wade, 1998; Cloonan, 1999). Meanwhile, although a considerable corpus of musicological studies has examined the potential links between 'national schools' of composition and nationalist ideologies, this work has been characterized by an overriding tendency to represent 'national' music in exotic and peripheral terms (M. Murphy, 2001: 7). Arguably though, the bulk of contemporary musicology simply regards nationalism as an obsolete concept. Incredibly, an entry on nationalism in the 2001 edition of *The New Grove Dictionary of Music and Musicians* concludes with the suggestion that the end of the Cold War in Europe did not lead to any 'resurgence or rehabilitation of music nationalism'. In contrast, a volume of essays edited by Slobin (1996) would suggest that the very opposite has been the case. This assumed collapse of music nationalism is attributed to the 'post-modern deconstruction' of concepts such as serious music and national essence (Sadie, 2001: 703). Even if we agree with the view that the 'grand narrative' of modern nationalism is on the wane, this analysis fails to offer alternative accounts of how the formation of musical identities may be related to culturally and/or politically bounded entities. It is a matter, then, of supplanting the narrow concept of (political) nationalism with a more flexible perspective on national identity that does not limit its purview to any one set of ideological and/or material contexts. Among other things, this enables us to regard the interrelations between the different musical practices and forms that might obtain in any culturally and/or politically defined entity.

For the most part of this discussion, I choose the nation state as a primary site of interpretation, while at the same time acknowledging the necessary distinction between nations and states or, for that matter, between 'nation states' and 'nation-states' (Connor, 1994; McCrone, 1998). 'Nation-state' is conventionally used to describe independent states with some degree of ethnic and/or cultural homogeneity whereas 'nation state' suggests a more civically oriented conception of statehood. Whichever conception is applied, I argue that the field of national identity will inevitably involve more than one type of collective identity and that, furthermore, although some phenomena of identity and music might be considered as specific to individual nations, others again can be interpreted as transnational categories of collective identification.

Just as I challenge notions of a 'national bypass', I also question a tendency towards the theoretical erasure of the concepts of identity and authenticity in musical studies. While it is quite feasible and arguably important to critique the ideologies underlying these concepts, the fact remains that they continue to inform common-sense assumptions about music. As such, identity and authenticity are inextricably linked to music discourses and practices. However, the strategic use of these terms in an analysis of musical–national issues does not imply any essential racial qualities for nations/ethnic groups or for national/ethnic music. Music and national identity are never constitutive of each other; rather, they interrelate through processes of articulation and negotiation.

In the next section I argue how the ideas of nation and identity continue to have relevance in contemporary global contexts. Following this, I set out some theoretical approaches to the study of national identity and music. This leads to a consideration of other foci of cultural identification besides that of the nation state, including the geographical categories of global, regional and local, in addition to other collective categories such as scene and diaspora (Straw, 1991). Here, I suggest some ways in which these other levels can impact on the relations between national identity and music. Finally, I argue that the theorization of authenticity suggests an approach through which the transitional relationships between national identity and music in global contexts can be interpreted.

Globality and National Identity

Global Issues

The assumption that the categories of nation and nation-state have been superseded by a global/local nexus is critiqued by a number of cultural theorists including Robertson who proposes rather that 'the contemporary assertion of ethnicity and/or nationality is made within global terms of identity' (1995: 26). Similarly, Nederveen Pieterse (1995: 49) suggests that the formation of nations and ethnicities can be regarded as necessary functions and expressions of 'globality', and as such should not necessarily be considered as oppositional to globalizing influences. This national–global dialectic is not new to music production and consumption. For example, Adorno interpreted the 'national' music of some nineteenth- and early twentieth-century classical composers as an early form of global capitalism through which process 'the qualitative differences between peoples ... came to be transformed into commodity brands on the world market' (1976: 163).

Modernist and postcolonial critiques of nationalist ideologies have highlighted the problems of essentialism and homogenization that are inherent to extreme forms of cultural nationalism (Smith, 1991; Hutchinson and Smith, 1994; Miller, 1995). However, according to Graham and Kirkland (1999: 2), these very critiques and negations of nationalism may be no less ideology-free and could themselves be governed by covert political agendas (see also Friedman, 1994: 143–4). These authors advocate an alternative approach in which the various manifestations and processes of national identity and the negation of these are regarded in terms of negotiation and reinterpretation. Similarly, Nederveen Pieterse (1995: 51) argues that, as opposed to the globalizing that took place during the expansionist periods of nineteenth- and twentieth-century colonialism, we now have a constantly changing state of globality that cannot be interpreted simplistically through such binarisms as centre/periphery, cause/effect or homogeneity/heterogeneity. Rather, he puts forward the Gramscian idea of articulation as a more suitable theoretical perspective in the analysis of contemporary global processes and discourses. As will be discussed below, the same concept can be applied to studies of national identity and music.

Thus, it is proposed that the idea of nations has not been consumed by globality but is in fact a part of it. The levels of locality, nation and globality are interrelated in both real and 'imagined' terms. Here, I adapt Benedict Anderson's oft-quoted definition of nations as 'imagined communities' (1991), arguing that all ideas of community, be they local, national or global, are socially constructed through a range of discourses, beliefs and behaviours. However, such social constructions are contextualized by specific material conditions. Actual boundaries do exist between nation states and these are frequently invoked when discursive parameters are drawn, as is the case with 'home' news printed in the 'national' press or when members of the public phone in to debate 'national' issues on radio chat shows. The popularity of international mass-produced music is interpreted through national charts, both printed and broadcast. At the same time, 'national' music can be actively promoted through the intervention of broadcasting quotas or through levels of media interest that are disproportionate to the market share enjoyed by domestic artists.

It is also misleading to characterize nationalizing influences as promoting homogeneity and globalizing influences as promoting heterogeneity, as there are countertendencies in both instances. Music that is regarded as typical of a nation – say, Polish, Irish or Greek – might be nurtured equally through nationalizing and globalizing forces. It is quite plausible to suggest that in the colonial–global contexts of the nineteenth century, the indigenous music of these countries was to some extent appropriated by nationalist causes. Simultaneously, it could be argued that the same music was exoticized and fetishized by antiquarian–folkloristic movements arising from colonial anthropological interests. In the contemporary state of globality, ideas about music and nationhood have changed considerably, and yet the beliefs, discourses and practices that connect these phenomena continue to do so within a global–national dialectic. In some cases, it is in the context of globality that the homogenizing of national music takes place, such as with the 'bouzouki music' of international Greek restaurants and the canned 'diddly-eiddly' music that blends in with the décor of Irish theme pubs the world over.

Arguably, the designation of 'national essence' to particular music is more problematic within modern nation states where tensions between the homogenous and heterogeneous are often lived out. As Wade argues in the case of national identity and music, 'homogenization exists in complex and ambivalent relationships with the construction of difference by the same nationalist forces that create homogeneity' (1998: 1). The dialectic of the homogenous and the heterogeneous operates within specific material contexts that change over space and time. Thus, the various phenomena of national identity and music cannot be interpreted solely in terms of opposition to globalizing influences; as Manuel (1988) illustrates, slight changes in global conditions along with local cultural nuances and material circumstances can alter or even negate such relationships. Rather, the area of national identity and music needs to be viewed as a relatively bounded yet 'porous' field of meaning that is inextricably linked to the increasingly 'transnational flow' of musical identities (Connell and Gibson, 2003: 143). In this way, 'foreignness' and 'nationalness' can be seen as interrelated concepts in beliefs and discourse pertaining to the music production and consumption of any defined political entity (Magaldi, 1999: 324–6).

General Parameters for the Study of National Identity and Music

However flexible our concept of what 'nation' might be, it is necessary to delineate parameters through which national identity, or identifications connected to concepts of 'nation', may obtain. Miller (1995: 2–5) outlines five areas that distinguish national identities from other types of identities. First of all, nations are conceived as a consequence of shared beliefs. The second feature of national identity is that it 'embodies historical continuity' (Miller, 1995: 23), although 'history' in this sense involves an imaginative process that includes mythology or even 'selective amnesia' (Schlesinger, 1991: 44). Thirdly, national identity is an active identity – nations 'do things together' in symbolic ways, represented by institutions or through proxies such as athletes and others (a striking musical example would be the Eurovision Song Contest). The fourth aspect of national identity is that it links people to a particular geographical area. This can vary between, on the one hand, 'fixed' imaginings of nation states and, on the other hand, more fluid, mythological conceptions of place, as would be the case with 'the Celtic fringe'. Finally, national identity is distinguished from other identities in that it requires 'a common set of characteristics' among its people (Miller, 1995: 22, 25). In a sense, this is closer to notions of ethnicity and, arguably, should read as a belief in common characteristics in order to avoid assumptions about origins and essence. Imaginings of national identity usually require particular sets of material conditions in addition to purely symbolic resources. Of particular importance in this regard is the role played by communications media in nationally defined territories (McLoone, 1991; Malm and Wallis, 1992; Miller, 1995). Thus, national identity is partially framed and symbolically mediated by the various policies, institutional structures and cultural media that obtain in a particular country. The interface between these centralized mediating influences and domestic production and consumption represents an important focus for studies of national identity and music.

So far I have used the terms 'nation' and 'national' in the knowledge that there can be no ideal type nation or nation state. Furthermore, these terms infer a multiplicity of interpretations, the category of 'nation' often being conflated with those of 'ethnicity', 'state' and 'nation-state' (Connor, 1994). It is also useful to draw distinctions and interpret interrelations between ethnic, civic and economic constructs of nationality and the nation state (Smith, 1991; McCrone, 1998). In the case of music, the particular ideological constructs obtaining in any nation state are likely to impact on the relative status and/or support afforded to different musical styles. Although folk or traditional music has often been imbricated in the cultural–national ideologies of many European countries, reflecting an ethnic construct of national culture, more often than not statutory investment has been primarily directed towards 'international' classical music infrastructures, reflecting a civic construct of national culture. In this way, nationalism would appear to have perpetuated a deception in which 'native traditions' are employed in its rhetoric while simultaneously imposing the values of high art/modernity on society (Gellner, 1983: 57). However, this historical tendency does not necessarily apply to all nation states; moreover, it is arguable that, in recent decades, boundaries between the various 'levels' of culture have become obscured.

A recent increase in the national prominence afforded to non-classical styles of music is not unrelated to the rising significance of the global–national dialectic insofar as new conceptions of national identity and music appear to be at least partly predicated on the global economic success of domestic products. Furthermore, the type of music–national associations in any country will vary according to where any specific music lies in a 'continuum' of insider/outsider perspectives (Folkestad, 2002). This not only refers to the potential interface of emic and etic[1] views of particular cultures, but also to distinct functions of music identity within cultural groupings. Thus, we can differentiate between domestically

-produced music which may be employed emblematically (external identity) and that which serves catalytically to promote group cohesiveness and belonging (internal identity). The first of these ideas brings to mind the more obvious cultural flags such as national anthems, but it could also describe a process where traditional or 'ethnic specific' music is directed outwards to embody symbolic meanings of nation (Folkestad, 2002: 156).

Although the same or similar music may be employed in the 'insider' collective identities of a nation state, the construction of such identities is not necessarily confined to any one musical style. Indeed, identification with national unity can be achieved through the celebration of musical–cultural diversity. In many cases, though, it is not a matter of either/or but rather a dialectic of insider/outsider identities. As I shall report later, an accommodation of these seemingly opposing tendencies is articulated by identifying with internationally recognizable styles such as rock and pop – or, for that matter, classical –while at the same time retaining other musical elements that are believed to be culturally unique. However, as useful as distinctions such as internal/external, national/cultural or emblematic/catalytic might be, it cannot be assumed that either side of these dualistic concepts are realized in the context of one 'function' or another. Critically, there is a need to establish how the idea of national identity and music can relate to a dynamic view of musical experience and musical meaning.

Theoretical Approaches to National Identity and Music

Identity and Identification

National identity does not reside in music, nor is any music – not even the music used in national anthems – reducible to the function of national identity. However, while a variety of contemporary theoretical positions combine to question the ideological assumptions of nationalism, the phenomenon of nations and national identities nonetheless persists. Moreover, as several writers have illustrated, music continues to be involved in various ways with nationalist independence movements and/or struggles between and among different ethnic–national groups (Slobin, 1996; Wade, 1998). If we hold that all forms of cultural identity are socially constructed and yet have real consequences for people's lives, then any such identity needs to be regarded as a dynamic, experiential and ultimately discursive process. For while relationships between national identity and music are always socially constructed, it does not follow that all people in a particular society will respond in the same way to the proffered symbolic meanings of music that is deemed 'national'.

Hall proposes the term 'identification' as a more flexible theoretical concept than that of 'identity':

In common sense language, identification is constructed on the back of a recognition of some common origin or shared characteristics with another person or group, or with an ideal, and with the natural closure of solidarity and allegiance established on this foundation. In contrast with the 'naturalism' of this definition, the discursive approach sees identification as a construction, a process never completed ... Though not without its determinate conditions of existence, including the material and symbolic resources required to sustain it, identification is in the end, conditional, lodged in contingency. Once secured, it does not obliterate difference. (1996: 2–3)

We can say, then, that although national identity is often imagined as 'fixed', in reality it comprises multiple identifications that arise from a plurality of social contexts and subject positions. Accordingly, the term 'national identity and music' can be understood as a general process by which individuals and groups may come to perceive, cognize and articulate associations between, on the one hand, specifically musical phenomena and, on the other hand, wider socio-cultural formations associated with national culture and/or the nation state. This allows us to consider diversity in the way that national identity and music may or may not be perceived.

A strategic and flexible approach to the interpretation of collective musical identities avoids assumptions concerning the nature or essence of either music or people. Nevertheless, the process of identity formation or identification takes place in specific contexts that involve a range of material and symbolic conditions. While both types of conditions are available in music, these interrelate in complex ways. Let us imagine a repertoire of songs popular in a particular country over a historical period. If this country is strongly regarded in terms of a nationalist narrative, then many of its traditional–popular songs might be symbolically identified as anthems or revolutionary songs or as part of a distinct ethnic heritage. In other words, it could be postulated that, given the particular historical–social contexts of the country and the values espoused by nationalist ideologues and/or national elite groups within it, one or more of these categories would constitute the 'identity' of songs in the traditional–popular repertoire. Yet, as strongly associative as these forms become, there may be real circumstances where the intended public meaning or 'identity' of the song is altered or even wholly appropriated. Striking examples of the latter would be the 'alternative' interpretations of religious or national anthems by 'anarchic' rock musicians – Jimi Hendrix, The Sex Pistols and Sinéad O'Connor being notable examples.[2] Furthermore, political song forms sometimes overlap with general expressive categories that are made up of specifically musical elements. For example, the identification of a traditional–popular song as 'rebel music' might not only arise from the particular political sympathies associated with the genre but could equally represent the apprehension of lively tempi, dotted rhythms or other such musical features. At the same time, any moment of collective identification in regard to the same music would be contingent on the 'extra-musical' conditions of time, location and the social organization of performers and audiences.

Interpreting 'National' Music

Although national identity and music can be regarded as a socially constructed field of meaning, it nonetheless remains that people's beliefs about any music are dialectically related to its intra-musical elements – that is to say, to the actual sounds of music itself (Green, 1988). However, while the analysis of particular musical texts might well tell us something about specific cultural identities, it would be erroneous to assume that the music(s) of a nation state is (or are) somehow representative of that cultural–political entity or of the social structures therein. As attractive as homology theories or other culturalist interpretations of collective identity in music might be for studies of musical–national identities, they can be questioned on a number of counts (Middleton, 1990: 127–71; Frith, 1996:108; Wade, 1998: 4). First of all, this type of approach does not take account of the complex nature of mediation in the wider nexus of social relations, not least the diversity of musical genres and practices that is typical of modern societies. Secondly, reducing the idea of any type of music to the reproduction of a 'unique' culture or subculture denies the potential that music holds for individual development, cultural renewal and social change (Swanwick, 1999: 25). Furthermore, if, as often happens, the music associated with a particular socio-cultural group comes to be culturally appropriated and integrated by groups external to it, then the assumed 'expressive fit' between musical styles or substyles and particular groups of people is no longer tenable (Middleton, 1990: 152–3).

An attractive counter-argument to those theoretical positions describing the relations between national identity and music in homogenizing and/or controlling influences is suggested by the idea that music is constitutive, rather than reflective, of identity (Stokes, 1994: 12; Wade, 1998). Indeed, music is often a primary agent in the construction and maintenance of national identity (Connell and Gibson, 2003: 118). However, even in cases where music does appear to be an active agent in the (re)construction of national identity (for example Baily, 1994; Manuel, 1998), we can never wholly interpret the processes of musical–national identification in unidirectional terms. Rather, the relationship between music and national identity needs to be considered as an interpenetrative process. Accordingly, while the textual analysis approach fails to present a complete account of the identification process, we still need to retain some musicological perspective in our discussion.

To illustrate this approach, I now briefly consider how the music of Irish pop-rock group The Corrs may or may not be interpreted in terms of its 'Irishness'. The international profile and success of this band presents us with a case where identification can be interpreted simultaneously in both national and global terms. The output of The Corrs could be described as international, radio-friendly music that includes a number of musical elements commonly perceived as 'Irish' (ethnic-specific). A typical Corrs' song combines the pop-rock line-up of female vocals, electric guitar/keyboards and drum kit with the sounds of fiddle, tin whistle and other instruments associated with traditional Irish music. Structurally, their music also forges the verse/refrain formula of the pop-rock genre with a highly repetitive use of four- or eight-bar instrumental motifs. These motifs are redolent of traditional Irish dance tunes, albeit played at slower tempi and without any identifiable regional style of playing. I give this brief analysis not to suggest that music by The Corrs is or is not essentially Irish, but rather to speculate on how some of its intra-musical elements may be involved in any identification of the music as Irish.

Suppose we do believe that Irishness inheres to this music. Such a belief might lead to a celebration of the music as an expression of modern Irish identity. Conversely, while regarding the music as Irish-sounding, we might not identify with it because we perceive it to be stylistically inauthentic or because we regard its Irishness to be artificially produced for consumption in global markets. Another possibility would be that the Irish-sounding elements are not perceived but nonetheless the music is identified as Irish by virtue of extra-musical aspects such as the band members' nationality and the symbolic global success that they have achieved thus far. So, while we can 'read' a certain degree of national and musical specificity in these cultural forms, the extent and type of identifications made will depend on the contexts in, and the values with, which people perceive the music.

But where does the idea of musical–national identity stand in relation to the notion of individual aesthetic experience? While a distinction can be made between collective and subjective identifications in music, these are never separable in actual experience (Frith, 1996: 109). Another way of looking at this is to differentiate between moments of identification (aesthetic experience) and positions of identification (normative views and/or collective associations of music) (Frith, 1996: 122). As separable as these are at a theoretical level, it is questionable whether individual aesthetic experience negates essentialist views about music, as Frith (1996) argues. If we accept that common-sense views pertaining to essence and identity in music actually exist, then the common-sense views of any one individual must be considered to be at least partly constitutive of that individual's holistic musical identification(s). Musical identification can at once be experienced individually and socially and, as was suggested earlier, identification is cognized as opposed to being received as an essence. At the same time, each musical identification will have its own determinate conditions of experience made up of specific material and symbolic aspects.

Adapting the Concept of Hegemony

National identity and music constitutes a complex field of meaning that revolves around contested concepts of both music and nationhood (Connell and Gibson, 2003: 123). Rather than capitulating to a wholly relativist interpretation of the area, the Gramscian concept of hegemony enables us to regard the various discourses and practices of a society's music as a unitary cultural field (Middleton, 1990: 7–10; Diamond, 1994). Under this view 'disparate cultural and ideological elements are nevertheless held together by an articulating principle or set of central values' (Wade, 1998: 4).

There are a number of hegemonic strata to consider in the case of national identity and music. To begin with, we have the interlacing and often contesting ideologies underlying the articulation of civic, ethnic or economic national identities along with the institutional structures and dominant social groups that may support some constructions of musical 'nationalness' over others. A number of these 'national' values and articulations may find resonance in everyday musical practices and beliefs, but arguably these are unlikely to represent the diversity of beliefs and practices pertaining to music in any given society, no matter how dominant or prevalent they may appear to be. Any interpretation of music-identity power relations in a particular nation-state would also need to consider a range of insider/outsider contexts, not only in the symbolic cultural terms referred to above, but also with regard to material matters such as the commodification or 'mediatization' of indigenous musical forms (Malm and Wallis, 1992). Hegemony, then, allows us to theorize aspects of the musical–national field in the knowledge that each political entity will have its own specific configuration of musical practices, values and articulations that are constantly subject to processes of (re)negotiation from both endogenous and exogenous sources. The potential range and scope of these is now illustrated with reference to a number of cross-cultural studies.

The agency of the nation state. In many jurisdictions, the nation state continues to exert a considerable and visible influence over what music is produced, transmitted and consumed within its own territory. We might expect this to be the case in 'ethnically' constructed nations with exclusivist notions of identity (see Baily, 1994), but this influence can also be seen to operate in 'civically' constructed nations where identifications arising from 'essential', national forms of music do not appear to be of central concern. For example, Cloonan (1999) describes how a combination of broadcasting policies, censorship and copyright laws, and other cultural or legal structures serve to promote home-produced music in Britain. Likewise, Shuker and Pickering (1994) report on the impact that state interventions – particularly in regard to broadcasting quotas – have on the production and consumption of domestic forms of popular music in New Zealand. Both of these cases point to the inevitability of the nation state's involvement in ongoing constructions of national identity and music. The interventions themselves may be cultural in aspiration, or they may be motivated primarily by national industrial concerns. In either case, notions of a 'national' music or musics are perpetuated.

The articulation of nationalness in international musical forms. From a national/ international perspective, Regev (1996) describes how rock culture in Israel, originally rebellious towards accepted identities of Israeli music, was subsequently altered through processes of 'Israelization' or 'ethnicization'. The interplay of factors bringing about this eventual reversal of position vis-à-vis national identity is summarized here:

1   *socialization* – indirect conditioning by the surrounding sounds and culture (including traditional or 'ethnic-specific' musical practices);
2   *ideology of authenticity of rock* – dictating a fusion of rock with local and individual identities;
3   *discourse of national identity* – celebrating the achievements of home-produced rock music;
4   *institutional validation and recognition* – rock music featuring in symbolic national events, rock music featuring in national media presentations of domestic music (adapted from Regev, 1996: 279–80).

In this analysis, a local musical subculture with international continuities appears to have been subsumed into national culture and identity. This has not been as a result of any authoritarian regime or overt policy of cultural homogenization, but rather has been a much more subtle process arrived at from a number of planes, at national, local and international levels. The 'appropriation' is not one-sided, however, since the national identity itself has been modified by the integration of an international musical style. Though not put forward here as a 'universal' theory, it is arguable that aspects of these findings will have resonance in other national contexts (for example McLaughlin and McLoone, 2000). The idea of authenticity as an articulating principle in the interface of global and national identities will be revisited towards the end of this chapter.

Multinational interests. Multinational music industries can also become involved in the formation of 'national' music styles. Homan (2000) describes how the interests of multinational recording companies had both empowering and constraining influences on the Sydney rock scene during the 1980s. Paradoxically, he states, it was through global marketing strategies that the identity of Oz Rock was forged, and this exploitation of local identity which involved the invention of 'tradition' partially explains the problems of identity that are now associated with Australian rock (Homan, 2000: 43–4). This is reflective of a process of 'glocalization': that is, the promotion and production of localized difference for global consumption, or as Robertson more glibly puts it, 'diversity sells' (1995: 29).

Although global corporate interests may become involved in processes that foster national identity through music, it does not always follow that performers and audiences will engage with these proffered symbols of identification. Duffett (2000) describes how in 1992 a number of multinational beer companies organized and sponsored a 'national' festival of Canadian popular music. Duffett reads this situation not only in terms of the blatant exploitation that was behind the corporate sponsorship, but offers some analysis as to how the festival was used and interpreted by the performers and audience at the 'Great Canadian Party'. He states that, because the corporate sponsorship enabled domestic-based musicians to overcome the huge geographical and financial constraints involved in making national tours, the festival did leave an impact on the live music industry in Canada (Duffett, 2000: 1). Furthermore, the festival engendered a degree of national identity in this vast and culturally diverse country. Duffett, however, concludes that although there was a clear and dominant ideological message arising from this event, alternative individual and/or collective positions of Canadian identity were 'actively socially negotiated' rather than being simplistically determined by the event itself. Thus, the same event led to a range of readings summarized by Duffett in terms of 'positive', 'negative' and 'ironic' (2000: 7).

The studies referred to above illustrate that the broad category of the 'national' can have a bearing on how identifications of music are constructed or reconstructed. As a corollary to this, music practices and discourses can play a role in constituting or reconstituting national identity. However, although the same range of conditions might apply across a variety of cross-cultural settings, the interplay of these conditions combine through specific interrelations in different places and at different times. This brief review of national identity and music studies suggests an increasing significance of factors that intersect the boundaries of nation-states. Accordingly, it becomes necessary to situate any consideration of national identity and music within the less bounded contexts of globality.

Transnational Categories, National Identity and Music

In the introduction to this chapter it was argued that, far from being redundant or extinct, the idea of 'nation' continues to be rearticulated and reconstituted within global terms of identity. At the same time, concepts such as 'local in global' and 'global in local' (Robertson, 1995: 40) present an alternative range of interrelated categories with which to consider processes of identification and music. Like 'nation', these 'spaces' and 'places' are fluid concepts of identification that are supported by material and symbolic conditions. They may be connected to actual locations, but differ from the term nation insofar as they refer to transnational categories. Paradoxically, however, if national diasporas are factored into the concept of 'nation', then it could also be said that 'nation' itself has transnational continuities. Accordingly, I would suggest that alternative conceptions of music and place might in fact inform and develop a theorization of national identity and music.

Musical Intercultures

Slobin proposes the term 'interculture' to outline 'a plane of analysis that extends beyond the issues of the lively, charged, and even tumultuous interaction of parts of a "society" within nation-state bounds' (1993: 61). Three types of interculture are proposed by Slobin: namely, the 'industrial', the 'diasporic' and the 'affinity'. While industrial intercultures are often cast as homogenizing, commodifying agencies, their interaction with local consumers and with the state can also lead to nation-specific popular music forms, in a process described by Slobin as the 'local domestication of Anglo-American rock music' (1993: 61–2). This underlines an earlier argument made here on the Irishness of The Corrs and also Regev's analysis on the 'Israelization' of domestic rock music. The diasporic interculture meanwhile 'emerges from the linkages that subcultures set up across national boundaries' (Slobin, 1993: 64). Here, Slobin eschews the idea of nation and diaspora being related along the lines of a centre/periphery model. This suggests that identity formation between nations and diasporic communites are more fluid and interactive processes. For example, it has been argued that a 'renaissance' of traditional Irish music in Ireland from the 1960s onwards was fostered in no small way by an opening of communication between musicians and audiences from both the north-eastern United States and Ireland (O'Connor, 1991).

Slobin's third category of interculture, the 'affinity', may be used to describe the phenomenon of 'transnational performer-audience interest group(s)' (Slobin, 1993: 68). This is similar to the idea of 'scene' in which musicians and/or audiences from a diverse range of localities connect through mutual interest in particular substyles, musicians or repertoire (Cohen, 1999). We can also use the idea of affinity interculture to interpret how aspects from one national–musical field come to be replicated or adapted in other national–musical contexts. This is a theme fictitiously explored in the book/film *The Commitments*, (Alan Parker, 1991) in which an underprivileged young man living in Dublin has a vision of forming an American-style soul band. He sets out on this project not only because he likes the sounds and groove of soul, but also because he identifies with what he believes to be the dominant narrative and values of 'Blackness'. On the other hand, cultural affinity might also arise from conceptions of difference or alterity; the recent and spectacular growth in the consumption of 'world', 'ethnic' and 'roots' music suggests a pattern where, for some social groups, musical 'difference' has become closely associated with cultural identity (Taylor, 1997).

Visibility and Level-shifting

Slobin also proposes the analytical perspective of visibility – 'the quality of being known to an audience' – and he suggests three types of visibility: local, regional and transnational (1993: 17). Of particular relevance to studies of national identity and music is the extent to which the same musical practices and/or products can be interpreted differentially in any of these three contexts, a phenomenon referred to as 'level-shifting' (Slobin, 1993: 21). Level-shifting may occur simultaneously or over a period of time. In the latter instance, this often coincides with the career paths of musicians. The idea of level-shifting is adumbrated by Regev (1996: 282–3) in his analysis of different phases in the production and reception of music by the Israeli–Yemenite singer Ofra Haza. Respectively, these can be characterized as a middle-of-the-road domestic pop period (national/regional level of visibility), a Yemenite 'musical roots' period (local level of visibility in addition to reception among a Yemenite 'diasporic interculture') and a final period of 'Israeli-contemporary' fusion when Haza was based in the USA (transnational level of visibility). While the earlier 'roots' records might have accommodated ideas of difference and authenticity in domestic articulations of 'nationalness', the sense of national identity engendered by the 'fusion' records was mediated by a globally managed version of 'Israeliness'.

Similar patterns of change can be observed in the career path taken by Clannad in Ireland. This family group from the Donegal *Gaeltacht* (an Irish-speaking district) began in the 1970s as a folk–traditional ensemble that also integrated classical resources and practices into their music. Success in Irish-language and culture festivals brought them to national attention, where they retained an emphasis on folk song repertoire (in both English and Irish) accompanied by a progressive, traditional-oriented instrumental base. Clannad 'shifted' abruptly to an international level in 1983 with the number one success in both Irish and British charts of the theme tune for the British TV drama series *Harry's Game* (Lawrence Gordon Clark, 1982). This was a haunting choral piece in the Donegal dialect of Irish (unintelligible to most Irish and British listeners) sung *a cappella* by the members of Clannad over a minimalist synthesized string backing. Later, by abandoning much of the acoustic instrumental base of their original arrangements and by relying less on traditional songs, Clannad's music could be classified under the more global labels of 'New Age' and 'Celtic music'. Arguably, this level was the starting point for the former Clannad member Enya, who capitulated to a global market with the production of her 1988 album *Watermark*.[3] Even if we regard Enya's transregional ('Celtic') visibility as somehow originating from her musical and cultural roots, there is no evidence to suggest that this has refracted onto specifically local and national identifications of her music. In other words, while some Irish people might enjoy Enya's music and take pride in the artist's international success, the same people are more likely to identify with the assumed 'Celtic' qualities of this music than regard it in terms of a 'uniquely Irish' sound.[4]

It should be remembered, though, that international success does not necessarily supplant an artist's national or local level of visibility; indeed, it may very well enhance it. Sinéad O'Connor presents an example of a musician who had a meteoric rise as an international rock star in the early 1990s. Since then, the Irish-born musician appears to have consciously sought out more intimate and informal modes of performer presentation (eschewing the persona of a rock star), a choice not unrelated to her gradual return to 'musical roots'. Arguably, O'Connor's most 'Irish' recording to date has been the 2003 album *Sean-Nós Nua*,[5] a musical memory of the (mainly Irish) traditional songs experienced in her own lifetime. The very different patterns revealed by the respective careers of Sinéad O'Connor and Enya suggest that the interplay of local, national and international levels is best understood in dialectical terms, rather than as some inevitable trajectory or continuum of success. Although the international visibility of domestic music and musicians can play an important role in the construction of national–musical identifications, as I shall now argue, any such potential relationships are contingent on beliefs about musical authenticity.

Authenticity

Authenticity, Identity and Music

Notions of authenticity are closely linked to those of identity (Stokes, 1994: 6). We can speak of authenticity or authenticities as assumed qualities that are 'given' in specific cultural contexts and, indeed, this approach is strategically used below when I argue that the rearticulation of old authenticities and the construction of new authenticities combine to redefine relationships between national identity and music. However, this needs to be regarded as a speculative analysis since ultimately any occasion of musical authenticity or authentication will depend on the agency of performers and listeners. While authenticity can be said to occur wherever there is discourse about music, it is 'an area that is marked by radical differences depending on the style of the music, the ethnicity and nationality of the musicians and other factors' (Green, 2001: 103). Furthermore, people's beliefs about musical authenticity can be addressed to such different factors as setting/ context, repertoire/material, 'style'/'soul' or combinations of these – discursive parameters that are reflected in much academic folklore and anthropology (Johnson, 2000: 283).[6] Moore proposes three possible modes of performance presentation that offer different levels of authentication (and identification) for listening subjects:

> *First person authenticity:* Artists speak the truth of their own situation.
> *Second person authenticity:* Artists speak the truth of the situation of (absent) others.
> *Third person authenticity:* Artists speak the truth of their own culture, thereby representing (present) others. (2002: 209)

The idea of third person authenticity is particularly applicable to our discussion here, though the other modes will also bear on issues of national–musical identity. For example, if Sinéad O'Connor's performances are considered to be authentically Irish, such a view might arise not only from the perceived Irishness of some of her material and/or performance practices, but also from her public/ private persona along with her views on a range of social issues in contemporary Irish society.

While agreeing with Martin Stokes' description of authenticity as 'a discursive trope of great persuasive power', it is difficult to concur with the assertion that 'authenticity is definitely not a property of music, musicians and their relations to an audience' (Stokes, 1994: 7). As with identity, I do not suggest that authenticity might somehow reside 'in' the music, but if the authentic is significant in music discourse then it follows that it is involved in relations between and among producers and consumers of music. As Taylor (1997: 22) describes, for musicians and listeners alike, authenticity can be real insomuch as it is believed in, talked about, and can actually influence musical behaviours.

In critical theory, authenticity has been negatively associated with the commodification of music products, and with the mythologization and fetishization of 'ethnic' and 'folk' musics. Indeed, the very idea of authenticity is premised on assumptions of wholeness, truth and organicism, but it is an ideology that fails to provide the material basis for such claims (Adorno, 1973). Ordinary people may also question the proffered authenticity of some types of 'national' music by considering it in such terms as exploitative, manipulative, 'touristy', kitsch and so on. In the context of globality, musical authenticities can be simultaneously celebrated and negated. Taylor (1997: 125–43) paradoxically describes how the West's demand for authenticity from idealized, 'pre-modern' music cultures is coupled with the strategic 'in-authenticities' of non-Western musicians and music cultures that choose to incorporate modern elements into their music. The global search for, and celebration of, local musical authenticities can impact on the identification of that music at a national level. For example, most of the traditional Irish 'supergroups' that were popular in the 1960s, 1970s and 1980s produced what might be called a generic traditional sound. However, the subsequent signing of musicians with more local-based styles by major 'world music' labels in the 1990s actually helped to increase the popularity of such substyles at a domestic level. On the other hand, the commercialization of traditional music is viewed by some as an inauthentic practice, through what might be referred to as the 'discourse of selloutism' (Taylor, 1997: 23).

The discourse of authenticity is also concerned with hybridization. Hybridization is a concept that tends to be associated with the postmodern condition of globality, but it does in fact have a history – a summary glance at the history of music in Europe bears this out. However, whereas colonial and extreme nationalist perspectives regarded hybrid cultural forms as inauthentic, the discourse of globalization tends to regard hybridity and syncretism as an antidote to essentialist notions of identity and ethnicity, a 'celebration of surfaces', as it were (Nederveen Pieterse, 1995: 54–5). However, this may be to oversimplify the matter because, as we have already seen, pre-modern musical products can be highly valued in postmodern cultures of consumption. Yet the very consumption of these cultural products changes how they are received, 'while engagement authenticates, its consumption de-authenticates' (Friedman, 1994: 104).

A Transitional Model of Authenticity

From the internal perspective of nation-states, authenticity can be employed to construct, deconstruct and reconstruct identities. To illustrate how this might happen in the case of music, I adapt Colin Graham's theoretical model of old, new and ironic authenticities in the negotiation of national identity (Graham, 1999).

First of all, an old authenticity would refer to nineteenth- and early twentieth-century notions of 'national music' that represent the 'essence' and 'natural characteristics' of the nation's people (combining ethic and civic conceptions of national identity). New authenticities might include some of old authenticity's beliefs about music's inherent ability to reflect the spirit and outlook of the people, but they eschew a direct link with 'nation' in the narrow cultural sense. From the perspectives of new authenticities, links with other cultures are desirable and, therefore, hybrid forms arising from the nation's traditional music are validated. New authenticities would also incorporate the idea of 'economy', in addition to those of 'nation' and 'state'. Under this view, the nation-state's music can also be regarded in terms of exportable products. The third type of authenticity is the ironic. Ironic appropriations of nationally celebrated musical forms construct alternative perspectives on national identity that may or may not involve implicit and/or explicit statements of social critique.

These three categories of authenticity for music and national identity are presented here as ideal types. Arguably, the predominant site for the negotiation of national identity and music takes place between old and new authenticities, as these may be seen to reflect a state of transition from a bounded, cultural and political view of the nation-state to one that might include supra-national configurations and the nation-state's place within a global economy. That said, ironic musical authenticities may play a pivotal role in 'interrupting' the traditional–progressive hegemony. The discourse of musical authenticity can be viewed as a complex site of contestation involving civic, ethnic and economic conceptions of national identity. Arguably though, some articulations of authenticity are less subtly arrived at than others. Indeed, it could be said that many cultural–economic entrepreneurs set out to appropriate collective imaginings of ethnicity or 'nationalness' in music to promote the idea of a 'national market brand' – for example Ó Cinnéide (2002) equally regards Riverdance and Guinness as economic signifiers of Irishness. The formation of these more globally oriented authenticities represents an altered hegemonic balance insofar as old authenticities and/or ethnic conceptions of national identity are subsumed within its discourse.

'Dúlamán'[7]

I now present one example of how music can be centrally involved in the process of constructing new authenticities within the context of national identity. The cultural product in question was a commercial that was broadcast for several months on Irish TV in 1999 to promote the privatization of Telecom Éireann, the then state-owned telecommunications company. This was the first time that the Irish public had been invited to buy out a state-owned company and on such a large scale. Music featured highly in the TV commercial, so much so, in fact, that it closely resembled a music video production. The piece of music was based on 'Dúlamán', a traditional song associated with the west coast of Ireland, and it was arranged and produced by Dónal Lunny, a well-known musician who has been performing, arranging and producing music in Ireland for over three decades. The basis of Lunny's music is traditional Irish, but he also incorporates elements of modern production along with other 'folk' or 'ethnic' genres. At a national level, Lunny is both commercially successful and critically acclaimed. However, because his music includes syncretic genres, the authenticity of his music often features in the traditional–progressive debate within Irish music discourse.

The musical product of 'Dúlamán' represents a highly sophisticated level of post-production and includes musicians from a wide variety of genres (including classical). This cultural product is significant in a number of ways. First of all there is an almost complete integration of the musical and the visual elements; if anything, the visual is subsumed by the musical. Secondly, music that is derived from 'authentic', Gaelic, traditional and non-commercial sources now appears to be appropriated by the interests of modernity, prosperity and plurality. The sense of plurality is communicated by the skilful layering of voices and textures, and also, perhaps, by a gradual build-up to a grand unison finale. We could also speculate that the advertisement aims to be as inclusive as possible in promoting this new form of 'privatized' Irish identity. The initial images show 'real' people with different types of Irish voices: young and old, traditional and progressive, rural and urban. And, as if to emphasize the new sense of modernity, Lambeg drums (symbolic of Northern Ireland Protestantism) are included in the musical fabric, perhaps as a further emblem of inclusiveness and reconciliation. Gradually, the number of voices and instrumental layers grows, and as this momentum gathers, a sense of transition from state-owned to private-owned seems to be articulated by the introduction of a progressive beat and sound, tempered by the retention of an overall acoustic effect.

It would appear that the creators of this TV commercial were consciously attempting to link in to some kind of collective consciousness, an Irish TV nation or 'imagined community'. The function of this advertisement was, of course, to sell a particular product but in order to achieve this objective it needed to endorse a transitional image of Ireland and Irishness. To do this it was necessary to propose a new type of 'authenticity', a process that was, in part, facilitated by a syncretism of traditional and contemporary musical ideas that would be identifiable as 'Irish'. As slick (and enjoyable) as the production of 'Dúlamán' was, the commercial poignantly failed to deliver on its promise of shared national prosperity: less than two years after this major publicity drive, Telecom Éireann's many thousands of investors were forced to sell their shares at a substantial loss as the recently privatized company was purchased by a multinational telecommunications group.

Conclusions

In spite of the growing influences of global contexts, the idea of national identity continues to be of importance in musical discourses and practices. Music can be involved in the construction or reconstruction of national identities in both material and symbolic ways. Nation-states continue to promote the idea of music as cultural symbol and/or national product, just as global markets have an interest in perpetuating and commodifying musical difference at the level of nation. Conceptions of national identity and music can range from exclusivist notions of musical essence and origin to those that celebrate diversity and hybridity. The negotiation and articulation of such contesting identities in any one music–national field can be interpreted through the theoretical concept of hegemony. Within this perspective, the construction of identity and difference can be seen as part of the same process. Thus, at both national and global levels, the diachronic tendencies of musical homogenization and musical heterogenization are dialectically linked.

Although identity and authenticity can be viewed as ideologically loaded concepts, people's common-sense beliefs around these qualities impact on musical experience. Identification with or in music is at once individual and collective. Any moment of engagement with music may be interpreted in terms of its aesthetic import, but aesthetic experiences cannot be completely divorced from positions of collective identity, including those of national identity. At the same time, music does not simply reflect or, for that matter, constitute national identity. Music–national identifications are discursive constructs, articulated through specific material and symbolic conditions. These include the sonic and structural properties of music and the social contexts in which it is sounded or heard, the mediating influence of national and non-national agencies, and the sets of values with which individuals or groups experience music.

While the category of nation presents an appropriate focus for studies of music and collective identity, an analysis of this kind cannot be divorced from a consideration of transnational categories and the relative fluidity between various levels of music production and consumption. A common thread in much of the interplay between national and global contexts of musical identification is the idea of authenticity. The theorization of 'transitional authenticities' suggests a strategic approach for interpreting the evolving relationships between national identity and music within the context of globality.

Notes

1 Terms used to distinguish the perspectives of those directly involved in particular cultural contexts and/or practices from the perspectives of those who observe and analyse the same contexts and/or practices.

2 Rock guitarist Jimi Hendrix (1942–1970) gave an ironic performance of 'The Star Spangled Banner' at the Woodstock festival of 1969; in 1977 The Sex Pistols had a UK no. 1 hit with their punk version of 'God Save the Queen'; Irish rock singer Sinéad O'Connor provoked US audiences in 1992 by her refusal to sing at concerts where the national anthem was played and by desecrating a photo of the pope on national TV. Paradoxically, much of O'Connor's subsequent work appears to have been inspired

by a 'post-feminist' interpretation (or appropriation) of sounds, images and beliefs from Irish /Catholic identities.

3   Eithne Ní Bhraonáin (Enya) left Clannad in 1982.

4   This was one finding to emerge from interview data gathered between 1999 and 2002 as part of my own doctoral research on the theme of national identity and music in Ireland.

5   *Sean nós* is a Gaelic term used to describe a traditional style of singing practised in some parts of Ireland. The title for O'Connor's album *Sean-Nós Nua* roughly translates as 'old-style songs sung in a new way'.

6   These categories emerged from the analysis of interviews conducted at music events between 1999 and 2002 as part of my doctoral research.

7   'Dúlamán' was an instrumental–choral version of a traditional Gaelic song arranged by Dónal Lunny and produced for an Irish TV commercial in 1999. It was subsequently released in the same year as a single CD/cassette recording.

Discography

Clannad, *Clannad, The Ultimate Collection* (BMG UK and Ireland/RCA, 74321 48672, 1997).

Corrs, The, *Forgiven not Forgotten* (WEA/Atlantic, B00005J7, 1995).

Enya, *Watermark* (WEA/Warner, B000002LR, 1988).

Lunny, Dónal, Coolfin and Friends, 'Dúlamán' (CD Single) (Dublin: Hummingbird Records, HDCDS004, 1999).

O'Connor, Sinéad, *Sean-Nós Nua* (Dublin: Hummingbird Records, HBCD0030, 2002).

Filmography

Clark, Lawrence Gordon (1982) *Harry's Game*.

Parker, Alan, (1991) *The Commitments*.

Chapter 2

Where Does World Music Come From? Globalization, Afropop and the Question of Cultural Identity[1]

David Murphy

World Music, Afropop and 'Otherness'

The term 'world music' was coined in the 1980s as a means of categorizing popular music that does not fit the mould of contemporary international rock and pop, which is dominated by music from the United States and Britain. In particular, world music became synonymous with music from the non-Western world, which was beginning to find its way into the consciousness of a number of influential Western music producers. However, as Martin Roberts (1992: 231) has pointed out, the precise meaning of 'world music' remains extremely fluid. For example, in Britain and the United States, the classification of music as 'world music' is often a question of language, generally – but not exclusively – referring to songs not in English. However, in France, the situation seems to depend less on linguistic than on racial or ethnic criteria: French music is, understandably, not categorized as world music but music from the French Caribbean is, even though this region is governed as part of the French nation.[2] Whatever criteria are used, it becomes clear that, as a category, world music is concerned with marking out 'otherness', whether linguistic, racial or ethnic.[3]

This concern with otherness is particularly evident in relation to popular music from Africa, generically termed Afropop.[4] For many Western critics, the strength of Afropop resides precisely in the fact that it is seen to be radically different to Western pop music, which is regarded as increasingly commercial and homogenized. Alongside otherness, 'authenticity' ranks as the other major recurring theme in the work of African music enthusiasts, many of whom view African popular music as an authentic expression of cultural identity, against which the commercialized music of the West pales in comparison.[5] Paradoxically, Afropop is also criticized in some quarters for its lack of authenticity, due to its use of certain Western instruments and musical conventions. However, there are many dangers in positing an authentic African music (from either of these points of view): musical styles can vary widely from one region of Africa to another, and most contemporary African popular music demonstrates a hybridity of form, based on borrowings from different cultures within and without Africa.

An informed discussion of Afropop must recognize this complexity as well as confronting the issues raised by the ways in which the music is mediated for the West. Accordingly, this chapter will examine the role of contemporary African popular music as an expression of cultural identity in Africa, focusing on the particular case of Youssou N'Dour from Senegal, while also analysing the means by which this music is repackaged and reinvented for consumption in the West. In particular, Mark Hudson's novel *The Music in My Head* (1999) will provide a useful insight into Western critical attitudes towards African popular music. This chapter will also explore the connection between world music and the influential theories of writers such as Homi K. Bhabha (1990, 1994) and Paul Gilroy (1993) on the cultural hybridity produced by the process of globalization. Basically, it will attempt to provide some tentative answers to the following questions: is world music the popular expression of a newly emerging, hybrid 'global' cultural identity? Or is it necessary to examine this music in its national or local contexts?

Popular Music in Africa: Syncretism and Hybridity

In the opening chapter of his influential book *Popular Musics of the Non-Western World* (1988: 1–3), Peter Manuel discusses the difficulties in defining popular music and, particularly, in distinguishing it from folk music as an expression of cultural identity. When it comes to defining the popular, it has proven extremely difficult to theorize the difference between what is sometimes referred to as the 'authentically' popular and the 'commercially' popular: does it refer to culture as produced within specific communities or culture as commercial product sold to the 'masses'? Generally speaking, most critics agree that, in the modern world, forms of popular music emerge in societies where there is a clear distinction between producers and consumers of music, and where there is also a mass media complex capable of relaying this music to a wide audience. On the other hand, folk music is seen as a form passed from one generation to the next within specific communities, although this does not necessarily mean that folk music is 'simple' and 'unchanging'; on the contrary, folk music is often more complex in form than much popular music (even though such working distinctions are useful, the distinction between different types of music – pop, folk, classical, jazz – remains highly problematic, and the boundaries between such categories are highly fluid). For the casual Western listener, it is easy to assume that all African music is folk music. The dominant Western vision of Africa as a backward, underdeveloped continent holds little room for the notion that Africa might possess either the capital or the sophisticated urban culture necessary for the development of a popular music in the Western sense of the term. However, contemporary African popular music is often very different from traditional ethnic folk musics. As various critics have shown, African musicians have proven adept at borrowing instruments and styles both from the West and from other parts of Africa. Timothy Taylor has commented that 'the very malleability of music makes possible local appropriations and alterations ... resulting in all kinds of syncretisms and hybridities, which themselves syncretize and hybridize' (1997: xv), and it has become commonplace to speak of the hybridity and syncretism of Afropop, of its seemingly boundless capacity to adapt and merge with other musics (see Stapleton and May, 1987; Ewens, 1991). In the course of this chapter, I will be using syncretism and hybridity as largely synonymous terms: the specific vision of hybridity proposed by Bhabha will be examined below.

However, a number of critics, both Western and African, have rejected this idea, arguing that Afropop is an alien cultural form in Africa. The work of the Cameroonian novelist and ethnomusicologist Francis Bebey is typical of this approach. In his influential work *African Music: A People's Art* (1975), Bebey sets out to discuss 'authentic' forms of African music, which he interprets as traditional African folk music. In fact, nowhere in the text does Bebey even acknowledge the existence of a contemporary popular African music, at one point warning about the dangers of imported music that might endanger the purity of 'authentic African music' (1975: 33).

As Neil Lazarus argues in *Nationalism and Cultural Practice in the Postcolonial World* (1999: 196–9), such essentialist notions about African culture can be countered on a number of fronts. For a start, much of the so-called 'alien', 'foreign' music that has shaped Afropop is, in fact, African in origin. For example, the first great pan-African popular music was the Congolese rumba, which emerged from the two Congos – the Democratic Republic of the Congo, formerly Zaire, and the Republic of the Congo, formerly the People's Republic of the Congo – in the 1950s. (One of the leading exponents of the Congolese rumba from the 1950s until his untimely death in the mid-1990s was François Luambo Makiadi, known to one and all as Franco: for a sample of his work, see Franco, 2000). In a classic example of Paul Gilroy's 'Black Atlantic' axis of cultural hybridity between the black cultures of Africa and the Americas, this music borrowed heavily from Afro-Cuban music, particularly son, which had been developed by the descendants of African slaves.[6] Equally, African musicians of the 1960s and 1970s were heavily influenced by African-American soul, jazz and funk stars, particularly James Brown, who was a huge star on the African continent, where he embarked on a major tour in the mid-1970s. One can also question Bebey's vision of African folk music as an unchanging, timeless cultural form. Cultures are constantly evolving, borrowing and adapting materials from other cultures, and African folk music is no exception to this rule. For example, in West Africa, the Islamic influence on certain forms of folk music is obvious but, in many cases, the Islamic presence is barely a century old, which does not exactly constitute time immemorial.

Rather than searching for an imaginary 'authenticity' in Afropop, one must recognize that this music is the expression of a modern and predominantly urban

African sensibility that merges various Western and African elements to form something new.[7] As Graeme Ewens argues:

> It is pointless to condemn any kind of 'fusion' music for a lack of authenticity. The authentic music is the music people listen to and live with, not that which is preserved in a state of near-death to be pulled out each year to mark some 'traditional' festival or other in a tourist village. (1991: 24)

African pop music is marked by syncretism of diverse 'African' and 'Western' elements in terms of musical style and lyrical content, as well as in the image projected by bands to their audience. For example, in the 1970s and early 1980s, the famous Malian musician/vocalist Salif Keïta, in his work with the Rail Band and, subsequently, Les Ambassadeurs, helped to create a startlingly hybrid form of music.[8] Keïta's lead guitarist, Manfila Kante, led many of their songs with a lilting guitar sound that modified the phrasing of the previously dominant Afro-Cuban son, quickening the pace of the music to create a cascading spiral of notes in imitation of the sound of the *kora* (a 24-stringed West African instrument, often compared to a harp). Kante's guitar was punctuated by Afro-Cuban brass sections, and the songs were driven by Keïta himself with his soaring, melismatic vocals and often deeply traditional lyrics, expressing the values of Mande culture: for instance, the Ambassadeurs' best-known track, 'N'Toman' ['My Namesake'], is a celebration of love and marriage in a series of Malian towns (see Keïta, 1997). In terms of lyrical content, these groups might have appeared traditional but their syncretic music projected an image of vibrant modernity that was very attractive, particularly to a young African audience, both in Mali and other parts of West Africa (the Ambassadeurs had moved to the regional economic capital of Abidjan in the late 1970s to reach a wider audience).

African pop music can thus be seen as a constantly evolving and highly complex form of cultural expression in contemporary Africa. Indeed, the influential critic Abiola Irele has argued that, 'it is the wide appeal of [African] popular music that makes it the most important single source of sustenance for millions on [the African] continent' (1993: 71). It is virtually omnipresent in the modern African city, forming the backdrop to everyday life: on the radio, the television, in the streets as teenagers blast out their favourite tunes on ghetto blasters, and especially at night in nightclubs and at concerts. In the harsh, competitive world of the African city, Afropop creates an 'imagined community' of listeners, providing a sense of shared cultural identity.[9] For instance, during the 1980s, in then Zaire, the exuberant soukous music of Papa Wemba (one of his best-known albums is *Le Voyageur* [The Traveller]; see Wemba, 1992) and his fellow *sapeurs*, with their designer clothes and glamorous public personas, provided a much-needed escape from the dourness of life under the dictatorship of Mobutu Sese Seko, who had imposed a strict code of national dress in the 1970s as part of his 'authenticity' drive.[10] Although it is a war-ravaged country in which the state has almost entirely collapsed, the Congo has a rich musical culture that is highly influential in other parts of Africa, and is one of the few sources of national pride for many Congolese.

Essentially, for its African audience, Afropop constitutes a dynamic and effervescent cultural practice that is both resolutely 'modern' and engaged in an intercultural dialogue, while also recognizably 'African'. I do not wish here to elide the major cultural differences between different regions of Africa. For example, the melismatic vocals and pounding polyrhythms of much Senegalese music do not travel well in central and southern Africa. This fact was brought home to me forcefully at a double-header concert in Dakar in December 1995, featuring the Senegalese singer Baaba Maal, and the Congolese soukous star Koffi Olomide. I attended with a Congolese friend who was deeply unimpressed by the Senegalese star's music, which he found alien and complex, a response this music often meets in the West. However, many African popular musics cross ethnic and political boundaries within Africa and come to be seen as an expression of a popular 'African' culture, as well as acting as expressions of specific ethnic or national cultures. For instance, the soukous of the 1980s and 1990s – a direct descendant of the trans-African Congolese rumba but with a souped-up beat – borrows from Latin rhythms, calypso and even includes some Hawaiian guitar. However, within much of Africa, soukous and its latest variant, ndombolo, are widely seen as 'archetypical African' music, as it has become *the* main popular music of many African countries such as Kenya and Tanzania. National identities may be relatively weak in Africa, but many Africans have a strong sense of their own ethnic identity, as well as of their identity as 'Africans'. Afropop with its myriad forms and styles provides a fascinating example of the way in which the local/national and the 'African' are negotiated in Africa itself. Indeed, as the African market for popular music has expanded, dominant styles such as soukous have increasingly become the 'African' norm, making it more difficult for new, 'local' forms to break through to a wider African audience.

The tension between the global and the local has been at the heart of much recent debate on popular music. In his study of world music, Tony Mitchell uses Appadurai's concept of the five spheres of influence, which govern the processes of globalization – ethnoscapes, mediascapes, technoscapes, financescapes, ideoscapes (Appadurai, 1991) – to explore the global and the local aspects of music in various locations: 'Ethnicity and ideology are important aspects of contemporary popular music, giving it a sense of defining local community, particularly when it is confronted with broader narratives of globalization and nationalism' (Mitchell, 1996: 1). Equally, Timothy Taylor has argued that theories of globalization have often been too abstract and generalizing: 'many analyses of globalization more often than not fail to take into account experiences of real people' (1997: xvi). I agree entirely with these attempts to nuance the analysis of globalization and, in the remainder of this chapter, I will follow the approach outlined by Mitchell and Taylor, paying attention to the local, in attempting to understand the global.

'Mediating' Afropop: The World Music Market

Most critics argue that Afropop is a genuine expression of African popular culture(s), despite their disagreements about the nature of these cultures. However, the issue of its reception and status here in the West raises a series of problematic questions.[11] Taylor comments incisively on the way in which world music is marketed as 'both timeless and new at the same time' (1997: 28), an antidote to 'the tired' popular music of the West and the expression of an 'authentic', uncommercial culture. He convincingly argues that many critics construct African cultures as 'natural' in contrast to the complex 'civilizations' of the West; Africa and Third World countries in general are seen to share a 'single', monolithic culture while Western culture is diverse and multi-layered (Taylor, 1997: 125–6). Equally, it would be wrong simply to assume that the Afropop marketed in the West as world music is an 'authentic' expression of contemporary popular African cultures. As Charles Hamm perceptively argues, 'mediation' is a key concept in understanding how African music is transmitted to the West:

> [M]ost Europeans and North Americans know this music mostly from performances in the West or from recordings produced for export; and anyone who has heard African pop music in Africa itself understands that mediation usually takes place when this music is performed abroad, through the intervention of entrepreneurs and managers and the intrusion of musicians from other parts of Africa or even the West. (1989: 214)

The African popular music that is heard in the West sometimes bears little relation to the music widely available in Africa, and as we shall see with the case of Youssou N'Dour below, such mediation can produce a completely different style of music altogether. One should also note that the impetus for such mediation is not necessarily the result of record company pressure but can also be the result of the African artist's desire to break into the lucrative Western music mainstream of 'international' pop. Either way, it is 'the global market' that influences these changes to the music.

This attempt to repackage the music for consumption in the West is one of the chief ironies of world music, as it is usually marketed precisely for its exotic otherness, its distinctly un-Western, uncommercial qualities. However, this view of African popular music ignores certain fundamental realities of the music scene in Africa, the most fundamental of which is the fact that Afropop is deeply enshrined within a commercial, capitalist system. In fact, its often blatant commercialism would shock many of its 'alternative' fans in the West, who see in it a radical cultural practice. The militant, oppositional music of the late Nigerian musician Fela Kuti is often taken as an example of the radical nature of Afropop but, in many ways, he is the exception that proves the rule. (The songs 'Zombie', 'Coffin for Head of State' and 'ITT' are classic examples of his attacks against the corruption of the various Nigerian military and civilian regimes of the 1970s and 1980s; see Kuti, 1999.) For example, other Nigerian musicians, such as Chief Ebenezer Obey, the king of juju music, often praise wealthy businessmen in their songs (for examples of his 'good time' music, see Obey, 1998). In fact, these businessmen often act as sponsors for bands, providing instruments and other equipment (see Waterman, 1990 for a history of juju music). In Senegal, musicians often sing the praises of wealthy, Islamic holy men, known as *marabouts*, in return for spiritual, but also financial, rewards.

The emphasis on Afropop's difference from Western pop music also runs the risk of seeing influence purely in terms of the West's influence on Africa. As was mentioned above, the Congolese rumba and its successor, soukous, had a profound influence on popular music throughout much of sub-Saharan Africa. In a brilliant analysis of popular music in West Africa, John Collins and Paul Richards challenge the vision of 'traditional' Africa as a continent of isolated villages, turned in on themselves, which was revolutionized by contact with the West. Instead, they stress the fact that Africans have long been open to influences from other parts of the continent, and they believe that African music is a classic example of this cultural dynamic (Collins and Richards, 1989: 36–7; see also Lazarus, 1999: 203–4, 214).

Youssou N'Dour: From Senegalese Icon to World Music Star

The career of the Senegalese pop star Youssou N'Dour provides a fascinating example of the evolution of African popular music since the 1970s, and also of its reception and mediation in the West (for accounts of N'Dour's career, see Stapleton and May, 1987: 119–22; Bender, 1991: 35–40; Ewens, 1991: 72–5). He is a member of the dominant Wolof ethnic group and he was born into a family of *griots* or in Tukolor *gawulos*, a caste of storytellers and musicians, who are charged with the important task of preserving the myths and values of their society, and also of singing the praises of certain noble families to which they are attached.[12] However, even though his mother was a well-known musician and performer in Dakar, his parents were reluctant to let him enter the unseemly world of popular music. His remarkable, piercing voice, with its tremendous vocal range, attracted the interest of several groups but, in 1975, when he was just 16, he ended up singing for the biggest Senegalese band of all, the legendary Star Band. This group had been formed in 1960 to perform Afro-Cuban music and Congolese rumbas at Senegal's independence celebrations. Throughout the 1960s and early 1970s, the Star Band continued to play Cuban-style music, often translating the Spanish lyrics into Wolof. However, as the 1970s progressed their sound became increasingly 'Africanized', introducing more percussion instruments (particularly the *tama*, the talking drum), which are integral to local folk musics, each drum playing a specific role in different rituals and festivals.

This process of 'Africanization' must be seen in the wider context of the strongly 'nationalist' post-independence period in Africa. Across the continent, many scholars and artists were engaged in either the revival of old cultural forms or the search for new, distinctive 'national' modes of cultural expression, which modified and adapted various ethnic traditions and cast them as 'national culture'. For example, countries such as Guinea and Mali created national and regional *orchestres* (a term which refers to 'pop bands' rather than 'classical' orchestras) to express these new, national popular musics. Effectively, this cultural project sought to break with the colonial period through the assertion of an 'authentically African' identity. In this atmosphere, the desire to adapt popular music to 'local' culture grew ever stronger. Afro-Cuban music, although established as a 'popular' form of music in Africa, increasingly came to be seen by many as a 'foreign' style of music. For example, the celebrated Senegalese filmmaker Ousmane Sembene associates Afro-Cuban music with the despised African bourgeois elite in his satirical film *Xala* [The Curse] (1974). The real Star Band is even shown playing at a high-society wedding (this was shortly before N'Dour joined the group) in a plush suburb of Dakar. Throughout the film, the lilting sound of this Afro-Caribbean music is pitted against the sparse sound of the xalam (a three-stringed guitar), played by one of the beggars who are constantly harassed by the police on behalf of their bourgeois masters. The xalam is accompanied by a harsh, guttural voice, singing a political allegory in Wolof, denouncing the bourgeoisie. In this musical duel, the traditional xalam is victorious, being presented as the cultural expression of the masses while Afro-Cuban music is dismissed as appealing solely to a Westernized elite. Sembene's critique of Afro-Cuban pop music is deliberately overstated and forms part of his polemical assault on the African bourgeoisie, possibly also betraying a rather conservative attitude towards 'youth' culture on the part of the then 51-year-old director. However, it is nonetheless indicative of much cultural thinking in 1970s Senegal, and elsewhere in Africa: rather than looking outside for cultural influences, Africans were increasingly turning towards local cultures for inspiration (see Murphy, 2000: 98–123, for analysis of *Xala*'s representation of the socio-cultural situation in 1970s Senegal).

The Star Band went through various mutations at the end of the 1970s and early 1980s, first being reformed as Etoile de Dakar and subsequently as Super Etoile (these names, 'Star of Dakar' and 'Super Star' play on the anglicized name of the original band). As N'Dour took the leading role in these new bands, the 'Africanization' of the music gathered pace, with up to seven types of drum being used. This fusion of Afro-Caribbean music, Western pop and Wolof folk music was christened mbalax, its name referring to the distinctive rhythm of the pounding music played at wrestling matches in Senegal.[13] The link to wrestling has not disappeared. N'Dour provided the television soundtrack for the major Senegalese wrestling match between 'Tyson' and 'Bombardier' on Christmas Day 2002 (N'Dour, 2002). However, mbalax is primarily a dance music, based on complex polyrhythms and abrupt changes of tempo and it has proven to have an enduring appeal in Senegal, spawning a whole range of dance crazes. When in Dakar, Youssou N'Dour regularly plays six nights a week at his nightclub, the Thiosane, and he has no difficulty in attracting crowds of 100,000 people to his stadium gigs. According to Wolfgang Bender (1991: 40), by the mid-1980s, his cassettes released in Senegal were selling up to 150,000 copies each, which is a remarkable 'official' figure in a country where cassette piracy is such a common feature – if Bender's figures are accurate, the real number of cassettes sold must be far higher than this.

Youssou N'Dour's role in the 'Africanization' of Senegalese pop music, and his lyrics, which often invoke Senegalese history and culture (particularly that of his own ethnic group, the Wolof), have placed him at the heart of Senegalese popular culture. This does not mean that mbalax can be seen as *the* national pop music. Over the last 20 years, N'Dour has faced challenges to his supremacy on the Senegalese pop scene from the likes of Omar Pène, Super Diamono and Ismaël Lô (himself a former member of Super Diamono), who have deliberately projected a rebellious, streetwise image in order to counter the appeal of the more respectable N'Dour (see Omar Pène and Super Diamono, 1993). Moreover, mbalax is not representative of all ethnic traditions in Senegal, a country where there are seven major ethnic groups. Musicians from smaller ethnic groups have come to the fore in the 1990s; for example, Baaba Maal sings in Pulaar, evoking Fulani traditions and culture. In Ousmane Sembene's 1992 film *Guelwaar*, which deals with issues of inclusion and minority cultures in Senegal, it is highly significant that Baaba Maal sings a number of songs, in Pulaar, on the soundtrack.[14] Despite these rival claims to his popular supremacy, Youssou N'Dour remains extremely popular with both a young and an older audience. Equally, his international success, although modest by Western standards, is a source of immense national pride, which appears to transcend ethnic and religious barriers. One Senegalese academic has even written a book comparing elements of N'Dour's work with the verse of both canonical French authors Baudelaire, La Fontaine and Racine and Senegal's former poet-president Léopold Senghor (Sankhare, 1998). His wealth has allowed him to become a major player in Senegalese society, co-owning a newspaper and a radio station as well as running his own recording studio in Dakar, Xippi [Eyes Open], which is used to promote young Senegalese groups. For example, Youssou N'Dour helped to launch the career of Cheikh Lô, producing his album *Né la thiass* [Gone in a Flash] (1996). Above all, N'Dour is seen as a symbol of an emerging, dynamic and modernized Africa, which is self-confident and successful. In January 2003, a video and audio piracy scandal involving N'Dour's production company brought the singer severe, and sometimes vitriolic, criticism in certain parts of the Senegalese press. However, in the same week, he played a series of sell-out concerts in venues throughout Senegal, indicating the depth of public affection for him.

Youssou N'Dour was thus already a major popular music star within Senegal, and further afield in Africa, when he was 'discovered' by the West in the mid-1980s at the beginning of the world music boom. He signed a deal with Virgin Records and gained massive media exposure through his performances on the Amnesty International World Tour with Bruce Springsteen, Sting and Peter Gabriel, the last of whom he also supported on an extensive US tour in 1986. During this same period, other African acts such as King Sunny Ade, of Nigeria, and Salif Keïta were also signed to major Western labels: the arrival of Afropop in the Western mainstream appeared imminent. However, the threatened breakthrough never took place. Youssou N'Dour was released from his contract by Virgin Records after three albums that achieved only modest sales. In the 1990s, he signed a new deal with Sony and had a number one hit in several countries with the song 'Seven Seconds', a duet with Neneh Cherry, which was quite an interesting and atmospheric, international pop tune, but one totally divested of any overtly 'African' elements. Although parts of the song are in Wolof, there are none of mbalax's trademark changes of tempo or swirling polyrhythms. Despite this brief but lucrative success, Youssou N'Dour has remained on the margins of the Western pop market, unknown to the average pop consumer.

The Music in My Head: Staying 'True' to the Music?

Mark Hudson's novel *The Music in My Head* provides an intriguing portrait of Youssou N'Dour, thinly disguised as Sajar Jopp, the widely proclaimed king of African music. The novel's narrator is Litch, an English record producer, A&R man and general world music authority. Much of the novel's action is set in N'Galam, the capital of the fictional country of Tekrur. Despite this fictional device, Hudson makes little attempt to disguise the fact that Tekrur is actually Senegal, and N'Galam is Dakar. Many of the key issues concerning the reception of Afropop in particular and world music in general are dealt with brilliantly and often comically in the novel by Hudson, primarily a journalist who has published widely on African popular music. He presents Litch as a deeply complex character. On the one hand, he is a cynical record industry type who does not hesitate to blow his own trumpet, basically claiming credit for launching the whole world music phenomenon, and particularly for bringing Sajar Jopp to the attention of the West. However, he is not merely a cynic out to make a fast buck from the latest musical fad. On the contrary, his deep love for African pop music has caused him to have his house repossessed, seen his production company go bankrupt, and almost destroyed his marriage.

Litch's passion for Afropop is born from his deep disillusionment with Western pop music. More than a decade in the music industry, managing Country and Western, rock, punk and new wave bands, has left him feeling 'empty and defeated' (1999: 35). Attempting to escape from the London music scene, one day in the mid-1980s, he takes a package holiday to Badiya (which is clearly the Gambia). At his lowest ebb, he hears the music of Sajar Jopp, the music that will give his life meaning again:

> Then, one day, I heard music. I heard a voice speaking to me inside my head. A voice tender, intimate, crooning, stroking a song into insistent animation. Against a lilting, Cuban-sounding backing of liquid guitar and slapping congas, the singer teased out

an exquisitely haunting melody, with that kind of yearning ... What was it? Arabic? Andalusian? Something vaguely Islamic. And while the singer himself sounded almost heartbreakingly young, there was behind the voice a sense of knowledge, ageless, mysterious, *other*. (102; emphasis in original)

This quasi-spiritual experience has a profound effect on Litch's life in a number of significant ways. Afropop excites his curiosity and passion because it is both strange and familiar at the same time (the mixture of 'newness' and 'authenticity' described so well by Taylor, 1997). On the one hand, the 'discovery' of Afropop is like finding the missing piece in a jigsaw puzzle that explains the origins and development of Western pop music: blues, rock 'n' roll, soul, funk are all there already in African pop music acting as an illustration of Gilroy's 'Black Atlantic' hybridity. He has found the source and the inspiration for the music that he has always loved, and he sets out on a mission to sell Afropop to the West. More importantly, the 'otherness' of this music, of which he speaks in the passage above, causes the jaded and cynical Litch to reassess his opinion that he has seen and done all there is to see. Discovering this music has opened up another world, a whole new way of being to him. Litch, the boy from New Malden, a grey suburb of London, has achieved the ultimate escape from suburban life. The novel is littered with short scenes from suburban England – shopping in Tesco's, domestic disputes, money worries – that act as reminders of all the things he feels he has escaped through his African 'adventures'. Just as Western teenagers form bands to escape the mundane world of the suburbs, Litch finds something 'real' and worthwhile in Afropop.[15] This passion for the 'otherness' of Afropop is not presented by Hudson as the fetishization of 'difference' or the 'exotic'. In fact, the novel goes to great lengths to illustrate Litch's knowledge of the specific 'local' signification of this music. Litch's love and appreciation of Afropop, and his friendship with Sajar Jopp, allow him to become a cultural insider in Africa. Litch feels an affinity with Sajar, despite all their cultural differences, because he feels that they are from similar backgrounds:

[Sajar's] still basically of the people. He never has been into *things*. He's into doing, not having. He's got his own sense of style, but he's never been into the Armani suits, the perfumes and accessories, the high life in Paris, New York and Rome ... He's only interested in football, music and women. He's just a working-class bloke. Like me. (102; emphasis in original)

Music is the common bond that joins Litch and Sajar together (at least in Litch's mind). Afropop is presented as a 'real' form of cultural expression that escapes from the cultural commodification of the West.

Litch's position as a cultural insider becomes one of the recurring motifs of his narrative. However, what makes it such an urgent issue is that his status is threatened by a row with Sajar over money. To fall out with Sajar is to lose his privileged perspective on African popular culture. He wonders if he will go to prison over this money trouble but that would not be the worst thing he can imagine: 'something far worse could happen. I could lose Sajar's good will. And with it the access, the uniquely privileged *in* I have to Tekrurian life and culture' (80; emphasis in original). Litch does indeed lose his privileged position within Tekrurian culture, finding himself pushed into the ignominious position of being just an average white man trapped on the surface level of Africa, viewing life from the outside. This is a personal tragedy for Litch because his access to African culture from the inside is what he sees as the distinction between himself and other Europeans drawn to the continent. Litch knows the 'reality' of Africa while everyone else remains on the outside. He is scornful of what he sees as manipulative Western record companies who promote African pop music but know nothing about the culture. Litch, on the other hand, has not only been allowed inside African culture, he has been allowed to view Africa from within the entourage of Sajar Jopp, the man whom he sees as Africa's leading pop culture icon. As the novel progresses, Litch becomes a fearful, paranoid figure, remaining isolated in his hotel room, afraid to go out and experience the 'reality' and exuberance of Africa that he had previously loved so much.

Through the character of Litch, Hudson thus provides us with a fascinating example of the dilemma facing those who wish to mediate the culture of Africa for the West. For all his self-centred, egotistical ranting about his status as the world's greatest living expert on African popular music, Litch does genuinely seem to feel a great love for this music, as well as displaying an in-depth knowledge of Senegalese (and, more widely, African) culture and society. He knows the legends and the historical figures that inspire the lyrics to Sajar's songs. He knows and loves the traditional folk musics that inform and shape the African pop scene, and he can trace the entire history of Afropop, charting the various trends and influences that have shaped it. Litch never loses sight of the fact that he is from *outside* African culture but he makes a sincere attempt to understand what African popular culture means *within* Africa. His love for this culture inspires him to promote it in the West, trying to bring to musicians like Sajar Jopp the international fame and success that he feels they deserve. However, this is not the only motivation behind Litch's promotion of Afropop. As was mentioned above, Litch is tired of the Western pop music scene, and he feels that Afropop is the perfect antidote to the insipid, bland synthesizer pop of the 1980s. Consequently, we can see that Afropop takes on a different cultural meaning and significance as soon as it is transferred to the West. It is an alternative to the mainstream pop that Litch despises, whereas in Africa it is the mainstream. He longs for Afropop to be commercially successful in the West but finally comes to believe that it is simply too different, too 'exotic' for the Western pop market. While on his current trip to Tekrur, he is invited to listen to a new band, which has developed an exciting style of rap, mixed with Tekrurian rhythms. However, after his initial excitement, he becomes pessimistic. If he were to go to the concert:

> [A]ll the time I'll be thinking, how can I translate what's good in this into something that'll appeal in the Western context – which is what they, of course, want – without

losing the funk, the feel and the taste that make it inimitably Tekrurian? And the answer is you can't … Somehow the magic is always lost, *and* it doesn't appeal in the Western context. Because it was in the first place only ever something for the Tekrurian or whoever-it-is people and the few fond and foolish souls like myself who bother to take an interest – that is the context in which it has real meaning, and it should really be left like that. (244–5; emphasis in original)

After so many disappointments in trying to 'translate' African music for the West, while remaining 'true' to its origins, Litch appears to have given up hope of Afropop ever breaking into the Western mainstream. Indeed, if bringing African pop music to the West means altering it beyond recognition, he would prefer it not to be brought to the West at all.

However, Litch's purism is not shared by African musicians themselves. If we look more closely at the preceding quote from *The Music in My Head*, we realize that cultural mediators such as Litch are important to African musicians precisely because the latter feel that the former can tell them what the West wants. Even minor success in the West can bring wealth to these musicians that would be next to impossible to achieve in the African pop market. For Litch, to alter the music in such a way is too high a price to pay, not only because it makes the music bland, but also because it will not make it popular in the West. Despite seeing him as 'Africa's greatest musician', Litch believes that Sajar Jopp's Western records 'are, in fact, extremely dull' (143) and:

although [Sajar] craves international fame and acceptance more than anything else, it's the very things that make him a genius – the things I would personally want to listen to in his music – that will never in a million years translate to a mass global audience. That's the tragic paradox of Sajar Jopp. (144)

Litch feels that the West is simply not interested in Africa so Africa should keep developing its own music rather than succumbing to the temptations of international pop. As he comically puts it: 'I've always said that African music's going to progress by looking ever deeper into its own traditions, not by making albums with Brian Eno' (201). In a more recent article on Congolese music, Mark Hudson is dismissive of the attempt by African musicians to alter their music to Western audience's tastes: 'Some musicians, notably Papa Wemba, flirted with rock and the Western middle class "world music" audience – with limited success' (2000a: 4).

Much of the novel's criticism of Western appropriations of African music is centred on the character of Michael Heaven, a transparent and wonderfully malicious parody of Peter Gabriel.[16] For Litch, Michael Heaven is just another cultural tourist 'skating over the surface of things in a Mitsubishi jeep' (250), who refuses to, or who simply cannot, enter into the 'reality' of Africa. As was mentioned above, Youssou N'Dour was given great exposure in the West by his association with Peter Gabriel, who brought him on tour and recorded a single with him, entitled 'Shaking the Tree' (see N'Dour, 1994a). Various commentators have analysed the ambiguous relationship between African popular music and Western musicians such as Peter Gabriel, Sting, Paul Simon and David Byrne (for a brilliant analysis of the 'explorer' motif in certain Western musicians' work with world music artists, see Taylor, 1997: 28–31). African musicians are happy to gain the support of Western artists as this guarantees them media exposure. However, as Graeme Ewens has argued, 'Africans get scorned for compromising their music, while people like [Paul] Simon and [Peter] Gabriel are praised for enriching theirs. And they get credit for "discovering" African music once again' (1991: 207–8).

Global Markets, Global Music?

Paul Simon's 1986 album *Graceland*, which brought together many different musicans and musical styles from across Africa (and beyond), has perhaps been the most fiercely criticized project in the brief history of world music. At the time of the album's release, Simon was criticized for breaking the embargo on contact with apartheid South Africa. He was also accused of cultural imperialism in appropriating 'exotic' African sounds in an attempt to revive his flagging career. Moreover, his use of slightly outdated styles of music from South Africa effectively pushed these styles to the forefront of the South African pop music market as producers tried to cash in on the *Graceland* sound (similar arguments have been put forward about the excellent work of Ry Cooder with Buena Vista Social Club in reviving older forms of Cuban music).[17] Much of the criticism of Simon has been wildly exaggerated and underplays his apparently genuine embrace of cultural pluralism, and the extent to which he sought to promote African artists on the *Graceland* tour, giving almost half the stage time to Ladysmith Black Mambazo, Miriam Makeba and others. For example, Neil Lazarus (1999: 204–7) attacks Simon for espousing 'one-worldism' in the music on *Graceland* while remaining resolutely 'first-worldist' in his lyrics, refusing to engage with African society and culture in any way. It seems unfair to criticize Simon personally for this approach: are African musicians criticized for not addressing the realities of North–South relations in songs where they borrow from Western pop music? However, I agree entirely with Lazarus's fundamental point that it is the nature of the economic and political imbalance between the First and Third Worlds that allows Simon to become such a key figure in the development of music from another continent. As Lazarus puts it, 'exploitation under capitalist social relations is rarely (and even then only incidentally) a matter of *personal* calculation or intent. Rather, it is *structural* in nature, simultaneously marked and masked by its relative *impersonality*' (1999: 217–18; emphasis in original).[18] For Veit Erlmann (1999: 179–98), *Graceland* is the classic example of how the West wishes to mediate the process of globalization, understanding and explaining 'otherness' in terms of its relationship to Western culture.

Should we conclude, then, that world music is simply another cultural commodity created by the insatiable appetite of the Western pop market, always anxious to create new products, and attract new consumers? For instance, Martin Roberts argues that world music differs from previous Western encounters with non-Western musics such as the bossa nova craze of the 1950s and 1960s. World music is supported by a commercial framework of specialist record companies and magazines which simply did not exist before the 1980s, leading Roberts to argue that 'world music may best be defined … as a new kind of commodity in the global marketplace of the popular music industry' (1992: 232–3). How does such a conclusion tally with world music's claims to promote a cultural pluralism that reflects a 'multiculturalist' reading of the process of globalization? In this latter view, globalization is argued to have produced a more cosmopolitan culture in Western societies, through the mass migration of Third World immigrants, lured by the West's economic dominance. In this positive reading, globalization is also widely argued to have advanced intercultural dialogue, through progress in travel and communications.

Much of the discourse surrounding the world music phenomenon attempts to be genuinely inclusive in nature, presenting a cosmopolitan vision of global relations. For example, this is how Tower Records, one of Britain's most committed commercial promoters of world music, sells its product in the *Tower Guide to … World Music*: 'just as Asian, Latin, Mediterranean and African restaurants have immeasurably improved the British palate, world music offers [a] rich, varied, fat free alternative to the stodgy musical diet [Britain] seems stuck on' (Cartwright, 2000/1: 4). However, the shortcomings of liberal models of 'pluralism' have been clearly exposed by JanMohamed and Lloyd (1990: 8) as a form of exoticism that neglects economic and social considerations. Many cultural theorists have sought to provide more thoughtful models for understanding questions of identity in what is often described as a 'post-national' world, and Appadurai's notion of interrelated spheres of influence within the process of globalization (see p. 43) is perhaps the most complex and insightful of these. Within the discussion of globalization, there has increasingly been an emphasis on the empowering nature of a globalized hybridity. Homi K. Bhabha's notion of a 'third space' being produced by globalization and mass immigration from the Third World to the West has been very influential in questioning the construction of national identities. Bhabha frowns on notions of 'authenticity', viewing all cultures as 'always already' hybrid, before any 'contact' with another culture. His notion of hybridity thus represents a complex vision of fundamental cultural ambiguity, which he places in opposition to the arguments of both theorists of authenticity and 'liberal' supporters of 'cultural diversity' (Bhabha, 1994). Equally, Paul Gilroy's theories on the culture of the 'Black Atlantic' (1993) as an axis of globalized (counter)modernity that exists in a complex and at times oppositional relationship to 'Western' thought and culture have been particularly illuminating, stressing the centrality of dynamic, intercultural communication to 'black cultures'. These cultural critics reject reductive characterizations of globalization as the active exploitation of one part of the world by another, preferring to see it as a process that affects the entire world, but which is not controlled by individual nations (see Tomlinson, 1991). Arguing from a left-wing perspective, George Lipsitz (1994: 14) claims that globalization is an ambiguous process that creates links between oppressed groups around the world at the same time as it spreads the power of international capital. The 'national', and to a lesser extent the 'local', as categories for analysis have thus been seen in some quarters as increasingly outdated as the role of the nation-state wanes, and theories of globalized identities come to the fore.

The 'Limits' of Globalization: In Defence of the Local/National

The work of Bhabha, Gilroy and others on the limits of nationalist (and also Marxist) ideologies, has been insightful and intelligent. However, I would argue that their work in its turn can sometimes neglect to examine the 'limits' of the 'global' as a category for analysis of cultural identity. As Kwame Anthony Appiah (1992) argues so convincingly, the espousal of a postmodern condition of hybridity, such as that of Bhabha, ignores the fact that the experience of this phenomenon might not be the same in the West as it is in the Third World, just as the Third World immigrant's experience of hybrid Western societies might not be the same as that of white Westerners. Equally, critics such as Tim Brennan, Neil Lazarus and Ella Shohat have argued that contemporary theories of cosmopolitanism generally give support to universalizing notions of hybridity at the expense of any adequate theorization of the economic and political processes that currently underpin globalization, namely the ever-growing economic power of a small number of predominantly 'Western' nations and the multinational companies based in them, although the rise of China and India may alter the picture quite radically over the next 20–30 years (see Shohat, 1992; Brennan, 1997; Lazarus, 1999; also Negus, 1996: 176–9). Even Gilroy's vision of the Black Atlantic is heavily biased towards the 'New World' experience of this phenomenon, saying little of African modernity/hybridity (for a materialist critique of Gilroy's ideas, see Lazarus, 1999: 51–67). Bhabha and Gilroy both prioritize the hybrid and the diasporic in their discussions of a globalized, postcolonial world (a trend that has come to dominate in recent postcolonial criticism); however, on a very basic level, the African memory of slavery or empire will not necessarily be the same in Africa as it is in the diasporas of the Caribbean, the Americas or Europe. In refusing to view Africa and the West as binary opposites, we must not forget the concrete economic and political differences between them. I would argue that theories of globalization must remain attentive to the 'national' and the 'local', in order to avoid generalizations that simply gloss over material differences between countries and continents (see Taylor, 1997 for similar ideas).

As an illustration of the necessity of retaining the categories of 'local' and 'national' culture, I would like briefly to analyse Youssou N'Dour's album *Joko: From Village to Town* (2000). This is N'Dour's fifth album made for the Western market and it is the one in which he makes the most significant alterations to his music in an attempt to break into the Western mainstream. I am not attempting to contrast a pure, African Youssou N'Dour sound with a Westernized form of his music. As I have consistently argued above, his music has always been based on a rich and varied mixture of cultural influences. However, *Joko* betrays a deliberate effort to purge his music of its most 'difficult' African elements in an attempt to attract a significant Western audience: the numerous abrupt changes of tempo, the complex polyrhythms, the piercing, melismatic vocals are all toned down or simply omitted altogether. In their place, N'Dour introduces a steady 4-4 tempo and banks of moody synthesizers that could have come from a recent Peter Gabriel album, and indeed Gabriel and Sting both make guest apearances on *Joko*. The difference between N'Dour's 'Senegalese' sound and his 'Western' sound is best illustrated on the album's final track, 'New Africa', an impassioned plea to Africans to unite, invoking the names of the great African figures of Cheikh Anta Diop, Kwame N'Krumah and Steven Biko.[19] Just two minutes long, this heavily produced song maintains a slow tempo throughout, N'Dour's vocals accompanied by a great bank of synthesizers, underlining the epic nature of the lyrics. However, the same track also appears on N'Dour's 1995 cassette, *Diapason plus* [Extra Groove], a live album that was released for the Senegalese and African markets (my copy of the cassette gives no details of producer or distributor). The song begins in similar fashion with moody synthesizers and N'Dour's prophetic lyrics. However, at the point where the Western version ends, the Senegalese version bursts into an explosion of polyrhythms as N'Dour continues to invoke the names of great African figures but in a joyous and exuberant celebration of Senegalese dance music.

I have not made this comparison in order to condemn N'Dour's Western albums.[20] Rather, I want to illustrate the point that the Afropop we hear in the West is not necessarily the popular music of Africa. In Senegal, 'New Africa' is a very popular dance track that conveys a sense of exuberance, of Senegalese, and more generally African, self-confidence, while in the West it is transformed into a middle of the road, new age evocation of Africa, in which cultural difference is safely packaged for Western consumption. However, despite Youssou N'Dour's desire to crack the mainstream Western pop market, his remains a marginal product in the West, trapped within the ghetto of world music. As was argued above, the 'local', popular musics of Africa take on a different meaning when 'translated' to the Western context. However, increasingly, as the case of 'New Africa' shows, it is not just that Afropop means something different in the Western context, the music is genuinely not the same.

Afropop has always been what might be termed 'creatively hybrid' but I would argue that the world music market has at times led African musicians to produce forms of music that are 'hybrid' primarily in the sense that they are attempting to woo Western consumers through a sanitized, and often bland 'Westernized' sound. In so arguing, I part company from Timothy Taylor, whose work I have quoted so approvingly throughout my chapter. In his excellent study *Global Pop* (1997), Taylor analyses N'Dour's previous 'Western' album, *Wommat* [The Guide], often in extremely incisive fashion (see N'Dour, 1994). However, Taylor goes on to accuse those critics of N'Dour's 'sanitized' Western albums of 'demanding local, premodern cultures of Africans' (1997: 135); the likes of Peter Gabriel and Paul Simon are allowed to '"Africanize" their music', while 'N'Dour is not permitted to work with them and "westernize" his music' (135). Effectively, Taylor concludes that '[p]ost-colonial/postmodern attitudes allow N'Dour a culture, as colonial ideologies did not, but it is a natural culture, while the west's culture is civilization, technological culture, premised on development, expansion, progress and artifice' (135). I admire Taylor's work greatly but I find a troubling lack of nuance in this particular statement. As I argued above, the notions of a static, 'natural culture' versus a progressive 'civilization' are extremely useful in thinking about the ways in which certain Western critics view the 'Third World', but is it not possible to criticize (or even merely to remark upon) the sanitization of N'Dour's Western albums while avoiding the trap of seeing his music as the expression of a 'natural culture'? To my mind, it is not a question of whether his music is 'modern' or 'premodern' – it is unquestionably modern and hybrid – but rather of the terms on which Africa is obliged to engage with late capitalist modernity. Taylor rightly speaks of the 'strategic' inauthenticity of N'Dour's work but he is in fact talking solely about his albums for the Western market, as those released in Africa are still firmly embedded in a dynamic, hybrid, urban, Senegalese culture, which is far from 'natural': N'Dour has been using 'Western' sounds in innovative ways for almost 30 years but in the last decade, his Western albums have adopted an increasingly homogenized, soft rock style. There may well be artistic decisions behind the recent musical choices taken by N'Dour – as Taylor suggests – but there are most definitely economic decisions too (a point brilliantly illustrated by Hudson in *The Music in My Head*). Seeing the process of globalized hybridity primarily in cultural rather than economic terms, Taylor claims that 'those who express reservations about the [world music] label tend to be those westerners whose desire for the real means that anything smacking of the popular, mass-mediated, or generic is unacceptable' (143). It could be argued that N'Dour's recent mbalax cassettes for the African market have also employed a 'popular', 'generic' sound, but it is patently not the same sound as on his 'Western' albums. In many ways, this is an illustration of a point that Taylor makes earlier in his book, where he speaks of 'the limitless ways capitalism constructs centers and margins' (14): world music is a 'marginal' product for the Western 'centre' but a strong argument could be made that, in terms of creative musical expression, N'Dour in fact views Senegal (and Africa) as the 'centre' and the West as the undifferentiated 'margins' to which he offers a 'sanitized' version of his work.

Conclusions

The growth of world music since the late 1980s has led many African musicians to move to Paris and London and has meant that much African pop music is now being created in the West. The financial rewards of success in the Western market are an entirely understandable attraction for African musicians, and this has undoubtedly led to the transformation of certain African musical styles and the adoption of less innovative and more streamlined, sleekly produced pop styles. This does not mean that Afropop in Africa is more 'authentic': the African pop market is no less determined by the 'commercial' appeal of artists than its Western counterpart. However, 'local' popular musics, far removed from the norms of the Western pop market, continue to emerge from various corners of Africa. The African musicians who make it to the West have almost always done so on the back of popular success in their own part of Africa. Afropop in Africa remains an integral part of the expression of, generally, urban African cultures, and, in the case of the most successful acts, it can forge imagined communities of 'local', 'national' or even 'African' listeners, sharing a fragile but nonetheless real sense of 'African' cultural identity.

In conclusion, I would argue that it is far too simplistic to view world music as a genuine example of a hybrid, cosmopolitan, globalized culture. World music is a primarily Western phenomenon: the music is 'different' to Western pop music but increasingly repackaged in a more digestible form, and it is marketed towards an educated, liberal, middle-class audience. The argument which claims that world music is a reflection of multicultural societies in the Western world only holds true up to a certain point, as immigrants are simply not targeted by the record companies as the main consumers of world music. In fact, immigrant communities in the West often have their own cultural networks, including music shops in which tapes from the home country are distributed. However, despite my misgivings about the often bland, universalizing discourse that surrounds world music, I would argue that it still retains the potential to establish a genuine cultural dialogue between the West and the 'Third World' or between 'North' and 'South', to use an equally problematic set of terms. As Neil Lazarus (1999: 221–2) argues, the syncretic nature of Afropop is usually what attracts Western enthusiasts to this music: it is both strange and familiar at the same time, as Litch discovers in *The Music in My Head*. World music, and in our particular case Afropop, offers an occasion to question the assumptions of Western popular culture, particularly its claims to be *the* international culture. Above all, Afropop illustrates the complex nature of intercultural relations in the modern world. Despite the influence of Western musical styles, Afropop is not simply a by-product of Western culture: it is the product of African, national, ethnic and regional cultures, and it is given specific meaning within these contexts. I am not claiming that 'local' music is of greater social or cultural value than 'global' music. As Keith Negus argues, it is more useful 'to ask how the local is given meaning in specific circumstances' (1996: 183). The work of Bhabha and Gilroy – amongst others – has been vital in addressing the transnational nature of much cultural dialogue but their incisive and intelligent attempts to forge global theories can at times lead them to overlook the specificity of local/national cultures, as well as the crucial role of economic factors. We may all be part of a global culture but this culture is expressed in very different ways in different societies: the 'local' and the 'national' still have a resonance that the cultural commentator cannot choose to ignore.

Notes

1   The author would like to express his gratitude to the British Academy and the Leverhulme Trust for their financial support, which allowed him to undertake much of the research for this chapter.

2   Note that France was a key location in the early 1980s for the development of world music through the work of African and Caribbean musicians based primarily in Paris.

3   In arguing that the USA and Britain highlight linguistic difference in classifying music as 'world music', I am not forgetting about examples such as the Caribbean musics soca and calypso, which, although invariably in English, are categorized for marketing purposes as 'world music'. However, the USA and Britain are usually quite systematic in placing popular musics from all non-English-speaking countries – and not just 'exotic', 'Third World' countries – in the 'world music' section of record shops. For example, the Portuguese singer Mariza is a world music singer in Britain but she is part of 'international rock and pop' to a French audience. And Manu Chao, a current world music favourite in Britain, is most definitely 'pop music' in France. As for folk musics of the world (whatever their origin), they are generally thrown into the 'world music' category as irredeemably different to the hegemonic Anglo-American rock and pop. The best account of the complexities and contradictions of the development of world music is to be found in Taylor (1997: 1–37).

4   Bernardo Bertolucci's excellent 1998 film *Besieged* features Thandie Newton as an African refugee in Italy. Her nostalgia for her unnamed homeland and the husband she has had to leave behind are, in part, evoked by the African music that she listens to in her room. However, this evocation of an African 'home' is somewhat ambiguous: Newton listens to music by Papa Wemba from the Democratic Republic of the Congo (formerly Zaire) and Salif Keïta from Mali, amongst others. In a film that is elsewhere so attentive to issues of cultural difference, it seems that the music is simply used in a generic fashion to evoke Africa as a distant, 'other' location that is foreign to Europe. The difference between Sahelian Mali and sub-equatorial Congo is lost on the average Western spectator to whom the film is addressed.

5   See Feld (1994) for an analysis of how Western discourses of authenticity and tradition have been applied to non-Western musics, and Taylor (1997: 21–8) on different forms of authenticity (authenticity of positionality, of emotionality and of primality) in relation to world music.

6   The principal Afro-Cuban influence in the two Congos and Senegal is not the generic complex of rumba (including guaguancó, yambú and columbia), which developed out of the secular dances of Congolese slaves, but son in its diverse forms. However, initial exports of son were catalogued as 'rhumba', which came to denote Latin in

style rather than a particular genre. Congolese rumba, whilst borrowing heavily from son, is a mix of Caribbean and Congolese rhythms. Afro-Cuban rumba, as a genre, became more influential in the 1970s on the back of the success of salsa. For a brief description of the generic features of Afro-Cuban rumba and son, see Manuel (1995b: 20–29, 35–44).

7   In describing this music as the expression of an urban African sensibility, I am not excluding rural African communities from the development of African popular music. Indeed, the African city is where the musics of rural communities are mixed together to form new musical styles. Migratory flows between country and city have brought the two areas into close contact; also, the growing use of transistor radios, and to a lesser extent television, is now bringing urban culture directly to many rural areas.

8   For a discussion of Keïta's career, see Stapleton and May (1987: 111–13). Keïta appears in *The Music in My Head* as Cherry Jatta Samba; see Hudson (1999: 57–64).

9   This notion of an 'imagined community' is of course borrowed from Anderson (1991).

10   The term *sapeur* comes from the notion of 'la sape', an abbreviation of Société des ambianceurs et des personnes élégantes [roughly translated as 'Society of Hip and Elegant People'], which puns on the colloquial French phrase 'bien sapé', 'to be well dressed'. The society originated in the People's Republic of the Congo in the 1970s, but took off as a social movement in Zaire in the early 1980s. For a discussion of the *sapeurs*, see Friedman (1994: 105–9, 157–66) and Wrong (2000: 173–9). Mitchell (1996: 79–80) describes the appropriation of formerly colonial bourgeois practice or Western styles as a liberating act of defiance.

11   The decision by Bob Geldof not to invite African musicians to take part in the main Live 8 concert in London (2 July 2005) is yet another example of the nature of the unequal relationship between Africa and the West; even at an event designed to promote the notion of Africa's right to govern itself (freed of the burden of international debt), Africans were excluded.

12   Although many of the structures of Wolof society have undergone profound changes, particularly in the period since independence, this notion of a higher and a lower caste still persists, with all its inherent social prejudices (in general, it remains socially unacceptable for people of different caste to marry each other). For a comprehensive study of the structures within Wolof society, see Diop (1981).

13   The evolution of mbalax is clearly illustrated on Stern's African Classics four-volume CD set of Etoile de Dakar's recordings from 1979 to 1982 (Etoile de Dakar, 1993–98). Ironically, the Senegalese rumba was revived in the 1990s when the group Africando, with Papa Seck (one of Youssou N'Dour's collaborators from the Star Band) as lead vocalist, enjoyed a major hit in the USA, topping the New York Latin music charts for seven weeks with the song 'Yay Boy' in 1996, thus reversing the process of influences that had launched the African rumba in the first place. This group, produced by Ibrahim Sylla and directed by the Malian flautist Boncana Maïga, is composed of musicians from Africa and the Caribbean.

14   Baaba Maal has shifted back and forth between heavily produced albums aimed at attracting a 'crossover' market in the West, such as *Firin' in Fouta* (1994), and 'traditional' works, which are more recognizably based on Fulani culture, such as *Missing You [Mi Yeewnii]* (2001).

15   For an analysis of the role of popular music for urban/suburban Western teenagers, see Frith (1992).

16   Lazarus praises Peter Gabriel as a 'sensitive' listener to world music (1999: 224). However, my knowledge of Gabriel's collaborations with Youssou N'Dour and his work with other African musicians for his Real World label leaves me highly sceptical about such a claim (the calculated remixing of Papa Wemba's music to appeal to a Western audience on his Real World albums is a particularly disappointing case of the sanitization of Afropop for the West).

17   See Fairley (2001: 283–5) on the Cooder and Simon paradigms of music-making.

18   See Hutnyk (2000: 127–9) for a critique of the unequal power dynamics involved in sampling.

19   Cheikh Anta Diop was a Senegalese anthropologist who argued that ancient Egyptian civilization was primarily a 'black' civilization: his theories have been seen by many Africans, and particularly the Senegalese, as a powerful source of black pride in their history. Kwame N'Krumah led Ghana to independence in 1957: as Ghana was the first black African colony to free itself from European rule, N'Krumah, a charismatic proponent of 'African unity', became a hero to many on the continent. The black South African Steven Biko was an anti-apartheid activist murdered by his country's security forces: his death saw him become a martyr for the anti-apartheid cause.

20   The question of the audience and reception of world music is made even more complex by N'Dour's latest album *Egypt* (2004), which employs a very moving and hybrid mixture of Senegalese musical traditions and 'classical' Egyptian orchestration. The album has been a major success on the world music circuit and has been heralded as N'Dour 'returning to his roots'. However, somewhat paradoxically, it has not met with his usual popular success at home in Senegal because, although the lyrics deal with the particular brand of Islamic Sufi mysticism prevalent in Senegal, the music is perceived by many Senegalese music fans as 'alien' and belonging to a religious sphere that is in many ways the antithesis of the popular music scene.

Discography

Africando, featuring Papa Seck, 'Yay Boy', *Volume 2: Tierra Tradicional* (Stern's Africa, STCD1054, 1994).

Buena Vista Social Club, *Buena Vista Social Club* (World Circuit, WCD050, 1997).

Etoile de Dakar, featuring Youssou N'Dour, *Volume 1: Absa Guèye* (Stern's Africa, STCD3004, 1993).

Etoile de Dakar, featuring Youssou N'Dour and El Hadji Faye, *Volume 2: Thiapathioly* (Stern's Africa, STCD3010, 1995).

Etoile de Dakar, featuring Youssou N'Dour and El Hadji Faye, *Volume 3: Lay Suma Lay* (Stern's Africa, STCD3012, 1996).

Etoile de Dakar, featuring Youssou N'Dour, Mar Seck and El Hadji Faye, *Volume 4: Khaley Etoile* (Stern's Africa, STCD3014, 1998).

Franco, *Franco: The Very Best of the Rumba Giant of Zaire* (Manteca, MANTCD013, 2000).

Keïta, Salif, et les Ambassadeurs, 'N'Toman', *Seydou Bathily* (Sonodisc, CDS7004, 1997).

Kuti, Fela, 'Zombie', 'Coffin for Head of State' and 'ITT', *The Best Best of Fela Kuti: The Black President* (FAK, Universal Music International, LC00126, 1999).

Lô, Cheikh, *Né la thiass* (World Circuit, WCD046, 1996).

Maal, Baaba, *Firin' in Fouta* (Island Records, CIDM1109, 1994).

Maal, Baaba, *Missing You (Mi Yeewnii)* (Palm Pictures, PalmCD2067-2, 2001).

N'Dour, Youssou, *The Best of Youssou N'Dour* (Virgin, CDV2773, 1994a).

N'Dour, Youssou, *The Guide (Wommat)* (Sony Music, 'Columbia', 476508-4, 1994b).

N'Dour, Youssou, 'New Africa', *Diapason Plus* (no production details given on cassette, 1995).

N'Dour, Youssou, *Joko: From Village to Town* (Sony, COL489718-2, 2000).

N'Dour, Youssou, *Lamb-bi* (Action 2000, 2002).

N'Dour, Youssou, *Egypt* (Nonesuch, LC 00286, 2004).

Obey, Chief Ebenezer, *Juju Jubilation* (EMI, Hemisphere, LC0542, 1998).

Pène, Omar, and Super Diamono, *Fari* (Stern's Africa, STCD1051, 1993).

Simon, Paul, *Graceland* (Warner, 7599254472, 1986).

Wemba, Papa, *Le Voyageur* (Real World, CDRW20, 1992).

Filmography

Bertolucci, Bernardo (1998), *Besieged.*

Sembene, Ousmane (1974), *Xala.*

Sembene, Ousmane (1992), *Guelwaar.*

PART II
LOCATIONS

Chapter 3

Voicing Risk: Migration, Transgression and Relocation in Spanish/Moroccan Raï[1]

Parvati Nair

Ever since Cheb Khaled's well-known cry of 'El harba wayn?' ['To flee, but where?'] came to voice the violent dissatisfaction with the Algerian authorities experienced by rioters in the 1980s, raï music has been overtly charged with political controversy.[2] Like rock 'n' roll or – more recently – rap, raï (the word itself means 'opinion' in Algerian Arabic) signifies a popular opposition to the status quo, breaking open instead a space for the articulation of difference lived and experienced at collective levels.[3] Traditionally, in the case of raï, this difference, both in Algeria and in France amongst the *Beurs*[4] or Algerian communities, has been perceived by its practitioners in terms that are at once cultural, economic and political. In this context, the recent emergence of raï music amongst Moroccan immigrants living in Spain comes as a sudden interjection into Spanish concert halls and recording studios, yet its arrival was no doubt foreseeable. Since its inception in the cities of Algeria some 30 or more years ago as a result of increased rural to urban population flows, raï has been a musical form arising from the experience of migration. As such, it opens a space for the articulation of displaced, uprooted North African identities and is marked by traces of both difficult and disjunctured encounters with newness. Also present in the music is the confrontation with cultural and political boundaries that are hard to cross. Furthermore, like the economically motivated migratory processes that it accompanies, raï, in its more recent permutations as well as in its undeniable commercial popularity as a particular ethnic expression of 'world music', is a specific cultural product of late modernity and therefore shares the latter's mobilities and fluid adaptabilities.

Raï as a form of urban music is nevertheless a reworking of traditions that are rural and largely folkloric. Its early manifestations can be heard in the urban rearticulations of *meddahas* or wedding songs sung by women in and around the city of Oran as well as in the music of the *cheikhat*, or young female singers, singing for men in cabarets and brothels. In Algeria over a period of two decades or so, raï has increasingly become synonymous with anti-establishmentarian attitudes amongst the young working classes, displaying resistance to state authorities and the dictates of Islam alike.[5] In its transnational formulations which emerged in France among the *Beurs* from the 1980s onwards, raï both expresses anxieties about assimilation and opens a space for resistance to such erasure of difference. Nevertheless, in French/Algerian raï, such resistance is seldom verbalized literally but, rather, discourses of love and desire in the lyrics serve largely to enunciate identities that are both different and in processes of flux.[6] In its crossings of national and other boundaries, raï displays late modernity's hybrid reinventions of cultural memory through what are largely collective experiences of deterritorialization and relocation.[7] In its latest Spanish form, however, it is also expressive of the contingency of representations of national and ethnic identities, displaying aspects of experience that are particular to given historical and cultural contexts. Thus raï, as it is currently being constructed in Barcelona, offers a discourse for immigrant Moroccans living in Catalonia and other parts of Spain with which to construct specific transnational and transcultural identities in their new socio-cultural and economic surroundings. In particular, this new strand of raï emerging from the culturally cosmopolitan city of Barcelona moves beyond lyrics of love to underline in no uncertain way the unmistakably physical risks attendant on illicit migration. Thus it marks the immigrant experience as different from, and more life-threatening than, the larger context of cultural pluralities that accompany postmodernity. Raï, therefore, highlights an important distinction which must be made between displacement and migrancy as key features of modernity, on the one hand, and, on the other, the dispossession and personal dangers experienced by many migrants who undertake transnational crossings without economic or political certainties. In this sense, it is through the explicit articulation of risk as lived experience which is inscribed on the body and foregrounded by the voice that this music seeks to construct any kind of dialogic encounter.[8]

In recent years, risk as a defining feature of modernity has been the subject of considerable theoretical exploration. In the light of such theorizations, this chapter will therefore seek to examine the first raï CD released in Spain, *Chab Samir* (Afro-Blue Records, 1999) by the group of the same name. While Ulrich Beck (1992) elaborates the notion of 'risk society', this can be distinguished from 'risk culture' or the experience of cultural movement as risk. Deborah Lupton (1999) in turn stresses that the subject of risk cannot be presented as universal, but should be considered in the context of cultural otherness in order to be perceived in terms of a specific history.[9] My claim here is that Beck's theorization of risk society centralizes risk as a key feature of late modernity, and hence of the industrialized West. In so doing, the uncertain vulnerabilities experienced by those whose claim on the benefits of capitalism is at best tenuous, such as illicit immigrants arriving on European shores in flimsy vessels, is somewhat ironed out and lost from view. Instead, risk, when lived as embodiment in terms of the stranger whose location is tentative and borderline, presents dangers that are experienced in terms of immediacy and the imminence of death.

The analysis presented here of this CD is also reliant upon personal interviews with the lead singer, Samir, and other members of his band, as well as on press reviews of his music and interviews with Moroccan immigrants living in Barcelona who frequent his concerts and live performances. Central to this effort, however, are the limitations that affect interview processes in the course of fieldwork. In this sense, there is little doubt that my status as an academic visiting Spain coloured the way in which I was perceived by interviewees. On the one hand, it defined the boundaries of my approximation to what I had defined as the 'field' and indeed raised some questions from my informants with regard to my motivations in obtaining the information that I sought; on the other, perhaps my own non-white, migrant identity afforded me glimpses into what might otherwise have been excluded from my line of vision. Equally, my preconceptions of immigrant identities somewhat determined my choice of demarcations for the 'field' of study. The threshold from which I operated was the boundary dividing my apparently 'licit' academic inquiry and the 'illicit' status of many of those whose migratory experiences formed the subject of the CD and hence of my study. The question of legality therefore implicitly lurked behind most exchanges as did the question of how to transcend the boundary that demarcates the licit from the illicit. As Samir's songs show, the kind of immediate and overwhelming risk faced by illicit immigrants in their transnational movements cuts through the fabric of late modernity's cultural climate of general risk, speculation or reflexivity and venture, highlighting their own liminality and otherness to the very contexts that they seek to enter. Thus, migrants, caught up in and driven by the globalized sweep of late capitalism, seek to become members of the risk society by engaging in risk-taking, but are all too often forced to pay the price of such risk with the currency most available to them, that of their bodies and even their lives.

The Raï of Chab Samir

Samir El Quichiri, who migrated to Barcelona from northern Morocco in 1992, is the lead singer and songwriter of the mixed Catalan–Moroccan group Chab Samir. His music aims to provide a forum for the articulation of immigrant experiences of displacement, underlining in particular the struggle to relocate in Spain, both in legal and cultural terms. Singing as one immigrant to another, Samir makes references to supposedly common experiences of racism and other kinds of social ostracization faced by Maghrebians in Spain. Calling on raï's well-established sense of defiance to established authorities, its alliance with the working classes and its transgressive impetus propelled both by economic and cultural migrant crossings, Samir launches forth to construct a voice that is at once in keeping with previous raï concerns and also quite specifically different. In fact, what is different about Samir's music is that this new form of raï refers back in its musical 'roots' not merely to Algeria, but more specifically to Morocco. By shifting the focus westwards from Oran across the border to Morocco and, from there, across the

Straits of Gibraltar to Spain, the violent history of French colonial interventions in Algeria, and Algeria's subsequent chequered and sometimes bloody trajectory as an independent nation, is somewhat overshadowed in this new raï by the more immediate and immensely pressing economic concerns shared by the majority of Morocco's youth in the face of widespread unemployment. Nevertheless, this cultural memory of trauma and violence acts as an important backdrop to these new constructions of raï, marking them with a historical depth of dissent. As Samir's songs show, and indeed as the current course of emigration from Morocco reveals,[10] economic concerns felt by much of Morocco's disaffected present-day youth can often only be addressed in the short term by engaging with risk at a personal and immediate level. At stake here, of course, is that often unvoiced memory of perilous crossing by *patera* or raft across the Straits of Gibraltar which, even if not shared by all illicit immigrants from the African continent, nevertheless figuratively acts as a metaphor to foreground their precarious and fragile entry to Spain and hence the West. The music both calls upon a shared cultural memory of Maghreb and stresses the difficult move to Europe; equally, it suggests an identity constructed in terms of struggle, one that is borderline, resistant and vulnerable. Thus, Samir's musical borrowings hail from his native Morocco, where he trained and recorded as a singer and musician in traditional Moroccan music, as much as from raï's own musical roots in Algeria, as also from the immediate cultural context of late modernity in Barcelona. Equally evident in his music, though, is the rebellion and subalternity that so clearly defined raï in Algeria during the tumultuous 1980s and rendered it, as Marc Schade-Poulsen argues in his *Men and Popular Music in Algeria* (1999), emblematic of popular experiences of masculinity lived at a collective level against the grain of state-sanctioned national identity. Samir's song thereby positions itself on the border zones of past and present, as well as across cultural and national boundaries – a transcultural, frontier position which, as any migrant knows, is inevitably shifting, unreliable and dangerous.

Risk, Migration and Music

Beck's development of the concept of 'risk society' bases itself largely on his perception of late modernity as typified by reflexivity or a pervasive tendency towards cultural self-consciousness. He views global social change as taking place within the context of a reflexive modernization, whereby change occurs through the calculated taking of risks. Beck states that:

> The concept of risk is directly bound to the concept of reflexive modernization. *Risk* may be defined as a *systematic way of dealing with hazards and insecurities induced and introduced by modernization itself.* Risks, as opposed to older dangers, are consequences which relate to the threatening force of modernization and to its globalization of doubt. They are *politically reflexive.* (1992: 21; emphasis in original)

While Beck acknowledges the risks that have always accompanied human existence, he nevertheless underlines the global scale of present-day hazards arising from the sweep of modernization. Risk society, for Beck, is in many ways post-industrial, in that it refers to the social realities of living within contexts of large-scale risks or threats. The effects of modernization on society are, of course, well charted, leading, in Beck's view, to numerous new 'social risk positions' which cover a range of class, gender or other positions. Thus, Beck views Western society as transitional, marked by a cultural relativism whereby the experience of risk marks all reflexivity with uncertainty and doubt. The everyday, in Beck's analysis, partaking of the large-scale hazards which accompany global modernization, must now therefore be thought of in terms of two key notions that accompany one another: risk and self-critique or reflexivity.

Both these concepts come to the fore in a consideration of the factors surrounding migration and identity. The issue of migration into and through Spain from the African continent is one which has been the matter of considerable political and journalistic debate since the mid-1980s. In particular, Spain's ambivalent relation with Morocco, its southerly neighbour across the Straits of Gibraltar, displays many of the factors which connect processes of uneven modernization, globalization and transnational migration. Spain's own rather abrupt emergence into cultural plurality following the transition to democracy in 1982 coincided with rapid economic acceleration that rehauled the modernization set in place by Francoism.[11] The aim was alignment with Europe and entry into the European Community. Coincidentally, it is Spain's own much desired 'Europeanization', together with its location on the Mediterranean that has marked it out as a feasible point of entry into Europe.[12] Over the last 20 years, important Maghrebian communities and cultural centres have established themselves across Spain. This is so to the extent that a 'second' generation of Spanish Moroccans is now beginning to emerge in Spain. While much of the migration from Morocco to Spain remains legal (Harding, 2000), nevertheless, as the Spanish press eagerly remind us on an almost daily basis, the legalization of immigrants is a hot issue and the *Ley de Extranjería* (a law that has undergone numerous unsatisfactory revisions in its delineation of immigrant rights) arouses acute controversy. So too is the question of *reagrupación familiar*, whereby the immigrant gains rights to bring his or her family over – or is denied them, as the case may be. Equally under debate between the two governments is the practice of issuing only temporary or seasonal rights to workers brought over to agricultural areas from Morocco. Most poignant of all, though, is the recurrent mention in the press of bodies lost at sea. As Harding states in his book *The Uninvited*:

> No one knows how many illegal migrants setting out on small boats from Morocco have drowned in the Gibraltar Straits, but no one doubts a figure in the thousands. To the clandestine immigrant, however, the idea that the border may be permeable is more important than the idea that it may not be. For reluctant hosts, the reverse is true. (2000: 103)

The possible flaw in Beck's universalization of risk can perhaps best be appreciated in terms of Harding's statement. Beck's theorization of risk society functions within the demarcated terrains of Western late capitalism. As such, its focus is on the means and strategies by which power is accumulated, maintained and enlarged. However, the concept of risk society does not take into account the activities that take place on the margins of Western industrialized society. The movements of migrants from the peripheries of the West challenge the precepts of risk society, just as the normative structures of the latter fail to acknowledge the immigrant experience of disjuncture and displacements. The many who continue to disappear on an almost nightly basis in the waters of the Straits signal risk not in terms of the 'systematic dealing' with the hazards of modernization, but rather in terms of the failure of risk society to provide a reckoning of those lost lives in economic, political or cultural terms. Moreover, statistics and discourses on immigration fail to encompass these dead, as there is no satisfactory way of keeping count of them or even of knowing who they were. Lost at sea and nameless, the drowned then inhabit the silences and the gaps in between borders.

Thus risk, as opposed to being different and separate from 'older dangers', as Beck states, becomes synonymous at its worst with the oldest danger of all, namely death. In less extreme forms, risk entails not the speculative play of capitalist ventures but exclusion from such circles through the sole status available to the illicit immigrant, that of illegitimacy and hence isolation from risk society when understood as late capitalism. Without rights, the illicit immigrant becomes not merely nameless but also prey to substantiating the very structures that seek to isolate him or her through deportation or expulsion as the host nation's undesired 'other'. Thus, the illicit immigrant as transgressor of national borders ironically serves as a reason to reinforce the normative measures of risk society that aim to keep at bay the movement of culture as risk. Nevertheless, as Harding points out, it is this same threat of forced exclusion that spurs immigrants to probe the chinks in between borders and thus penetrate and so shift Western hegemonies. In this sense, risk society and the living of culture in terms of risk are mutually implicated.

Lupton develops a similar view of risk, not as society but as culture, when she writes of otherness as central to any theorization of risk. By contextualizing risk in terms of modernity, with its stress on order, regularization and control, yet confronted time and again by its own mobilities and displacements, Lupton explores the ensuing disjuncture as the point from which hybridity, and hence risk, emerges. Otherness, for Lupton, is a liminality, a 'transitional middle-stage' (1999: 133), that threatens social order. Therefore, Lupton constructs risk culture as that which is non-rational, non-normative, transgressive. Lived primarily through embodiment, risk creates both panic and desire through the possibilities for change that it presents. It can be deduced, then, that for Lupton liminality projects temporal finitude, the prospect of the death of the self as we know it, especially as the body becomes the locus where risk culture is lived and experienced. Embodiment for Lupton, therefore, serves as a metaphor for the borderline, that disruptive point of contact between social norms and cultural shifts.

Raï as Risk Music

It is at this very locus of risk that Chab Samir's music can be located, a hyphenated position between the normalized, on the one hand, and the unruly, dislocated peripheral, on the other. For Samir's voice to be heard above the multifarious ensemble of world music that floods most music stores in the West, it is important to make the distinction between risk, in Beck's terms, as a social, and hence regularized phenomenon of late capitalism and risk as the liminal threat that disturbs the boundaries of the normative. This same distinction is relevant to considering the emergence of his music in the culturally cosmopolitan and postmodern city of Barcelona. It would be easy to elide the CD into the larger kaleidoscopic picture of cultural multiplicity that is assigned to Barcelona – and, indeed, this may well be the case for many of his listeners. In the collection of short stories *Barcelona, un día* (1998), the writer Rosa Regás explores the synchronicities and fragments that make up this mosaic-like city. As a major European capital and as a long-standing host to immigrants from other parts of Spain as well as from various parts of the world, Barcelona is emblematic of Spain's transition to pluri-form European identity that is at one and the same time regional, national and continental. Equally it speaks of the foregrounding of localized as opposed to national identity, as was made evident during the opening ceremony of the Barcelona Olympics in 1992 when the Catalan and Spanish flags were flown side by side in an apparently unproblematic, though semantically contrary, display of plurality. The production of Samir's CD by Afro-Blue Records, a company that almost single-handedly controls the output of 'ethnic' music from the region, may somewhat confirm the group's appropriation by capitalist enterprise and thus render theirs just one more voice amongst multiple others to emerge on the music scene. Indeed, the presence of Catalan musicians in the group can be read as a multicultural display of heterogeneity typical of postmodernity, resulting in a musical fusion which, though culturally diverse in its origins, does not pose the threat of political dissent.

To do so, however, would be to reduce the CD to a mere example of packaged, kitsch ethnicity and so efface the nerve of disjuncture that bristles through it. What ties this music to the liminal is not the CD *per se*, but its symbolic significance for those who identify on a personal basis with both the lyrics and the locales where Samir sings. Indeed, as with much raï and other forms of politicized music, the symbolic impact of this music is not uniform. Thus, it can be said that Chab Samir's raï functions at two levels in terms of the music's dissemination: via live performances in clubs and larger, organized concerts in major Spanish venues and via the sale of the CD. Differentiating the dispersed world market of CD listeners as well as the heterogenous audiences of major concerts from the live audiences that frequent Chab Samir's club performances are deep divisions of class, normative legitimacy and ethnicity. Hence, the symbolic significance in cultural and political terms of this music to its respective audiences no doubt differs greatly. In this sense, the music inhabits a borderline position between sociations that are normative and regularized – that is, the music market, the organized venues where concerts take place – and cultural migrancy as disruption, that which is often illicit and marked by struggle. Club performances, which provide the group with their core, socio-cultural function, offer a sense of community for immigrants who are liminal, a spatial and temporal affirmation of specific socio-economic and political positions. The appeal the music makes on both sides of the boundary of licitness is articulated in terms of the performative, and hence the body – or, in other words, the voice – in motion.

Perhaps what is most remarkable about Samir's raï is not so much this binary opposition that it throws up between risk as a central feature of society and risk lived in terms of cultural struggle, but in fact his own impelling, though apparently unconscious, complication of this division. Chab Samir's borderline position both addresses different worlds and casts shadows on the boundaries which apparently divide them. This is particularly so because the music is contextually bound to the audience it addresses as much as it is to the contexts in which raï has historically arisen. Thus, on the CD and, as Samir stated to me in the course of my interview with him, in concerts that take place in large, public venues, the songs that are performed contain explicit lyrics of political protest aimed at inciting awareness of the immigrants' position in a hostile socio-political milieu: 'Of course, our music is about having a good time. But I also want it to make people aware of what it's like to be an "arra"[13] over here'. Thus the lyrics of many of the songs sung at these concerts and on the CD provide explicit narratives of social injustice, exclusion and oppression, graphically depicting the position of those who are both economically and legally on the periphery of mainstream society.

Two songs on Chab Samir's album stand out in particular for their political forcefulness. 'Alghorba' ['Problems'] voices the legal marginality of the immigrant 'sin papeles' (whose papers are not in order): unemployment, waiting in queues, insecurities and the 'fantasy' of the blue residence permit colour his days:

> The papers are the problem
> There are always excuses
> Running around day and night
> In search of the blue permit.[14]

The supposed 'freedom' and openness of post-Francoist Spain is put into question by Samir's statement in the song that it is impossible to walk down the main road in Barcelona, the Ramblas, without being stopped and searched by police. Indeed, he goes so far as to say that police have been stationed there specifically to stop the 'arras' or 'dark-haired' men. Racial difference is thus expressed as a visible boundary that leads to isolation. At one point in the song, Samir breaks into Spanish using a rap style, mimicking the police's demands to search the immigrant's van, presumably a reference to inspections for drugs, given the close links between the illegal trafficking of immigrants and drugs into and through Spain. The memories etched here are not specifically of Morocco;

indeed, they call up visions of uncertainty, aspects of the immigrant imaginary that evoke not visions of 'home', but rather the loss of roots and the chequered mixing of cultural influences. Identity is experienced here as displacement and insecurity. The use of rap as a musical style, juxtaposed to the softer melodies of more conventional raï, inject urgency and a certain defiance into the lyrics. The transcultural shifts in the style of music both recall earlier forms of raï and branch away from them to adopt a more radical tone. The explicitness of Samir's lyrics, in contrast to the more usual use of love as a screen for social problems, places a greater defiance and undeniability on the situation of those concerned and opens an arena for transgression in the face of the immigration policies of the West and the socio-economic struggles of the immigrant. The assertiveness of Samir's lyrics, in contrast to the more veiled insinuations of raï's Algerian counterparts, is striking for its openness. This is a voice that clearly avails itself of the freedom of speech existing with vehemence in post-Francoist Spain today in order to forge a social understanding of otherwise silenced and under-represented immigrant experiences. What is more, in the Catalan context, Catalonia's own history of struggle for a 'voice' in the face of Francoist oppression cannot be ignored.[15] Thus, in an ironic twist, the new immigrants of Catalonia force attention through their music onto the history of Catalan nationalism.

The unexpected adaptation of rap in terms of raï renders explicit the political emphasis and sense of defiance in Samir's music. Rap is a musical style which legitimizes the marginal and foregrounds a certain kind of identity aimed at disturbing that which is conventional by breaking down established borders of social centrality (see Krims, 2000). In the rags-to-riches stories of rap singers who move from the ghetto and become millionaires and in their songs about race and drugs, a new kind of subaltern identity is etched, carved out of memories of black slavery, the prison experiences of numerous blacks and the rough dismissal of white, middle-class values. Rap is disturbing – or alluring, as the case may be – most of all for voicing the 'unmentionable' histories of subaltern groups who have remained silenced or unvoiced in dominant historical narratives. This is a drive that is present in Samir's work as well.

In his song 'Patera' ('Raft', a word easily recognizable in terms of its connotations of illicit migration to those who read the Spanish press), Samir reconstructs the experience of the unsanctioned, risky crossings of the Straits of Gibraltar by raft or inflatable dinghy. Few members of a Spanish–Moroccan audience would also hear this word without mentally associating it with death. Seldom does a day pass, particularly in the summer months, without reports of people rescued at sea or, more often, bodies washed ashore in the attempt to migrate to Spain from Africa. It should be stated here that Samir himself did not arrive in Spain in this way, having first come as a tourist to attend the Barcelona Olympics of 1992. He then stayed on after marrying a Catalan woman. Despite his 'legitimacy' in Spain, the cultural memory of migration as risk, possible death and certain fear finds a voice:

... aged between 17 and 30,
Tarifa you are a cemetery ...
I have reached the beach, I have landed scared,
I have run to the woods
God!! I shall never forget this day
I have cried and my heart has shrunk.[16]

Samir's song 'Patera' clearly opens up a space for the articulation of forbidden aspects of immigrant experience. It lends authority to this experience that is normally denied expression and hence legitimacy. Equally, it draws on the backdrop of death that is attendant to a significant proportion of the immigrant presence in Spain, rendering it a key aspect of the imaginary in terms of new constructions of immigrant identity. The urgency of his lyrics and their forthrightness draw upon the risk of crossing borders, whether these be between diversely empowered nations or between life and death.

The experience of young men as immigrants in Spain is central to the narratives of Samir's songs. The CD liner notes include this statement from the producer Florenci Mas of Afro-Blue Records:

Canciones con influencias variadas, como corresponde a músicos de hoy, sean marroquíes o españoles. ¿Textos?: los normales en un joven cantante marroquí que vive en Europa desde hace algunos años y que mira la realidad de cara.

[Songs with various influences, as befits musicians today, whether they are Moroccans or Spaniards. The lyrics?: what you would expect from a young Moroccan singer who has been living in Spain for some years and who looks reality in the face.] (my translation)

This 'reality' that is referred to is underlined by one half of the reverse side of the leaflet, which is visible when the CD is shut. It shows the faces of the diverse members of the all-male group, Moroccans as well as Spaniards, one with an obviously Catalan name, pasted onto the coveted *DNI* or National Identity Card aspired to by immigrants. Names and roles within the group – saxophone player, voice, drums and so on – have been filled in. By aligning Catalans, Moroccans and Spaniards in this way, the CD's focus on legalizing and representing those without rights is rendered obvious. Furthermore, the document itself is proof that 'textual' representations of identity, be they on paper or in music, are necessary to invest authority in claims of identity.

Yet what becomes apparent after the initial introduction to Chab Samir's raï is not the finality of a political thrust, but the play of ambivalence, as the music projects shifting currents of cultural change onto its different audiences. When the CD was released, numerous press reviews stated that Samir sang regularly in a club, called Club Rubí, in Sabadell, a working-class district on the outskirts of Barcelona, long home to immigrants from other parts of Spain as well as from other countries. For the purposes of my project a good starting-point seemed to be a visit to the club in order to see the group perform live. However, when I went to Sabadell with this intention prior to arranging a meeting with Samir, no one in the area knew of such a club. It was not listed in the directory and there seemed to be no way of locating it. A visit to Nasifone, the main Arabic music shop in central Barcelona, led to more bewilderment. When I asked the shop attendants if they knew of a Club Rubí, the two Moroccan men behind the counter looked at one another and appeared to be amused. No, they said, the Club Rubí no longer operated, but Samir continued to sing in other clubs. They could not say, however, where these might be. Later, after I had got to know Samir, I was told by Hassan, a construction worker (whom I met via a Moroccan workers' organization and whose own legal status was not made clear to me) and member of his regular audience, that the club had no fixed location. Because so many of its members were illegally in the country and because it was hard to get licences for gatherings of illegal immigrants, the club moved place from time to time and it was only by word of mouth that audiences were able to follow its trail. Disused shop interiors, locales hired for a few nights by members of the local Moroccan community or venues such as church halls were transformed into a club when the group performed. They often sang in or near Sabadell, Hassan said, because so many factory and construction workers lived around there. Indeed, he said, they usually performed to a packed house somewhere in the Barcelona area on three nights a week.

The group's location, not at the helm of any kind of certainty but rather in the interstices of cultural transition, became even clearer in the course of my meeting with the members. Our interview took place in a small local bar in the suburb of Barceloneta, near the group's recording studios where they rehearsed. Here Samir stressed his chosen role of voicing immigrants' political concerns that were seldom heard in commonly circulating discourses. At the same time he showed ambivalence as regards his own position:

> I am both Moroccan and Spanish, I can be whichever I want. And, more to the point, sometimes when I am in Morocco, I feel Spanish and when I am here I feel Moroccan … My music is a bridge across the Straits; like the *pateras*, it makes its crossings. And yes, to some it is also outside boundaries of what is acceptable – to people who like more conventional music or to those who do not like mixes. There is a bit of everything in my music: flamenco, traditional Moroccan folk music, Algerian raï, jazz, blues, rap, even Hindi film music. Of course, it's raï, but then raï is not just one thing, it's a mix of many different things.

The transgressive impulse of Samir's music became even more evident when I asked about his local audiences, as did the background of dissent from which the music arises. How did they respond to the songs on the CD? Samir replied that he seldom sang songs such as 'Alghorba' or 'Patera' to audiences in the clubs around Barcelona. 'There is no need to', he stated. 'Most of us who are Moroccans already know what it's like to go through such things.' More to the point, Samir implied that a song such as 'Patera' was superfluous because death and loss were already a feature of the immigrant imaginary:

> Why should I sing to them of dying in the sea? They all know about it. I sing that to people who wouldn't think of it otherwise. Almost all of us who are here know of someone who came that way. Can you imagine what it must be like to spend fourteen hours drifting on a raft in the windy seas? Those fourteen hours are not just fourteen hours, there is no measure for them. It is to look death in the face eye-ball to eye-ball and then, when you come ashore, you come back to life ... but to a strange, lonely, new life, not the one you left behind or the one that you knew.

The experience of risk as cultural rupture lived in the face of finitude was tangible in his words, despite his own safety, and the normative grounds for risk society marked by reflexivity and cognitive measure become dispersed in the fearful, anxious turn of fraught, immigrant crossings. This club music emerging from the peripheries of Barcelona was, apparently, no mean extension of postmodern fusion or pastiche but, instead, an attempt to connect back to a place and time that had become scattered in the course of migratory displacements and, concurrently, an acknowledgement of that very disruption.

Ostensibly Samir stated that the club music was aimed at creating an atmosphere for dancing and relaxation. Many of the songs the group performed in such venues were, according to Samir, remakes of older raï hits, often from the repertoires of well-known Algerian singers, such as Cheb Khaled or Cheb Mami. Often, though, he stated, these revisions would contain Spanish words or would be rephrased to match the Spanish context, so as to reflect somewhat the identities and realities of those in the crowd. Improvisation was often the norm in live performances, he said. Clearly, the decision as to what to perform where was determined at least partly by contextual factors, as well as by the group's own perceptions of the audiences concerned. As opposed to the blunt exposure of social injustice present in more public performances, it appeared that in the more intimate settings of the clubs, the paramount focus was on pleasure.

Indeed, in the history of raï, this aim has been consistent. In raï, as Schade-Poulsen (1999) points out, lyrics of desire or *mehna* (suffering and longing) function as a veil for the restless strivings of the immigrant and the socio-economically underprivileged. By offering a canopy for representing popular subjectivity in terms of desire or love, raï both conceals and reveals social and cultural experiences. As the central theme of raï songs, love, in Schade-Poulsen's analysis of Algerian raï, acts as a cloak for the restraints of state, religion and gender. Equally, through its Westernization of Wahrani music (from Oran), audible in terms of the instruments used and imagined in terms of the lyrics of sexual freedom, raï adheres at least in part to the musical discourses of shifting identities in the West. Nevertheless, signification is doubtless not intrinsic to any 'text', musical or otherwise, but instead is culturally invested in it. For Lipsitz (1994), music provides minority communities with a means of countering the threat of assimilation in the context of immigration. It allows a paradigm of citizenship and identity that is multi-sited and allows for intercultural communication as well as serving to locate conflict. Clearly, Chab Samir's aim is to negotiate new terrain for raï, and by extension for Spanish-Moroccans like himself. As such, and as Stokes (1994) indicates, music transforms space, negotiating and generating new boundaries. The historical specificity of the factors surrounding the production of such music necessarily underlines the contingency of boundaries, so that any given musical or cultural 'stereotype' is reliant upon particular axes of space and time. The dynamics of the music provide space for numerous interpretations and attitudes, dissolving barriers that exist in normative society as well as the very socio-cultural limits attached to the concept of the mainstream. Raï thus allows for a 'double' existence, at once contradictory and irreconcilable, yet intrinsically bound by the tremulous borderline.

Perhaps this complexity became most evident in the pause that followed my asking Samir if I might visit whichever venue he was performing in that week. The silence that the question sparked underlined a sudden rupture both in our conversation and in my attempt at fieldwork. Skilfully, then, Samir turned the interrogative on me, asking about my background and my work. The conversation continued for a while, but the permission I had sought was neither addressed nor granted. His tacit refusal confined my academic pursuit to one side of the boundary of licitness that Samir clearly maintained, straddled and confounded. This chapter, then, arises from the imaginations of that location. It goes without saying, therefore, that in articulating the complexities of raï in terms of risk, the struggles between the normative and the transgressive become foregrounded. The restless urgency of this Spanish–Moroccan raï ensues, not so much from the CD *per se* or indeed the music's innovativeness, but from the fissures, the hidden spaces and the joints between the two levels at which the group and its lead singer operate.

Chab Samir dissolves boundaries between the structures of risk society and the less predictable fluxes of risk cultures and operates in both contexts. In so doing, the singer and his group both confirm and disturb the currency of the normative, revealing the transitionality and ambivalence of immigrant cultural identity. By extension, this raï music exposes the imbrications of the local, the national and the global. More importantly, such apparently defined categories as the local, the national or the global are seen to be themselves fissured and mutually implicated, both far-flung from one another and connected by this migrant music of challenge and change.

Notes

1 A version of this chapter, with more emphasis on fieldwork, is forthcoming in *Interventions: Journal of Postcolonial Theory*.

2 This song was adopted as the anthem of protesters in October 1988.

3   Lipsitz (1994) connects raï with reggae and bhangra as examples of immigrant music that coincide in their rise with hostility towards ethnic minorities in the capitals of the West. In this context, Krims (2000) writes of rap as a poetics of 'revolutionary' identity.

4   The word *Beur* refers to second generations of North African origin. See George in this collection.

5   The title 'Cheb' or 'Chebba' used by many singers denotes 'youth', a setting up of oneself against tradition in a rebellious posture.

6   An exception is the more recent raï of Rachid Taha whose lyrics often openly explore the ruptures that accompany the migrant experience, as well as the migrant's dream of homecoming, for example his 1998 chart success with 'Ya Rayah', his version of the traditional *Sha'bī* song.

7   George Lipsitz states in this context that 'many immigrants pursue cultural and political strategies that emphasize the heterogeneity of their group, the hybridity of their culture and the multiplicity of identities available to people who are not only immigrant or ethnic subjects' (1994: 120). Raï, as a hybrid mix of the folkloric, the urban and the cosmopolitan, then becomes a musical gesture of resistance in the face of state attempts at regularized homogenization, be these Algerian or French.

8   *In This World* (Winterbottom, 2002) is a film that charts the illicit movements of a young Afghani boy as he makes the arduous journey from Pakistan to London, a journey which exemplifies such risk.

9   Lupton (1999) constructs her concept of risk by reference to Mary Douglas's earlier work on this notion (1985, 1992).

10 See Crain (1999) for more details of migration from Morocco to and through Spain.

11 The exact date of the transition following Franco's death in 1975 is a matter of some debate, 1982 is the year in which the Spanish socialist party PSOE won the general elections.

12 Spain entered the European Community on 1 January 1986.

13 This is a Spanish racist term, meaning 'dark heads', used to denote immigrants.

14 My translation from the Spanish version of the lyrics sung in Arabic, as printed on the cover of the CD.

15 The regime imposed severe restrictions on the use of the Catalan language.

16 My translation from the Spanish version of the lyrics sung in Arabic, as printed on the cover of the CD.

Interviews conducted by the author

Samir El Quichiri, Barcelona, April 2001.
Hasan, Barcelona, April 2001.

Discography

Chab Samir, *Chab Samir* (Afro-Blue Records, B-16823-1999, 1999).
Rachid Taha, 'Ya Rayah', *Diwân* (Arabic forum for playing music) (Barclay, 314 539-953-2, 1998).

Filmography

Winterbottom, Michael (2002), *In This World.*

Chapter 4

Banda, a New Sound from the *Barrios* of Los Angeles: Transmigration and Transcultural Production

Helena Simonett

In the 1980s popular music scholars began to critically look at the powers of technology and the music industry in marginal countries and in the Third World and the apparent irrelevance of culturally-specific locations in the transnational and transcultural production and consumption of musics known as 'World Beat' (Wallis and Malm, 1984). The following decade witnessed a burst in the number of publications on transnational musical styles such as bachata, merengue, raï, salsa, soca, soukous and zouk, as well as an increased preoccupation with theoretical questions concerning the global flow of local musics.[1] Scholars have recognized the efficacy of transnational musics in creating new social relations and identities for both local and global audiences. Indeed, whether audiences will choose one music style over another does not depend on its availability and visibility alone, but on the consumers' aesthetic sensitivities (Taylor, 1997). Despite the efforts of multinational recording corporations to plan and control the music market, products and consumer desire cannot be entirely gauged in advance.

Accelerating processes of globalization, including mass mediatization and transmigration, encourage us to rethink our cultural concepts. What is needed when looking at contemporary musical landscapes is a mode of thinking that is open to such broader processes, one that not only includes at once the micro-world and the global cultural flow, but also accounts for the complex interplay between local and overarching music systems (Slobin, 1993). This chapter describes and analyses the (techno)banda phenomenon of the 1990s in Los Angeles, establishing its importance as a living and dynamic transnational music, while discussing the role of place, roots and memory in contemporary culture.

LA's hottest sound of the 1990s

The steady flow of immigrants from Mexico and Central America has changed and continues to change the face of California. The Los Angeles metropolitan region, more than any other place in the United States, is a magnet for immigrants, notably from Mexico. Latinos are gradually becoming a demographic majority.[2] From the historical Mexican *barrios* [neighbourhoods], East Los Angeles, Boyle Heights and Pico Union, Mexican newcomers have spread into the San Gabriel Valley in the east, San Fernando in the north and San Pedro in the south. Newcomers have also spilled into the traditionally African-American South Central, Watts, Compton and Inglewood areas. Moreover, many recent immigrants have settled in the former industrial heartland of the county (Acuña, 1996: 3; see also Clark, 1996; Waldinger and Bozorgmehr, 1996). Latinos form 80–90 per cent of the population of this extended neighbourhood or *mega-barrio*, also known as 'Nuevo LA' [the new LA]. The rapid transformation of metropolitan Los Angeles has created much anxiety and controversy among residents, in particular among white residents. Concerns about an 'invasion of brown-skinned people' and about the subsequent and inevitable erosion of 'American identity' have become frequent themes in the media. Ethnic minorities, immigrants and refugees became exposed to xenophobic attitudes, which, on the political stage, were expressed in propositions such as 'Save-Our-State' and 'English-Only', the former seeking to deny public education and non-emergency health care to undocumented immigrants and their children, and the latter requesting that bilingual education be abandoned (Acuña, 1996: 156–8; 293–4).

On the one hand, California's prevailing anti-immigrant climate of the early 1990s alienated the Latino communities in the US south-west, but, on the other, as young people of Mexican descent became more sensitive to racial discrimination and exploitation, they began to take an increased interest in their own and their parents' and grandparents' heritage and traditions. The musical replenishment from south of the border encouraged Mexicanos to reaffirm and bolster their 'ethnic consciousness', and to express their cultural loyalty. Their choice to affiliate with, and belong to, a particular subculture was not random.

The new sound that emerged from the burgeoning Mexican neighbourhoods of Los Angeles was called technobanda (or just banda), a modernized version of a regional band with roots in nineteenth-century rural Mexico (Simonett, 1999). In contrast to the traditional acoustic banda with its clarinets, trumpets, trombones, tuba, horns, tambora and tarola (double-headed bass drum and snare drum, respectively), technobandas are made up of electric bass, keyboard synthesizer, saxophones and trumpets, and feature a vocalist.[3] Yet until the extraordinary and persisting popularity of a new Spanish-language radio station, KLAX-FM, which aired ranchera (country or rural-rooted) music began to threaten the hegemony of the English-language radio industry in Los Angeles in the early 1990s, (techno)banda had been the music of an 'invisible minority' of recent Mexican immigrants and blue-collar workers. With the radio station's sudden and unexpected success, banda music was pulled out of the *barrio* and brought into the limelight. In 1993 the *Los Angeles Times* proclaimed boldly: 'The hottest sound in LA is banda', a 'Mexican music with German roots [that] has caught on big with young Latinos' (Oumano and Lopetegui, 1993: F1). The vibrant new sound that had emerged in 'Nuevo LA' began to reverberate amongst vast audiences both north and south of the US–Mexico border.[4]

Technobanda apparently found the right place, the right time and the right circumstances: a susceptible and favourable young audience for whom this new, catchy and danceable rhythm became a style of life and a strong force of cultural identity. The new music allowed its participants to raise their own voice, to make their presence visible and audible, and, at the same time, to create a liveable place for themselves in an environment that had not welcomed them and that grew increasingly more hostile to anyone of Mexican or Latino descent as California's economic condition further deteriorated.

Technobanda, a Promising Transnational Music

Soon after the first technobanda recordings, made by the Jalisco-based label Fonorama in the late 1980s, other Mexican labels also began to record the new groups. MCM (Metro Casa Musical, Monterrey), Disa (Monterrey) and Musivisa (Mexico City), companies which had already specialized in Mexico's 'rural-rooted sounds', norteña and ranchera, began to sign banda acts. Yet banda products from Mexico remained largely ignored in the United States. Without retail distribution, fans were forced to trade and copy tapes they had brought across the border from Mexico. In 1992 Fonovisa Records, which has a US distribution agreement with the Mexican label MCM, released two albums by Banda Machos from Jalisco, *Casimira* and *Sangre de indio* [Indian blood], which became instant sales hits in the United States. Both albums made it into the top 20 of Billboard's Top Latin Albums/Regional Mexican chart. Based on the sales success of technobanda recordings in the US, *Billboard* magazine declared 1993 'the banda year'.

After the unprecedented inroads of 'rural-rooted sounds' into Mexico City, sparked by technobandas' success in the USA, new labels were created, among them Raza by Warner Music Mexico in 1994. EMI Music Mexico showed interest in acquiring DLV, a company specializing in norteña music. BMG International (Bertelsmann, New York), Sony Discos (Miami) and Capitol Records' EMI-Latin (Los Angeles) signed norteña and banda acts. Mexican label Discos Musart (distributed by Balboa Records, Los Angeles) competed with labels operating in Los Angeles such as Fonovisa (Van Nuys) and La Sierra Records (Panorama City). Fonovisa made US distribution agreements with Mexican labels such as Musivisa, Disa, MCM, Fonorama and LMC (Luna Music Corporation, Los Angeles).

Televisa, the world's largest Spanish-language media company, had multiple interests in promoting grupos and bandas. The company owns Melody Records which is affiliated with Musivisa. Televisa also developed Río Nilo, a 540,000-square foot multi-purpose facility in Guadalajara, Jalisco, where music and dance shows featuring norteña groups, bandas and grupos routinely draw between 70,000 and 90,000 fans. Although Hispanic television contributed much to the popularization of banda music and technobandas through the dissemination of their images, it had been rather slow in 'discovering' and promoting the new groups. But, once discovered, Televisa turned banda into a commodity for the masses, propagating it nationally and internationally.

Technobanda's success in the USA indeed made multinational recording corporations take notice and sales managers look into the possibility of marketing technobanda in the 'Hispanic'/ 'Latino Pop' or even 'World Beat' categories. However, a few years after the initial boom, only a small selection of technobanda albums were to be found in national outlets such as Tower Records or Blockbuster. Unlike tejano (Texas–Mexican) music, technobanda had not burst out of its Mexican/Mexican-American boundaries as culture industry executives had hoped for when the new sound emerged in the early 1990s. The barriers against a smooth crossover into common-denominator Latin pop seemed impossible to overcome due to the music's rootedness in the particularities of its local culture.

For the many Mexican/Mexican-American fans, however, technobanda's appeal was grounded precisely in the tension between elements of nationalist resistance (the reinterpretation of regional Mexican music) and conformity to the hegemonic power of the culture industry with its MTV-inspired hi-tech music. Participation in banda events allowed both Mexican immigrants and Mexican-Americans to reclaim and renovate their own tradition while enjoying the commercial seduction and standards of MTV and its related industries.

Technobanda's Presence

In 1990 most Latin dance halls in Mexican LA featured *música tropical* (Caribbean music such as salsa and cumbia). When banda music began to gain ground and the dancing public asked for the electrifying novel rhythm, local musicians 're-banded'. Within a year, technobanda had given rise to dozens of groups, and the *quebradita* dancing fever spread rapidly.[5] To many young people who had been used to 'canned music' (disco), it was attractive that the music in these nightclubs was playing live.[6] One dance aficionado assured me: 'What draws me to the nightclub is the energy of the music. I dance banda because it's so fast and there are live instruments: it's a complete band.' The banda movement was carried by the music's danceability. Technobanda's accelerated tempo and powerful amplification enabled dancers literally to feel the music.

The nightclub scene drew more and more young people of Mexican heritage, most of whom had grown up in the United States. Participating in American popular culture, they used to listen to rock, rap, heavy metal or deep house, and they would never have imagined that one day they would tune into Mexican music and engage in a *vaquero* [cowboy] dance fad. One 18-year-old woman told me:

Before it started with Banda Machos, I didn't like Spanish music … I listened to English music, techno, etc. Then banda became popular and everybody started liking it. All these songs came out ... And when the clubs started, that's when I started too. And since then, that's all I listen to.

Because of an increasing number of violent, gang-related incidents in the 1980s and 1990s in and around youth dance clubs in Los Angeles's inner cities, authorities had closed one after another. Young people of these neighbourhoods were left with no place to gather and to dance. Thus, the main reason for youths hanging around at banda nightclubs may not necessarily have been the type of music featured, but the prospect of meeting and dancing.

Afraid of drive-by shootings, the security guards of the popular nightclubs had to prevent youngsters in baggy clothes from gathering in front of the nightclub. The *vaquero* dress code was imposed on those who wanted to enter. At first embarrassed to dress up as cowboys, many youths had a feeling that banda was forced upon them. Yet, the nightclubs' appeal was too strong to resist; eventually they exchanged baseball caps and oversized clothes for cowboy hats and tight jeans. Transformed into 'urban cowboys', but with a techno or hip hop past, they became a driving force in the modification of the dancing style. The manager of one of the large nightclubs confirmed:

> The way they dance it here is different from how it is danced in Guadalajara. Many people think that the real *quebradita* is how it is being danced here, and I agree because it was here where the dance got mixed, where the youths blended in their own steps. Elderly people don't like to dance the *quebradita*. They say that it ruins the banda music, that banda has to be danced differently. (Interview, 1996; translation mine)

Over the years, the *quebradita* style evolved and *el caballito* ('the little horse') began to dominate the nightclub scene, followed by *el brinquito* ('short-leaping'). To dance *de brinquito*, the cowboys had to take off their hats, exchange their boots for comfortable dancing shoes and their tight jeans for baggier pants. Accessories such as the *correa* (a leather strap engraved with the name of the Mexican home state of its wearer) and the *pañuelo* (a bandana with embroidery in the colours of the Mexican flag) that boosted regional and national pride disappeared. Instead, dancers expressed their regional self-esteem in distinctive dancing styles. People from central Mexico tended to be more innovative, adding new steps and gestures, while Sinaloans continued to dance in traditional posture.

In Search of Cultural Identity

In neighbourhoods where Mexicans constitute demographic majorities, many do not regard themselves as members of an alienated and marginalized minority. The proximity of Los Angeles to Mexico enables Mexican newcomers, as well as long-term residents, to maintain strong ties to their homeland. Rather than immigrants in the traditional sense, most of these people are transmigrants who remain attached to, and empowered by, a 'home' culture and a tradition.[7] Frequent travel back home and maintenance of multiple relations across the border facilitate a clinging to accustomed ways of life. Because of their sheer demographic mass and limited contact with other Angelenos, Mexicanos have not only retained a strong sense of cultural identity, they also fashion their new place so as to feel at home.

Although the sense of being a 'people' with historical roots was not new to Mexican-Americans, Chicano scholars celebrated Latinos' newfound confidence, claiming that now, on the verge of the twenty-first century, 'LA's culture comes full circle':

> Twenty years ago, sociological literature considered ethnic identification a deviant behavior ... Today Latinos have begun to value their own norms and ways of life. It is only the strength of our identity and our multirooted culture that can make the disaffected among us, particularly the youth, feel like they belong to the larger society. In fact, we are becoming the mainstream. (Hayes-Bautista and Rodríguez, 1994: B11)

Summarizing the ambience at a Los Angeles nightclub when the *quebradita* craze was in full swing, Rubén Martínez (1994) argued that the dance-and-music craze fuelled a latent feeling among the participants that they too had a right to succeed in the USA, where most of them had been born. The dimensions of the movement let them recognize that others too felt the need to belong. Indeed, like other youths of foreign descent, Mexicanos are often more hurt and troubled by their exclusion from mainstream society than are their parents. Faced with discrimination and an increasing openly expressed racism, children and young adults have tried more fiercely to assert their ethnic particularity and to search for a musical voice to state unequivocally who and what they are.[8] Banda music was something new for a generation of Mexicanos who had grown up listening to mainstream rock and rap music. By the mid-1990s, a large number of young Latinos engaged technobanda as a space for cultural affirmation. Instead of American popular music, the latest banda hits now poured out of open car windows: this was their political statement. A young banda aficionado told me:

> Have you noticed that the more that things turn against the immigrants and the more laws they make against the immigrants, the more they are coming out? They are dressing more expressive, they like to turn up their car radios more. They're proud of who they are, they are not intimidated any longer. The banda movement helped young people to address the issue of being Mexican. To tell who they are or to fight against injustice and discrimination. Definitely ... I have friends that were ashamed of their roots, they didn't want to admit that they are Mexican. And now I see my cousins' friend, they're going to dance banda: 'Yes, I'm Mexican!' Young people are aware of a lot of things – in a younger age.

Identity formation was encouraged by the mass media, in particular by the radio stations, which had not only developed a youth market among the teenage children of immigrants but also reached a young American-born audience.

Finding One's Own Place

While most traditional anthropological studies tended to favour representations of contained people, places and identities, many recent studies concentrate on highly diverse social groups in multicultural settings. Public controversies over 'multiculturalism' and 'English-Only' reflect a deep uneasiness among many Californian residents about contemporary conditions of life.[9] The election campaigns for the governor of California in the 1990s have not only shown how deep the division actually is between the opposed concepts of 'melting pot' (uniculturalism) and 'multiculturalism', but also proved Rosaldo right that '[t]hese days questions of culture seem to touch a nerve because they quite quickly become anguished questions of identity' (1993: xxi). The debate over multiculturalism has brought questions of conflict, change, inequality, disruption and difference onto centre stage, and with them questions of ethnic identity and self-representation.

Peter W. Preston proposes to 'think of identity as a shifting balance between what is remembered and what is currently demanded. Identity is thus always shifting; it is never fixed' (1997: 49–50). To stress the transformative aspect of identity, Stuart Hall (1990) has called identity a 'meeting point', a point of temporary identification that constitutes and re-forms the individual so as to enable that individual to act. Subject to the continuous play of history, culture and power, identity emerges as a continually contested domain. Questions of identity, as Gupta and Ferguson recently pointed out, 'demonstrate with special clarity the intertwining of place and power in the conceptualization of "culture"'. Moreover:

> By stressing that place making always involves a construction, rather than merely a discovery, of difference, the authors ... emphasise that identity neither 'grows out' of rooted communities nor is it a thing that can be possessed or owned by individual or collective social actors. It is, instead, a mobile, often unstable relation of difference. (1997: 13–14)

Analogous to the notion of identity as fluid and dynamic, ethnicity is not a given but 'something reinvented and reinterpreted in each generation by each individual' (Fischer, 1986: 195). Identifying oneself in ethnic terms is a basic human need to express social belonging. Moreover, some sense of identity is linked to a sense of place, to networks and to memory.

Much has been written during the last decade about 'the sense of place'.[10] The initial focus of inquiry into 'the sense of rootedness in place' has shifted in recent years to 'the sense of displacement' and to place as a site of power struggles. Yet, 'displacement is not less the source of powerful attachments than are experiences of profound rootedness' (Feld and Basso, 1996: 11). As Clifford Geertz has so keenly noted:

> For all the uprooting, the homelessness, the migrations, forced and voluntary, the dislocations of traditional relationships, the struggles over homelands, borders, rights of recognition, for all the destructions of familiar landscapes and the manufacturings of new ones, and for all the loss of local stabilities and local originalities, the sense of place, and of the specificities of place, seems, however tense and darkened, barely diminished in the modern world. (1996: 261)

Thus, the consciousness and worldview of a collective 'people' continues to be rooted in place, tradition and locality. For people, whether dislocated or not, memory is not a simple nostalgic longing for, or an illusion of, home, but 'a basis for ideas of continuity; a store of experience and knowledge to inform future activity; a sphere of reflective self-understanding; a fluid sphere liable to alteration in the light of new events or merely via the passage of time' (Preston, 1997: 52–3).

Although these statements are somewhat general, those who write about popular music usually assume a certain sense of 'community'. Yet, like 'subcultures' and 'ethnic groups', communities are not stable units of contained people, defined or self-defined. Perceptions of such groups are not only discursively and historically constituted, boundaries and contents are constantly negotiated and allegiances are shifting. Since people tend to identify with more than one musical genre, music as an 'identity marker' exemplifies the volatility and the multiplicity of such allegiances.

In the United States, (techno)banda was able to leave its marginalized confines and become the cultural expression of a very diverse people, thus transcending class boundaries. For many individuals who sensed their ambiguous social position as Chicanos/Mexican-Americans in the United States, the participation in banda events was an alternative musical activity that also affirmed their political standing. As one college-educated young woman asserted:

> I like the music, but it is also political. To me, a lot of it has to do with my parents' history. It is knowing my history. I like a lot of the lyrics, especially the old songs – the older lyrics talking about growing up in a small town. Banda Machos's 'Sangre de indio' [Indian blood] talks about moving away from the home-town, about being an Indian. They're talking of being proud of who you are. I know how it is to live in a small town because of my parents. I feel proud of listening to this kind of music. It reinforces what I was taught to believe.

Music embodies imagined worlds. Yet, the banda movement has shown that imagination is not a simple daydream or idle escapism but rather an empowering force. Because music offers strong images of characteristic identities, it is a source for identity and pride, as a young Mexican-American expressed:

[The music] also shows, in a political sense: 'Yeah, we're also here and we are proud of being here. We're strong people.'

In the diaspora, community, once understood as being rooted in particular localities, moves to the level of the nation. The shift from an explicit affirmation of regionalism to a cultural expression of nationalism was particularly noticeable at dance events in Nuevo LA. As one participant observed:

> It was very powerful when that article came out in the *L.A. Times* [*Magazine*, by Rubén Martínez, 1994]. I remember I was reading it at school. Three years later, it's still the same big crowd. In terms of clothes, it is different ... All these accessories are gone, but they still react to the *saludos* [salutes to Mexican states]. It's not so territorial anymore. Just Mexico. Maybe there is an unconscious influence because there are so many things going on against Mexicans [in the US] recently – they became the scapegoat for political reasons. It becomes secondary from what state you're from.

A Postmodern Synthesis

Technobanda allowed Mexicano youths to form an attachment to values shared with grandparents and parents and rooted in their 'homeland'. On the other hand, it also allowed for the incorporation of social conventions, fashions and aspirations derived from American youth culture into Mexicano culture. As with other recent popular musics of large migrant populations, technobanda's syncretic fusion of traditional elements and contemporary features is an expression of its listeners'/participants' own senses of identity. As pointed out by Peter Manuel, cultural expressions of migrant communities often show an inclination towards postmodern aesthetics, while simultaneously retaining ties to pre-modern ancestral traditions. The coexistence of post- and pre-modern cultural attitudes in lower-class urban subcultures, though, is not a 'postmodern pastiche' in the sense of a calculated play with elements from disparate discourses and subjectivities as employed by postmodern artists:

> [R]ather, subcultures are often born into struggles against poverty and discrimination, in which the reconstitution of a sense of personal or collective subjectivity is not a casual pursuit, but rather an urgent task crucial to psychic survival ... the migrant's search for a sense of identity, like that of modernising societies in general, is not necessarily a post-modern process, but one which synthesises traditional and contemporary subjectivities in an often profoundly emotional manner. (Manuel, 1995a: 229, 235)

California's socio-political circumstances have contributed much to condition the power and force of banda music. In its modern garb, technobanda appealed to hundreds of thousands of young people. As a 'traditional Mexican' music, it was a source of pride in one's own culture and race. Moreover, technobanda generated a taste for acoustic banda music. Indeed, banda's modernized version and the dance craze it triggered was a detour to learn about the existence of, and eventually to appreciate, Sinaloan banda music. As KBUE-FM DJ Rosy González emphasized, many young people found their roots, their 'home', in banda music: '*Banda de viento* is a feeling that people have of back home. When I hear banda sinaloense I get the chill' (personal interview, 1996). Another young banda fan concluded: 'Now, I like the tambora [regional designation for banda sinaloense] more than technobanda. It's the real stuff' (personal interview, 1996).

Concluding Thoughts

Music offers palpable data for understanding societies in transition because music has played and continues to play a crucial role in the transformation of societies. Yet music not only reflects existing social realities. If we listen carefully, changes in society may be audible before they become visible. As Lipsitz has noted, 'the relationship between popular music and place offers a way of starting to understand the social world that we are losing – and a key to the one that is being built. Anxieties aired through popular music illumine important aspects of the cultural and political conflicts that lie ahead of us all' (1994: 3).

For decades, Mexican newcomers who settled in the traditional Mexican *barrios* of Los Angeles and, more recently, in the industrial heartland of the city remained invisible (and inaudible) to the main population's political, social and cultural concerns. When politicians and the news media began to blame the state budget crisis and economic recession that California had suffered due to cutbacks in the aerospace and defence industries in the 1980s on the growing number of immigrants, technobanda exploded in popularity and became a unifying symbol of resistance and pride in one's own culture and traditions.

The new sound from the *barrios* constituted a powerful way of belonging, firmly rooted in local attachments, *la tierra* [the native land] and in local traditions. Holding on to a way of life informed by custom and history has become increasingly more significant to anyone trying to resist the uprooting and dislocating forces of our time. George Lipsitz thus urges us to see music as a part of the collective historical memory and continuing social dialogue, for 'one reason for popular music's powerful affect is its ability to conflate music and lived experience, to make both the past and present zones of choice that serve distinct social and political interests' (1990: 104). Among younger Mexicanos, technobanda was valued because it drew from Mexican roots, and because it made them feel *orgulloso* [proud]. For once, their presence in the United States was acknowledged by the media in a positive way. Their love of dancing to banda music had been transformed into an important tool of cultural politics. Not only had they become visible, they were also audible. Cruising around in their cars that vibrated with the rhythm of the new sound of Los Angeles was both a powerful statement of identification with their Mexican heritage and a forceful affirmation that they too belonged to this city and this nation. The vibrant and youthful new style was relevant to both their lifestyle and their cultural needs. With technobanda, the Mexicano youth of the 1990s had finally found its voice.

Notes

1   See Erlmann, Garofalo, Guilbault and Pacini Hernández in the special edition 'The Politics and Aesthetics of "World Music"' of *World of Music* (1993).

2   As of 1990, Latinos (including newcomers and American-born Latinos) made up 40 per cent of the Los Angeles area's 13 million inhabitants; over 3 million Angelenos, Los Angeles residents, speak Spanish at home. Labelling of ethnic groups in the United States does change over time, reflecting changes in how groups of people see themselves in relation to the larger society. Despite the fact that in the 1990s the word Mexican was often used in a derogatory way in California's political arena, some young second or third-generation US citizens of Mexican heritage began to refer to themselves as Mexican or Mexicano/Mexicana, even if they were more fluent in English than in Spanish. Thus, the term Mexicano is used here to refer to the population of Mexican origin residing in the United States, regardless of birthplace or generational status. Mexican is used when referring to those born in Mexico, while Mexican-American and Chicano are used to refer to the American-born population. The term Latino is employed to include other Latin Americans.

3   Technobanda may be best described as a grupo-version of a Banda Sinaloense, a brass-band type from Mexico's north-west coast, in particular the state of Sinaloa. The grupo ensemble with its synthesized instruments and lead vocalist is one of Mexico's commercially most successful popular musics; grupos' main repertoire consists of easy-listening Mexican and international pop ballads. Apart from novelty songs that most often address the new dance style and clothes, a great number of technobanda songs are reinterpretations of traditional Mexican rancheras and corridos (ballads) from the banda and norteña repertoires.

4   By 1993 banda music had become so loud that it was impossible to ignore it any longer. The print media was first to 'discover' (techno)banda. The new music-and-dance craze made headlines in major newspapers such as the *Los Angeles Times*, the *New York Times*, the *Wall Street Journal* and the *Washington Post*, as well as Los Angeles's Spanish-language newspaper, *La Opinión*.

5   The new dance style got its name from one of its distinctive gestures: dipping the female dancer backward into a *quebradita* [break]. Along with the music and the dance came a specific dress code, the *vaquero* [cowboy] style.

6   The following paragraphs are based on fieldwork done in Los Angeles during the years 1994–96. Excerpts are taken from interviews with a number of female dancers whom I met in Los Angeles nightclubs while gathering information for my dissertation project (Simonett, 1997).

7   Transmigrants are migrants who maintain active involvements with the people and places they left behind; thus, they create new kinds of communities that span the international border. See Glick Schiller, Basch and Blanc-Szanton (1992).

8   This tendency is also observable in Europe, where young second-generation immigrants have begun to articulate their ethnic particularities through new styles of popular

music. For British-born Indians, see Banerji and Baumann (1990); for German-born Turkish youth, see Greve (1997).

9   Assimilation used to be the main goal of US immigration policy for many decades. Newcomers were expected to strip off their distinctive inheritance and blend into mainstream American society as quickly as possible. In recent years, however, there has been a trend towards celebrating ethnic diversity. The contemporary ideal is not assimilation but ethnicity; the escape from origins has given way to the search for roots. Multiculturalism asserts that people with different roots can coexist and learn to tolerate each other's culture.

10 See, for example, Feld and Basso (1996), Gupta and Ferguson (1997) and Stokes (1994). Stokes's volume contains an interesting collection of ethnomusicological essays that address questions of how music is used by social actors in specific local situations to construct and mobilize ethnicities and identities.

Discography

Banda Machos, *Casimira* (Fonovisa Records, 1992).
Banda Machos, *Sangre de Indio* (Fonovisa Records, 1992).

Chapter 5

Rapping at the Margins: Musical Constructions of Identities in Contemporary France

Brian George

Une tchatche hargneuse et poétique.[1]

As a relatively new cultural form, rap currently plays a significant role in some of the challenges being posed to traditional, monolithic conceptions of what constitutes Frenchness. First among those challenges is the assertion of a new sense of identity among the young, multi-ethnic inhabitants of the *banlieues*[2] of major French cities. Less obvious, perhaps, is the way rap has been embraced by some of those challenging the linguistic and cultural hegemony of Paris and working towards the recognition of linguistic diversity in the nation. I want to look briefly at how genuinely subversive a medium rap can be construed to be, and hope to illustrate some of its linguistic features. A brief consideration of the work of two bands using the Occitan language in their work will involve a discussion of rap's eclecticism, its postmodern mix of the old and the new.

It has become a truism to state that rap has emerged as one of the favoured vehicles of cultural expression of young *banlieusards* in the course of the past decade.[3] Most rap group members come from the *quartiers difficiles* [difficult neighbourhoods] which encircle the major French cities, many of them from second-generation immigrant families. It is this layer of young people who are often demonized in political rhetoric, not just in the propaganda of the racist Front National, but also in the discourse of mainstream political parties. The young *banlieusards* have been condemned, feared, mistrusted, the victims of racist attacks and murders, and have been the subject of journalistic sensationalism. Periodically they have engaged in rioting which has confirmed the racists in their prejudices and administered a profound shock to the assimilationist ideology of mainstream liberal intellectuals.

These events have taken place in the context of a deep crisis in French identity. This identity crisis is predicated on the struggle to come to terms with loss of empire, the challenge of absorbing an immigrant population of diverse ethnic origins and a perceived loss of national influence and prestige on the world stage, especially in the shadow of the increased power of the USA and the predominance of the English language.[4] At the same time, there has been a growing interest internationally in exploring the experiences of the 'Black Atlantic' diaspora, and in the construction of new identities by second- and third-generation immigrants, on both an individual and a collective level. In tandem, there have been renewed attempts to protect and nurture 'minority' languages within European nations. Catalan, a close linguistic cousin of Occitan, has perhaps achieved the highest profile of these minority languages, a privileged position largely predicated on the political decisions adopted by the *Generalitat* (autonomous government) in Catalonia.

The most disturbing feature of the identity crisis in France has been the growth of racism, in both its crude, lumpen variety and its more insidious, sophisticated form. This has been accompanied by much lamentation on the part of left-leaning intellectuals that such xenophobia should have arisen in a country that has always prided itself on being a haven for refugees, with a reputation for welcoming and assimilating people from diverse ethnic backgrounds. Between 1998 and 2002 a limited optimism developed that France was learning to develop a more inclusive sense of national identity, one that was willing to embrace multiculturalism. This optimism was based on certain symbolic events, such as the ecstatic response to the successes of the multiracial French national football team, rather than on solid evidence of substantially changed attitudes in society at large. A commentator in the British press expressed scepticism about the depth of this supposed attitudinal change:

> In poll after poll, a majority of voters admitted to entertaining 'racist ideas' ... I knew that the FN was less attractive merely due to its squabbles ... The *banlieues* were still toxic dumping grounds where hatred was cultivated. (Fraser, 2000)

This writer's scepticism seems to have been vindicated by the political earthquake represented by the first round of the French presidential election in April 2002, when the Front National leader Jean-Marie Le Pen pushed the socialist prime minister Lionel Jospin into third place. Overnight the complacent optimism regarding the inevitable withering away of racism vanished. It is true, of course, that Le Pen's electoral 'success' prompted mass mobilizations and demonstrations, particularly of young people outraged by his propaganda, and that he was heavily defeated by Jacques Chirac in the second round of the elections. Overall, though, the 2002 elections dealt a heavy blow to hopes that racism was on the wane in France.

The Griot of the *Banlieue*

It is no accident that rap, and its associated musical forms, ragga and rub-a-dub, have achieved their relatively high profile in the popular culture of France during this period. Rap feeds into, and is nourished by, many of the social, political and cultural issues touched on above. While rap is not a native French form, it is quite possible to identify some recent cultural antecedents within France itself. Many of the issues rap articulates were anticipated in two cultural phenomena of the 1980s: alternative rock and community theatre. The alternative rock movement, of which the best-known representatives were the bands Mano Negra and Négresses Vertes, combined the defiant anti-establishment posture of punk with a promiscuous mixture of musical influences including Jamaican reggae, Algerian raï and Latin rhythms. Community theatre had proliferated in France in the aftermath of May 1968. In the hands of its best practitioners, such as Armand Gatti, André Benedetto and the Téâtre de la Carriera, it made sustained efforts to link theatre with the lives of people in deprived communities. Projects such as Benedetto's *Ville à vif* in Avignon in 1977 problematized the growing economic, social and cultural rift between city centres and the marginalized outer suburbs, where many minority ethnic families lived. Such projects sought to develop an alternative model of cultural expression, one in which ordinary people were involved as active participants and creators rather than merely as spectators or consumers. The growing political awareness of second-generation immigrants found one of its first expressions in a variant of community theatre, the *théâtre beur* movement of the mid-1980s.[5] Calio suggests that this movement, which was showcased at the 1986 Lille Festival, can be seen as French rap's 'elder brother':

En réaction à tout ce qui s'écrit et se raconte sur eux ... les enfants des maghrébins en France ont décidé de s'organiser, de prendre la parole pour dire qui ils sont réellement et ce qu'ils veulent. (1998: 23)

[Reacting against everything which is written and said about them ... the children of North African immigrants in France decided to get organized, to speak out about whom they really are and what they want.]

On a global scale, rap as a specific cultural form traces its roots to the New York of the late 1970s, being originally one component of a range of linked forms which included dance and graffiti art as well as music. Common to all three are a posture of defiant rebelliousness, a lack of respect for the surface of the surrounding milieu,[6] and an attempt to encapsulate the speed and discontinuity of modern urban life.

French rap practitioners have always identified closely with the American originators of the form. Rappers have sought to discover, in African America, an alternative source of identity to the Frenchness from which they feel forcibly excluded. This identification is revealed in a variety of ways. If we look briefly at symbolic features like band names, this becomes evident. Many band names are wholly or partly English, often modelled on American predecessors. A few examples illustrate how band names are far from neutral, being used to convey strong cultural messages. The name Massilia Sound System proudly advertises the band's place of origin and makes explicit their identification, not with

France as a nation, but with a region and a specific city.[7] The second and third words of the name foreground the Jamaican and ragga culture which defines the band's overriding musical style. The name dispenses with the French language altogether. IAM, the name of Massilia's Marseille rivals, again asserts the band's identification with English rather than French, but is polysemic, like many rap band names. The name is both a bold assertion of their individuality ('I am') but also an acronym, standing for 'Imperial Asiatic Men'. This second representation of the name is designed to assert the band's identification with non-white, non-Eurocentric traditions.[8] Other band names, while not disowning the French language in the same way, are equally defiant in the challenge they pose to polite French bourgeois society. One of the most uncompromising of all rap groups is NTM. Again, the name is an acronym, having at least two interpretations. Best known is 'Nique ta mère', a translation into French of both the worst possible insult in the Arabic language and the American epithet 'Motherfucker'. At the same time, the initials NTM stand for 'Le Nord Transmet le Message' [The North Transmits the Message], a reference to the band's origins in the northern *banlieues* of Paris as well as to their trenchantly ideological stance. Names are thus enormously important to rappers and are a crucial part of the forging of a distinctive identity. They represent one aspect of the importance of *code* in the language of rap, allowing the initiated to mark themselves off from the 'others'. Incidentally they may also allow bands to keep the more subversive aspects of their messages covert. TRIBU may well see themselves as a sort of separate tribe, but their name is also an acronym for the uncompromising message 'Tape la Race Inférieure des Bâtards en Uniforme' [Smash the Inferior Race of Bastards in Uniform].

It is not just the band's collective name which is central to identity construction, but also the nicknames or 'blazes' assumed by individual band members. These, too, are often anglicized (there are many 'MCs' and 'Daddys') and can fulfil radical purposes. The members of IAM gave themselves alternative Egyptian names to assert their solidarity with the idea that Egyptian civilization was created by black people and that it lies at the origins of world culture. Thus the lead IAM rapper Philippe Fragione supplemented his original Americanized nickname 'Chill' with 'Akhenaton'. This willingness to assume a double identity is nothing new, of course, having been practised for decades in the world of show business and in the criminal underworld, with both of which rap is connected. On a more serious level, this practice recalls similar steps taken by leading figures from American civil rights and black power movements, such as Malcolm X, who changed his name, after a visit to Mecca in 1964, to El Hajj Malik El Shabazz, Stokely Carmichael (of the Black Panthers and later pan-African movements), who became Kwame Ture, and, of course, Muhammad Ali, who renounced his given name of Cassius Clay in order to align himself with civil rights movements stressing black separatism and pride. This identification on the part of IAM with Egyptian culture also raises the issue of the key role played by Islam in Black Power movements since the 1930s. As Adam Krims (2000: 78–80) notes in his study of the poetics of identity in rap, within 'reality rap' or 'knowledge rap' in the USA, there is a prevalence of Afrocentric ideology that is clearly influenced by the rhetoric of movements such as the Nation of Islam and Five Percent Nation.[9] André Prévos labels IAM's stance as 'Pharaohism', suggesting that this choice of Egyptian culture has a pragmatic rationale as well as a degree of idealism:

> [It] may be seen as a means of underlining Arabic origins, all the while bypassing the popularly negative representations of North African countries gripped by Islamic fundamentalism and economic uncertainties. (Mitchell, 2001: 46)

As we have seen above, bands often exhibit a fierce pride in their place of origin. However, it should be noted that, even though most rappers are from immigrant families, this is rarely equated with their parents' country of origin, but is normally a specific neighbourhood of the Parisian suburbs, or a provincial French town. This assertion of a community identity does not necessarily mean that bands look at their home town or neighbourhood through rose-tinted glasses. Many rap songs speak in stark terms of the social problems and deprivation of the estates in which they live. Ministère Amer [Bitter Ministry], for example, describe a day in the life of Sarcelles in their song 'Un été à la cité', an ironic updating of The Lovin' Spoonful's classic hippy anthem from the 1960s, 'Summer in the City':

> Dans mes escaliers tout le monde a signé, d'autres ont pissé, les chiens ont chié.
> Il n'y a plus de respect donc la gardienne gueule sa mère, fait des simagrées.
> Ma famille crie (Trouve un métier).
> Je dois m'évader.
> ...
> On surveille ses arrières pour ne pas se faire serrer, c'est ça un été à la cité.
> (Ministère Amer, 1996)

> [On the stairs everyone has signed their name, others have pissed, the dogs have crapped.
> No-one shows respect any more, so the caretaker is shouting her head off, making a real fuss.
> My family are all yelling at me (Get a job).
> So I'm out of here.
> ...
> You watch your ass to make sure you don't get jumped, that's summer in the 'city' (estate) for you.]

Rappers are consciously aiming to set the record straight, providing an insider's view on life in the *banlieues* in contrast to those, whether derogatory racists or compassionate middle-class liberals, who speak and write about the estates from the outside. This can be seen as an act of reappropriation of territory. The *banlieues*, usually portrayed as bleak, unattractive, terrifying spaces, in both the physical and the symbolic sense, are reclaimed and have a certain value conferred on them by rappers. On occasions the rappers' attitude can veer towards the sentimentally nostalgic, even where the vision of the estates' problems is on the whole convincingly drawn and clear-eyed. IAM refer to the home estate as a magnet, a place which exerts an irresistible if demonic attraction, a place you can never escape, and as a quicksand, a place that drags you down to despair and death.

Certain key words recur in the language rappers use to characterize the estates. Prominent among these are 'enfer' [Hell], 'ghetto', 'Chicago', 'poubelle' [rubbish bin], 'jungle' and 'zoo'. The use of the words 'ghetto' and 'Chicago' reinforce the sense of identification with the experiences of African-Americans. 'Poubelle', 'jungle' and 'zoo' suggest not merely that the estates are inhospitable places but that they are being used as dumping grounds and that the inhabitants feel that they are under constant scrutiny, regarded from the outside as subhuman or exotic species. Timides et Sans Complexes explain the effects of growing up in such places:

> Nous avons grandi en enfer, flingués par le système ...
> Toi l'bourgeois, envoie ton gosse dans le ghetto.
> Il se transformera en chien.
> (TSC, 1994)

> [We grew up in Hell, screwed by the system ...
> Hey, you, bourgeois, send your kid to the ghetto.
> He'll soon turn into a dog.]

Thus many songs speak starkly of the life experiences of rappers on the estates – experiences of poverty, insecurity, drugs and, especially, racism. Many rap groups attack the Front National, with Le Pen, predictably, attracting particular vitriol. For IAM he is a 'gros blond haineux et stupide' [fat fair-haired guy, stupid and full of hatred], while Zebda see him as 'ce cochon de Bretagne au sourire maléfique' [that Breton pig with the evil smile] (Calio, 1998: 66). Racism is constantly attacked, not just when it emanates from the Front National. Zebda subject President Chirac's infamous speech about the 'noise and smell' of estates with predominantly immigrant populations to withering irony in their song 'Le bruit et l'odeur' ['The Noise and the Smell'] (Zebda, 1996). It is this experience of racism which leads many rappers to reject totally any identification with the French nation. Big Red, the mixed-race leader of Raggasonic, states that 'Bleu, Blanc, Rouge ne sont pas les couleurs de mon drapeau' [Blue, white and red are not the colours of my flag] (Raggasonic, 1995). The same song goes on to show how, for many rappers, their art is a means to exact symbolic revenge on the racists:

> Je me sers de mon micro comme je me servirais d'un Uzi
> Pour éliminer le FN, Le Pen et tous les fachos à Paris.

> [I use my mike just like I'd use an Uzi
> To eliminate the FN, Le Pen and all the fascists in Paris.]

This desire to distance themselves from any identification with the nation that produced Le Pen leads some rappers to reject the national in favour of the local. Massilia and IAM define themselves as Marseillais, inhabitants of a city which has existed for far longer than the French state and which has been subjected to various attempts at invasion by the latter. IAM's debut album *De la planète Mars* [From the Planet Mars] (1991) sought to portray their home city as a 'world apart', a port, historically characterized by immigration from many parts of the world, which was to all intents and purposes separate from France. The punning title of the album (underscored by the refrain 'Mars-Marseille' in the title track) reinforces this view of the *otherness* of Marseille and, only partly in jest, warns the rest of France to expect an imminent counter-invasion from this band of dangerous extra-terrestrials, led, of course, by IAM themselves. Le Pen is seen as simply the latest in a long line of would-be French invaders of the city of the Phoenicians, and the 25 per cent of Marseillais who voted for him are denounced as collaborators. In its turn, the Front National has well understood the challenge posed by rap to its xenophobic, exclusive version of Frenchness, and has responded by banning rap groups from using municipal facilities in some of the towns it controls in southern France.

Racism is just one aspect of conventional society against which rappers are in constant rebellion. The forces of law and order are an equally frequent target of rap's anger. The two targets are often combined: the police are seen as being among the worst perpetrators of racist abuse and violence against the immigrant community. The most infamous example of this conflict between rappers and the police remains, of course, the jail sentence imposed on members of NTM for inciting the audience to chant 'Nique la Police' [Fuck the Police] at a concert in La Seyne-sur-mer in July 1995.[10] The Marseillais crime fiction writer Jean-Claude Izzo, who vividly depicts in his novels the same neighbourhoods which nurtured bands like IAM and Massilia Sound System, has claimed that hatred of the police provides a common bond for working-class youth of all races, paradoxically assisting in the forging of a common identity.[11]

It is instructive to look briefly at the vocabulary used by rappers to refer to the police. Mostly consisting of slang, it is almost uniformly derogatory or ironic. *Verlan* (Parisian backslang) words feature strongly, including *keufs* (abbreviated from *keufli*, *verlan* for *flic*, an earlier, now almost mainstream, slang word for policeman), *guisdés* (*verlan* for *déguisés* – that is, those who wear uniform), and *kolbocks*, the derivation of which shows the rappers' willingness to 'verlanize' English words as well as their contempt for the police! Some rappers go as far as to assert that they live in a virtual police state:

On vit où? Dans un pays de flics.
On vit où? Dans un putain de pays de flics.
(Tout Simplement Noir, 1995)

[Where do we live? In a cops' country.
Where do we live? In a fucking country full of cops.]

As with the racists of the Front National, the very act of rapping about the issues can be seen as a symbolic act of vengeance against the police.

Is it, then, legitimate to see rap as a vehicle for a social group in total, insurrectionary opposition to the French State and all its institutions? Should we ascribe to rap a consistently revolutionary quality? On closer examination we see a more contradictory attitude to the defining features of the society in which rap has developed. Money is clearly identified as one of the driving forces of this society, with individuals being largely defined by how much of it they possess. Lack of money is one of the principal means of social and cultural exclusion. Rappers are fascinated by money and material signs of success. The tendency within the world of hip hop towards the ostentatious display of wealth and consumption has been taken to an extreme in the 'bling bling' aesthetics which originated with the New Orleans rap group Cash Money Millionaires in the late 1990s. The cynical boastfulness of this aesthetic is clearly present in the following lines by Expression Direkt from 'Mon esprit part en illecou' ['My Mind goes to Hell']:

> Car j'aime la tune et je veux faire fortune
> Sans travailler comme un iench et subir le stress
> Le ¾ Costela, racaille
> Et qui tape du bizness ici?
> Moi! Et j'ai longtemps opté pour ce choix
> qui de surcroît m'apporte la illasseca.
> (Expression Direkt, 1994)

> [Cos I love the green stuff and I want to make a million
> Without working like a dog and getting stressed out
> With my Lacoste ¾, scum,
> Just who is cutting the deals here?
> Me! I chose this path long ago
> And that's how I make my dosh.]

Other rappers see money and its pursuit as a source of corruption of youth and a potent symbol of the twisted value system of contemporary society:

> Si on se rapproche on voit qu'une Porsche
> Motive plus d'amour qu'une mère qui nourrit ses gosses.
> C'est fou de voir tous ces gens attirés par l'argent
> Comme le requin attiré par le sang.
> (Assassins, 1995)

> [If you look closer you see that a Porsche
> Inspires more love than a mother bringing up her kids.
> It's crazy to see all these people attracted by money
> Like sharks attracted by blood.]

It is possible to identify a certain hypocrisy in rappers who flaunt the material signs of their success, while at the same time professing to condemn society's obsession with commercialism. Some commentators such as Shusterman (1992) prefer to characterize this contradictory attitude to money and consumerism as a postmodern paradox. In this context Shusterman seems to be using the problematic term 'postmodern' in the sense of a knowing, ironical detachment, a refusal to believe too deeply in the validity of any professed ideal. This type of 'postmodernism' can seem little more than an escape clause, a convenient means of avoiding political or moral responsibility for one's actions and artistic statements. In reality there is a considerable tension between material success and the ideal of authenticity or 'keeping it real', of rap reflecting and giving voice to the experiences of the disenfranchized youth from the *banlieue*. This tension was heightened by the phenomenal commercial success of many French rappers during the 1990s. MC Solaar's second album sold over a million copies, while rappers have frequently claimed the top prizes in music industry awards and many have been signed to major record labels. Even the rebelliousness of hardcore bands like NTM has been used successfully as a marketing ploy to sell more records, regardless of how sincere or authentic the posture of defiance might be. Rap has been extremely adept at assimilating the language, style and techniques of advertising associated with advanced capitalism. The use of acronyms in band names is one illustration of this, facilitating a process of 'brand identification'. It could be claimed with some justification that rap, whose raw, angry edge provided an antidote to the pervasive blandness and inauthenticity of mass media and advertising, became internationally co-opted as the defining style of publicity during the 1990s.

Is the vaunted 'authenticity' of rap and the life experiences it reflects really a sham? Should rap not rather be seen as one of the consummate cultural products of late capitalism? There are at least two possible responses to these questions. On the one hand we could argue that rap inevitably reflects the society, warts and all, in which it exists. It feeds on and borrows from its cultural and social milieu, taking aspects of the publicity-dominated consumerism which surrounds it and subverting them for its own dissident purposes. According to this line of argument, rap uses the techniques of late capitalism to attack its cultural superstructure, altering people's hearts and minds irrevocably and making possible a series of profound social changes. Alternatively, it is perfectly possible to see the opposite process taking place, arguing that capitalism always and everywhere succeeds in taking control of social and cultural movements that emerge within it, however initially subversive their ideology, defusing them and perverting them to serve its own purposes. Rebellious, articulate young people are converted into harmless icons and used to further the process of selling goods and making profits, without having the slightest impact on the bedrock social problems that led to their emergence. Rap concerts provide occasions for letting off steam, while poverty, segregation, racism, drug abuse and violence remain constant features of life in the *banlieues*. Any 'reinvention of identity' that takes place around rap would be spurious, a diversion from a serious engagement with social and political realities.

This ambiguity in rap's socio-cultural significance may be explained with reference to Bakhtin's notion of the carnivalesque. For Bakhtin, carnival provided the occasion for the people to 'celebrate temporary liberation from the prevailing truth and from the established order' (1984: 10). The celebrations involved the symbolic overthrow of figures of power, the derision of those in authority and, inevitably, much profanity. There are clear parallels here with many of the features of rap outlined above. However, it is not totally certain that the established order is necessarily reasserted intact after the festivities, unaffected by the temporary inversion of hierarchies, the ridicule of officialdom and the violation of decorum attendant on the carnival celebrations. Recent French practitioners of community theatre have also grappled with this transgressive potential of the carnivalesque. André Benedetto (1980), for example, dramatized the real historical example of the carnival held in the town of Romans in 1592 to show how carnival could easily become the prelude to a period of 'real' insurrection and repression.

Whatever the definitive answer to these questions, rap's cultural role in contemporary France is not limited to the extent of its significance as a catalyst for social change. Its linguistic features are equally worthy of attention. To state the most obvious point first, the language of rap is not that of the Académie Française,[12] nor even that of the chanson tradition.[13] Rappers use the language of the street, of the *banlieue*, as their raw material. Some of the song extracts quoted above illustrate this well. The excerpt from 'Mon esprit part en illecou', by Expression Direkt (p. 100), incorporates relatively well-known slang expressions such as 'tune' [money] alongside more obscure examples of *verlan* ('iench' = 'chien' [dog]; 'Costela' = 'Lacoste') to construct a text whose full meaning would be available only to those initiated into the linguistic code. Alongside *verlan* and the even more devilishly difficult to decipher *veul* (a kind of 'reverse *verlan*' of which two examples are 'feum' for woman, and 'rebeu' for 'Arab'), rappers freely incorporate Parisian slang, Arabic slang, Occitan (of which more later) and, of course, English, into their texts.

This *métissage* [promiscuous mixing] of lexical items reflects the multi-ethnic, multi-linguistic milieu of the *banlieues* in which French rap had its origins. It also reveals an irreverent creativity, a willingness to play with language, to recombine apparently disparate elements in a genuinely original way. The texts are delivered at breakneck speed, in a heavily accented, perhaps even overarticulated phrase structure which reflects the material environment in which its practitioners live, as well as the speech patterns of their fellow *banlieusards*. Its rhyme schemes can convey alternating impressions of monotony and genuine surprise. Rap indulges in word play which can be both puerile and sophisticated, and its word play is accompanied by frequent alliteration which can prove enervating to the listener. It is a verbal art which has been likened to a form of *bricolage*:

Les rappeurs … assemblent leurs textes comme des ferrailleurs de la langue, valorisant le bric-à-brac lexical de la France d'aujourd'hui et recyclant les mots de fortune. (Pierre-Adolphe and Bocquet, 1997: 72)

[Rappers … put their texts together in the manner of scrap merchants who deal in language, enhancing the value of the lexical bric-a-brac of today's France and recycling makeshift words.]

It is also a practice which has been compared to that of the *griot* in traditional African societies:

certains rappeurs revendiquent une filiation avec le griot: 'Il y a toujours eu le rap en Afrique'.
　　Les griots devaient chanter dans la langue courante en utilisant les moyens d'expression de l'époque. Ils jouaient la Kora ou tapaient sur un tambour et racontaient tous les événements courants. Ils s'amusaient et informaient les gens de village en village. (Calio, 1998: 88)

[some rappers claim a direct line of descendance from the *griot*: 'Rap has always existed in Africa.' *Griots* sang in everyday language, using the means of expression of their own time. They played the Kora or banged on a drum and sang about everyday events. They had fun and kept people informed from village to village.]

In the 'Savannah Syncopators' chapter of *Yonder Come the Blues* (2001), Paul Oliver draws comparisons and traces possible lines of descent between West African griots and American blues singers. As well as discussing musical similarities, Oliver comments on the social and political role of *griots* in terms that bring to mind some of the key features of rap:

[Griots] must have the ability to extemporize on current events, chance incidents and the passing scene. Their wit can be devastating and their knowledge of local history formidable … Rather than being a perpetuator of attitudes (the *griot*) is an instrument for social change. (2001: 53)

Oliver also recognizes that in certain instances *griots* could be compared to 'the medieval king's jester … a comic fellow to whom every outrageous licence is permitted' (2001: 54).

This affiliation with the *griot* fits well with the tendency of certain rappers to identify with Africa, seen as the 'Terre Mère' ['Mother Earth'] and the source of an alternative, more authentic identity and lifestyle, in opposition to 'Babylon', the fount of corruption with which contemporary France is often equated.[14] These identifications are clearly influenced by Rastafari culture, in which Africa is equated with Zion, the promised land, while Babylon is equated with white European colonial and imperial oppressive power structures. However deep or meaningful this occasional identification with Africa, it is as an expression of the second-generation immigrant, caught between (at least) two worlds and two cultures, that French rap's true interest lies.[15] The rapper seizes on the language with which he comes into contact, whether in the speech of his parents, on the streets, on television, his favourite records or through the Internet, and combines its disparate elements in novel ways. The end result is, more often than not, a scathingly critical reflection of contemporary French society, but insofar as one could identify any positive core alternative values, they would probably boil down quite simply to anti-racism and cosmopolitanism.

Troubadours and Sound Systems

The tendency to mix the old and the new, to identify both with an Africa which has always existed and always will and with the French *banlieue* of the 1990s, can be seen as typically postcolonial. As Tony Mitchell explains, 'Hip-hop is about both where people are from and where they live' (2001: 32). He further discusses how hip hop, in many countries, increasingly serves as a vehicle for 'contestations about nationality and "hyphenated" identity' (2001: 32). Such notions of hyphenated or 'hybrid identities' are particularly relevant to any discussion of the work of some of the bands from southern French cities who combine rap and ragga musical styles with a fascinating linguistic mix, juxtaposing colloquial, contemporary street French with the apparently archaic language Occitan. I want to look briefly at the work of two of these bands, Fabulous Trobadors from Toulouse and Massilia Sound System from Marseille. The latter sum up their linguistic style in one of their songs:

> Ca tchatche en anglais, occitan ou français.
> (Massilia Sound System, 1999)
>
> [We talk in English, Occitan or French.]

Rapping can be seen as a contemporary manifestation of 'la tchatche', the ability to talk impromptu, at length and with a disconcerting fluency, on any subject. The name of the Fabulous Trobadors, meanwhile, uses a combination of English and Occitan words at the expense of French, and evokes both the contemporary world and the Middle Ages. This is not just a linguistic trick: the songs of both bands engage with contemporary social issues (racism, the Front National, the municipal politics of Toulouse, to give a few examples) while attempting to imbue their commentary on these issues with a modern interpretation of the philosophy of the troubadours, in particular its commitment to equality and tolerance through its central concepts of *paratge* and *convivença* which will be discussed in detail below.

On the surface the Fabulous Trobadors appear to have little in common with rap groups like NTM. Both members of the band are white, and the main writer,

Claude Sicre, is considerably older than most rappers. His background appears to be that of an intellectual 'folkie' rather than a 'ragamuffin' from the ghetto. Sicre is, in fact, sometimes unhappy about being classified as a rapper. Massilia Sound System are, superficially at least, more representative of the typical rap mould, a multiracial band from the *quartiers nord* [northern districts] of Marseille. They, however, also differ in many ways from the 'mainstream' of rap, and are more accurately described as a ragga band.[16] A relaxed humour permeates the band's songs and stances.

Despite some apparent differences, both bands have much in common with the rappers discussed previously and are normally classified under the rap umbrella, in both record stores and music journals. This affiliation can be seen in superficial features, such as the propensity of band members to assume nicknames, but also has more profound roots. The musical style is pared down and represents a kind of collage; above all, both bands have the staccato vocal delivery typical of rap and they (especially the Fabulous Trobadors) take rap's verbal inventiveness and love of word play to new limits. This can be illustrated by the following excerpt from 'High Tençon'[17] by the Fabulous Trobadors:

> Les vieilles élites se délitent/ les neuves sont dans nos quartiers/ hiérarchies renver c'est/ à nous de réveiller/ ce pays de sa torpeur ...
> Peur des U.S. Académie/ démission impossible/ n'est pas passé franc/ Ankylose l'ose plus/ plus d'invention extrême onc ...
> Extrême-onc Thelonius/ et cou tu me pièges
> (Fabulous Trobadors, 1998)

> [The old elites are falling apart/ the new ones are in our neighbourhoods/ overturned hierarchies it's/ up to us to wake/ this country from its torpor ...
> Fear of the US Academy/ resignation impossible/ did not go through/ Old and stiff no longer dares/ no more invention extreme unc ...
> Extremonk Thelonius/ and you've trapped me][18]

Where some rap bands seek an intellectual framework and a source of identity definition in ancient Egypt or Africa, the Fabulous Trobadors and Massilia consciously align themselves with Occitan traditions. In particular, both bands pay homage to the ideas of Félix Castan, the writer and Occitan activist from Montauban. Castan had already exerted a strong influence on an earlier generation of radical artists from southern France, particularly community theatre practitioners like André Benedetto and Claude Alranq in the 1970s and early 1980s. For 50 years, Castan has been an implacable opponent of centralism and Parisian cultural hegemony, which he has likened variously to a 'virus', a 'gigantesque moulinette' [enormous blender] and a 'dévoreur d'identités' [devourer of identities] (Castan, 1984). He believes that French culture is in desperate need of a revivification which can only come from its despised margins, where the culture and literature of its linguistic minorities have been ruthlessly stamped out. It is, of course, the historic language and culture of southern France, variously referred to as Occitan, Languedoc, Provençal or Gascon that Castan has been most concerned to rehabilitate.[19] In particular he has adopted an evangelical attitude towards the tradition of the troubadours, which he regards as having been one of the most significant formative influences on Western civilization, thought and culture. It is no exaggeration to say that his sense of historical injustice at the fate of this once great literary and cultural tradition parallels that felt by black artists and writers at the neglect and distortion of African history and culture.

It is interesting to note that Castan has absolutely no time for any agenda of political separatism, regarding attempts to construct a spurious Occitan 'nationalism' as contrary to the spirit and tradition of Occitan thought:

> Au cours de sa longue histoire, le peuple occitan n'a jamais cru que la Nation fût la seule forme d'existence d'un peuple, ni qu'un patrimoine linguistique et culturel, aussi fort soit-il, dût nécessairement engendrer une nation, encore moins un Etat. (1984: 26)

> [Throughout their long history, Occitan people have never believed that the Nation was the only form of existence for a people, nor that a linguistic and cultural heritage, however strong it might be, must necessarily give rise to a nation, even less a State.]

Both the Fabulous Trobadors and Massilia Sound System place themselves consciously in this tradition of Occitan thought. They have sought to combine the most up-to-date musical styles with the centuries-old tradition of the troubadours to explore the reality of contemporary France and to construct new local and regional identities. What they are emphatically not interested in is the preservation of a cultural archive for its own sake. Sicre was led to embrace rap as a medium partly through his dissatisfaction, in the early part of his career, with the milieu of folk music. He wanted to forge a music that bridged 'popular' and 'elite' cultures, one that was *functional* (my emphasis), able to support and serve as an expressive vehicle for the daily lives and the landmark events of whole communities. His frustration at the lack of a living oral folk tradition on which to draw for the creation of a vibrant contemporary culture in France led him on a journey of research and discovery among various examples of folk musics in different parts of the world. This journey led, via American country blues and the music of the Brazilian North East (where he discovered to his astonishment a strong historical influence of the Occitan troubadours), to rap and ragga. Sicre particularly appreciated rap's stripping away of layers of musical accompaniment to focus on its essential elements, voice and percussion, and the possibilities it offered for verbal inventiveness. Rap seemed to Sicre like a contemporary manifestation of both 'la tchatche' and the 'tençon', or 'joute poétique' [poetic joust] of the troubadours.[20]

Sicre has been for many years a social–cultural activist, organizing various events in the Arnaud-Bernard district of Toulouse, where he lives. To Sicre, this construction of a community identity is of crucial importance. Events organized include neighbourhood meals, carnivals which sought to be genuinely subversive events and even Socratic debates in the street involving figures such as Castan and the linguist Henri Meschonnic. The music of the Fabulous Trobadors and other bands they have supported and championed has been a central feature of these community events. In initiating such activities the Fabulous Trobadors demonstrate their affiliation with community theatre practitioners such as Benedetto and Alranq. The ideological inspiration for these practices is a determination to identify with the *périphérie* rather than the centre. Both Castan and Benedetto have theorized this as a contemporary version of the baroque, defined in opposition to a supposed classicism which is characterized by ordered hierarchy and dependence on the notion of a single, unique centre. According to this vision, the unique 'centre' becomes a repressive, sclerotic force tending to strangle the life and creativity of a city or country. Castan called for the creation of a whole series of cultural 'capitals' in France as a counterweight to the negative influence of Paris, while Benedetto saw inhabitants of the despised peripheral estates as furnishing the most vital human agents of the process of regenerating and recivilizing the city of the future.

This identification with, and championing of, Occitan language and culture may seem curious, even perverse, in musicians keen to embrace the contemporary world. At first sight, Occitan seems an archaic, perhaps dying, language. Evidence on the extent of its continuing status as a the preferred language for everyday use in specific communities is contradictory, but it has been argued that it has virtually died out in urban areas, and is confined largely to older people in the shrinking rural heartlands. With the remarkably rapid rural exodus eroding its natural community, and in the absence of governmental policies designed to protect and nurture the language, particularly in schools,[21] would it not be realistic to recognize that Occitan is a terminal case among languages? It is true that some of those who have professed an attachment to Occitanism since the 1970s have done so out of nostalgic sentimentalism, a vague dissatisfaction both with the hard-nosed values of contemporary French and global capitalism and with the failure of the heavily centralized and bureaucratic parties of the Left, particularly the French Communist Party, to carry through fundamental social change. There may be, therefore, a form of escapism associated with superficial attachment to the Occitan cause.

In the case of the Fabulous Trobadors and Massilia Sound System, despite the latter's apparent insistence on their role as mere 'entertainers', there is a deeper purpose involved in their engagement with Occitan language and culture. In the first place, they strongly believe that the values associated with the traditions of the troubadours have relevance for today. Chief among these would be the linked concepts of *paratge* and *convivença*. *Paratge* implies a commitment to equality, an acknowledgement of the common humanity of all, irrespective of class or ethnic origin. *Convivença* implies not just conviviality, the ability to enjoy life, to relax and party, even though this aspect is particularly important to Massilia Sound System. More importantly, it stresses the aspect of *living together*, an acceptance of all languages and cultures as having equal value. As such it contains the germs of an alternative value system to that of individualistic late capitalism and also to the exclusive, xenophobic definition of Frenchness which has led to the marginalization of those whose natural language or accent is not that of the centre.

Embracing Occitan culture, speaking and using the language in writing, theatre and song, thus constitutes an act of collective defiance. The Occitan rappers resent what they see as a tendency in France to stamp out not only minority languages,[22] but even regional accents. This pressure, they feel, leads people to internalize the values of the centre, to feel ashamed of their accent and perform what amounts to daily self-censorship on their mode of speech. Seen in this light, identification with Occitan language and culture acquires a political dimension which fits well with many developments in the contemporary world. It is a reaction against centralization and globalization, a rejection of the 'big is beautiful' mindset, a symbolic alignment, even, with social movements which stress participatory democracy alongside the importance of protecting and nurturing diversity in all aspects of human interaction with the environment.[23] In the philosophy of some of the artists who have been influenced by Castan, there is often a fairly crude binary opposition at work, equating France and its language with the imposition of order and a repressive police-state mentality, while Occitan, by contrast, is identified with the creativity of the repressed underdog. Massilia Sound System have attempted to go beyond this binary opposition and to recognize the more complex reality of contemporary southern France. They have made at least some effort to unravel the web of psycho-social factors which have led to the paradox of the Front National finding its most fertile terrain precisely in the territory formerly occupied by the tolerant, generous-spirited Occitan troubadours. At the same time the band has been outraged at the Front National's attempt to invoke Provençal traditions in municipalities they control, and have frequently hoisted the Provençal flag on stage at their own gigs as a gesture of symbolic reappropriation.

It is worth commenting here on a further paradox which has been widely debated in relation to rap, particularly the American variety: its attitude to sexual politics. For a cultural movement which vehemently opposes oppression and inequality, the misogyny and homophobia of many rap lyrics, particularly 'mack rap', is one paradox which has proved extremely difficult to swallow for some of its enthusiasts and cultural commentators. 'Big Willy-ism' describes the closely linked boasting of prowess with women with the flaunting of wealth discussed above (Krims, 2000: 154–5). French rap, while perhaps less virulently misogynistic than much American rap, has an undeniably macho quality: it is noticeable that, to date, few women rappers have emerged in France. A song by Massilia sums up this contradiction. Titled simply 'Marseillais', it argues powerfully for cultural pluralism, asserting that attachment to the local, the particular, can be a route to an acceptance of the other:

Nous agissons, nous pensons,
Nous parlons en marseillais!

Nous sommes fiers de notre ville,
Nous sommes fiers de nos quartiers!
Oui, c'est la différence qui nous permet de dialoguer ...
(Massilia Sound System, 1995)

[We act, we think,
We speak in Marseillais!
We are proud of our town,
We are proud of our neighbourhoods!
Yes, being different allows us to have a dialogue ...]

Yet this same song, in trying to pin down the defining quality of being Marseillais, cannot seem to see beyond the stereotype of the sweet-talking Mediterranean chat-up merchant:

De parler aux filles, c'est ça notre spécialité! ...
On leur parle en occitan,
Elles trouvent ça très érotique ...

[Talking to girls, now that's our speciality! ...
We talk to them in Occitan,
They think it's really erotic ...]

Massilia would no doubt protest that these lines are not to be taken too seriously, and others might claim that the lines merely reflect cultural attitudes endemic in the communities from which the band emerged. It is also likely that, given Massilia's debt to ragga, there is an underlying influence of the traditions of toasting or the 'slackness' inherent in much Jamaican dancehall music in the 1990s.[24] We are, however, left to wonder what the half-million or so *marseillaises* make of this definition of their supposedly unique cultural qualities. At the very least, one is entitled to draw attention to the striking lack of ideological consistency at the heart of rap which this example highlights.

A fuller exploration of these political and cultural issues is outside the scope of this chapter, but even the above summary will have indicated that the Occitanism of the Fabulous Trobadors and Massilia Sound System is not a quaint anachronism, but engages with issues of fundamental importance in contemporary France. These bands have also enthusiastically embraced new technologies. Many formerly marginalized groups have used the Internet to create networks and to establish 'virtual communities' of users of minority languages. Incidentally, this embrace of the creative, subversive possibilities of the Internet illustrates how the Occitan bands share other rappers' enthusiasm for many aspects of American culture. In this, too, they demarcate themselves sharply from the prevailing anti-Americanism of much contemporary French cultural and political discourse. It is the creativity associated with America and the English language which particularly attracts these artists. One of Sicre's most cherished concepts and achievements is the

Linha Imaginot, a network first established by the music sector of the Institut d'Estudis Occitans[25] and popularized as the title of the Fabulous Trobadors' most recent album. This Occitan phrase, which can be roughly translated as the 'Imaginot Line', puns on the 'Maginot Line' beloved of French historians of the first half of the twentieth century. The title thus mocks the pomposity inherent in the traditional teaching of French history, while simultaneously asserting that the real line of resistance, the real route to national salvation, will be through the exercise of artistic imagination. It is this inventiveness which characterizes the Fabulous Trobadors above all, a creativity which they claim to derive from the language spoken by real people in real communities in parts of France neglected by the dominant culture.

Conclusions

It seems indisputable that rap and its associated forms have played an important role in the ongoing process of identity construction on the part of those marginalized by mainstream French society and culture, whether they be disaffected youth from the *banlieues* or those who feel a sense of linguistic estrangement from the centre. Simon Frith has pointed out the fallacy of looking for direct reflections of identity or place in music, suggesting instead that we should look at popular music as a process 'through which identity is actively imagined, created and constructed' (Mitchell, 2001: 32). In France, rap has served as a vehicle for linking the local and the global, bringing the authentic voices and concerns of a new demographic section of society (multi-ethnic, second generation immigrant youth in the *banlieues*) to widespread attention, while at the same time allowing this relatively disenfranchised section of society to connect with wider issues of global importance and to claim their distinctive place, through the 'universal language of rap' (Mitchell, 2001: 12), in the worldwide hip-hop community. It also seems fairly clear that rap itself is passing rapidly into that very mainstream of contemporary cultural expression in France, becoming commercially successful and acceptable in many circles. When Minister for Culture Jack Lang declared in 1990 'Je crois à la culture rap' [I believe in rap culture], this marked a watershed in the status and public perception of rap (Labi, Daum and Crazy, 1990). We are therefore entitled to ask whether rap will continue to play the culturally subversive role it has up to now, being embraced by the marginalized as the means of creating an identity which allows a sense of pride and belonging. It is quite possible that its tolerance and acceptance by wider groups of people indicate that it has already contributed to a deep process of cultural and social change in France, a process that is leading to a radical redefinition of what it means to be French in today's world. It is, however, equally possible that rap will turn out to be an ephemeral phenomenon, that those who continue to feel marginalized will seek out and create new cultural forms through which to explore and create identities, feeling that rap has limited possibilities to offer them. Some American commentators have already concluded that rap is dead as a serious oppositional cultural force, claiming that its initial 'rhetoric of freedom' has been replaced by 'an ethic of abjection, male sexual predatoriness and male body introspection' (Mitchell, 2001: 3). While this trend may currently be dominant in its country of origin, the rapid spread of hip hop and rap to much of the world reveals a vitality and a capacity to connect with local roots and concerns. The development of rap in France clearly confirms its worldwide importance as an identity marker and a locus of identity construction for young people in revolt against the injustice perpetrated on their communities by mainstream society.

Notes

1 'Aggressive, poetic talk', a characterization of rap used in Pierre-Adolphe and Bocquet (1997: 74).
2 The standard English translation of *banlieue* – suburb – does not fully capture all the connotations which the French term has acquired. 'Bleak peripheral estate', though rather clumsy, gives a fuller idea of the preconceptions and emotions which the word *banlieue* conjures up for the French reader. It is hardly necessary to add that many *banlieues* contain a high proportion of residents of black or North African origin.
3 '[U]n des rares moyens d'expression de cette jeunesse pluri-ethnique' [one of the few means of expression of these multi-ethnic young people] (Calio, 1998: 11).
4 The strong opposition voiced by President Chirac to the war in Iraq in the spring of 2003 perhaps indicates the early stages of France carving out a new role for itself in world politics in the twenty-first century.
5 There is some dispute about the derivation of the word *beur* which refers to second-generation immigrants of North African origin, though it is now generally accepted that it originated as a *verlan* (Parisian backslang) version of *arabe*. Whatever its origin, the term was soon adopted as a badge of identity by young people of North African origin themselves.
6 The graffiti artist, or *taggeur*, appears to 'desecrate' the walls of his or her city; the DJ of a rap group samples and literally 'scratches' the records (s)he uses to generate the musical accompaniment to the vocalists. This apparently cavalier attitude to the given environment has been variously seen as a form of destruction on the one hand, or as an act of metamorphosis or transformation on the other.
7 Massilia is the Latin name for Marseille.
8 Though they all identify strongly with their home city of Marseille, the band members come from extremely diverse backgrounds, including Spanish, Italian, Senegalese and Algerian as well as French. The 'Imperial' tag in this second interpretation of their name is ambiguous: it implies an ironic posture in relation to contemporary Western imperialism, but can also be taken to indicate an identification with the imperial grandeur of ancient Egyptian civilization.
9 'Reality rap' maps the realities of inner-city or ghetto life, while 'knowledge rap' has a didactic aim, focusing on political or historical tales.
10 'Traquer les keufs dans les couloirs du métro
     tels sont les rêves que fait la nuit Joey Joe

Donne-moi des balles pour la police municipale
Donne-moi une flingue.'
(NTM, 1993)

[Hunting down the cops in the subway corridors
That's what Joey Joe dreams of at night
Give me some bullets for the local police
Give me a piece.]

11   'La haine des flics c'est ce qui unit les mômes' [Hatred of the cops is what unites the kids] (Izzo, 1995: 96–7).

12   The venerable body that seeks to preserve the purity and quality of French language and culture.

13   'Chanson', the French word for song, refers in this context to the popular song tradition which developed between the two world wars and continued as a powerful cultural force at least until the 1970s. While chanson frequently reflected the seamier side of contemporary social life, many of its best practitioners, such as Georges Brassens and Jacques Brel, have been recognized as important poets in their own right.

14   The rhetoric tends to focus on an ancient Africa disassociated from the politics of contemporary Africa.

15   The reduction of rap to an authentic Afro-American form of cultural expression in fact belies the racial diversity of its originators which include Latino and other Afro-Caribbean immigrants (Mitchell, 1996: 27–9).

16   Ragga combines traditional Jamaican reggae with digitally produced instrumental tracks. It is also indebted to older Jamaican rural forms such as mento and poco. A macho swagger is a common element in the lyrics, which are often in Jamaican *patwa*.

17   Typically, the title itself has at least two layers of meaning: there is a play on the English phrase 'high tension', but the Occitan word *tençon* refers to a sort of medieval poetic contest between troubadours: an event which can be seen as a predecessor of the 'poetry slams' popular in New York in the 1990s and which share many of rap's features.

18   It is impossible to capture in translation the word play, alliteration and internal rhyming of the original, while the breathtaking rapidity of the elliptical, eclectic stream of consciousness can barely be hinted at.

19   'Occitan' is now generally accepted as the correct generic term for this language. 'Provençal', 'Languedocien', 'Gascon', 'Limousin' and 'Auvergnat' are its main dialectical forms.

20   See the excerpt from 'High Tençon', p. 105.

21   Despite the lip service paid to protecting and nurturing minority languages in the Poignant report (July 1998) commissioned by Lionel Jospin, France lags way behind the support given to minority languages in countries such as Spain and the UK.

22   In Occitanist circles, there has been intense debate around the alleged centralist intolerance of regional difference supposedly deriving from the Jacobin republican tradition. Benedetto's play *Les Drapiers Jacobins* [The Jacobin Drapers] (1976) provides an interesting exploration of these issues in dramatic form.

23   'We should care about dying languages for the same reason that we care when a species of animal or plant dies. It reduces the diversity of our planet. In the case of language, we are talking about intellectual and cultural diversity, not biological diversity, but the

issues are the same ... Increasing uniformity holds dangers for the long-term survival of a species ... If the development of multiple cultures is a prerequisite for successful human development, then the preservation of linguistic diversity is essential, because cultures are chiefly transmitted through spoken and written languages' (Crystal, 1999).

24   'Slackness' refers to sexually explicit lyrics in dancehall music. There has been an intense debate about whether 'slackness' is degrading to women, objectifying the female body. Female artists such as Lady G, Junie Ranks, Sister Nancy and Sister Charmaine have contested sexism in dancehall culture. For an extensive discussion of gender and rap, see Rose (1994).

25   The Institute of Occitan Studies is an organization devoted to the preservation and propagation of the language and culture of Occitanie.

Discography

Assassins, 'Shoota Babylon', *Homicide Volontaire* (Delabel 724384039325, 1995).

Expression Direkt, 'Mon esprit part en illecou', *Ghetto Youth Process* (Night&Day, CDe0009456, 1994).

Fabulous Trobadors, 'High Tençon', *On the Linha Imaginot* (Mercury 558 772 2, 1998).

IAM, *De la planète Mars* (Delabel 07777 868952 2, 1991).

Massilia Sound System, 'Marseillais', *Commando Fada* (Shaman 073145281802, 1995).

Massilia Sound System, 'Reggae Fadoli', *Massilia Sound System London Experience* (Eve 99013/02422, 1999).

Ministère Amer, 'Un été à la cité' (Copyright Delabel Editions/Secteur A Editions, CD 45687-88890-345,1996).

NTM, 'Police', *J'appuie sur la gachette* (EPC 473630 2, 1993).

Raggasonic, 'Bleu Blanc Rouge', *Raggasonic 2* (EMI Music Publishing France, 1995).

Timides et sans complexe, 'Le feu dans le ghetto' (FNAC, 3456774, 1994).

Tout Simplement Noir, 'OP12FLICS', *Dans Paris Nocturne* (Night&Day, 259256, 1995).

Zebda, 'Le bruit et l'odeur' (Barclay, 56739993, 1996).

Chapter 6

The Quest for National Unity in Uyghur Popular Song: Barren Chickens, Stray Dogs, Fake Immortals and Thieves

Joanne N. Smith

Colonizers and Collaborators

This chapter focuses on the Uyghurs, a Turkic Muslim group living under Chinese political hegemony in an area currently known as the Xinjiang Uyghur Autonomous Region of Northwest China (or Chinese Central Asia).[1] The region is home to 17 nationalities, including the Uyghur, Han, Kazakh, Kirghiz, Mongol, Russian, Manchu, Uzbek, Tatar, Daur, Hui, Xibo, Tajik, Dongxiang, Tibetan, Salar and Tuvan peoples. However, only the first three are present in significant numbers.[2] To date, the Uyghurs remain the largest of these groups, though the number of Han Chinese immigrants in the region is likely to surpass the number of Uyghurs in the near future. Uyghurs have viewed the Han presence as an unwelcome encroachment since Qing rulers began to encourage mass immigration to the region in 1821, and the desire for self-determination – and, for many, secession from the People's Republic – has been greatly fuelled by socio-economic competition from Han immigrants in urban areas and by the collapse of the USSR and subsequent formation of independent Central Asian states adjacent to Xinjiang in 1991.

The concept of encouraging Uyghur national identity through cultural forms is not new in Xinjiang. In the 1920s, as the region groaned under the weight of heavy taxation levied by Chinese warlord governors, Yang Zengxin and Jin Shuren, Uyghur intellectuals had begun to employ elite culture (poetry and poetry recitation) as a means to disseminate political ideas and encourage Uyghur national identity. This 'poetry of resistance' has been explored elsewhere (Rudelson, 1997: 146–53). From the late 1980s and early 1990s, and parallel with the rapid strengthening of Uyghur national identity in response to particular domestic and international conditions, popular forms of culture such as popular song, jokes, storytelling and oral histories came to play an increasingly important role in the reproduction of that identity and the process of ethno-political mobilization.[3] In particular, the works of certain contemporary singers struck an emotional resonance with diverse sectors of the Uyghur populace, and began to transcend social divides of oasis origin, occupation, generation, political orientation, educational level and degree of religious observance. By focusing instead on the ethnic boundary between the Uyghurs and a monolithic Han 'Other', a boundary expressed daily in symbolic, spatial and social terms in urban Xinjiang in 1995–96, these singers were able to blur intra-ethnic divides to a significant degree.[4] At the same time, the hierarchical older/younger sibling relationship inherent in government rhetoric surrounding Han-minority relations was re-cast as a relationship of colonizer to colonized.

    Here, five songs released in 1995 by popular singer Ömärjan Alim are analysed as a means to explore the representation and reproduction of Uyghur national identity constructed in relation to the Han Chinese and the quest for Uyghur national unity. Exploring the singer's agency in group identity construction, I examine metaphorical representations of the 'colonizer' (the Han Chinese) and the 'collaborator' (those Uyghurs thought to place personal ambition above ethnic loyalty).[5] I show how these representations reflected popular perceptions held among disparate groups of Uyghurs across the region, forging a common sense of 'emotional unity', while reproducing relational configurations of Uyghur identity in the cities, and going some distance to create a broad-based Uyghur national identity with the capability to straddle both urban and rural communities. Conversely, it is suggested that by highlighting the perceived barrier to Uyghur national unity – a national character grounded in political passivity, self-interest and opportunism – representations of the Uyghur 'collaborator' may paradoxically foster negative self-identity and low self-esteem, this perhaps explaining why certain songs have avoided censorship by the Chinese government. Finally, I propose that in lamenting Uyghur national disunity, Ömärjan Alim (intentionally or not) assumes the role of 'illuminist', providing a timely source of national enlightenment.[6]

Geographical Origin and Migration to the Turpan and Tarim Basins, AD 840

To understand the foundations of Uyghur/Han conflict today, it is necessary to contextualize the relative histories of the Uyghur and Han peoples in the region known as Xinjiang. The first mention of a people called the Uyghurs refers to a Turkic nomadic tribe living on the steppes of today's Mongolian Republic. During the Uyghur Empire (744–840), the Uyghurs ruled the steppes from Qarabalghasun, a permanent city 'crowded with markets and various trades' (V. Minorski, cited in Barfield, 1989: 157), and stored silk extorted from China in their fortified capital. When in AD 840 the Uyghur Empire was destroyed by Qirghiz nomads, the steppe Uyghurs split into three separate groups that began migrations (Haneda, 1978: 5; Geng, 1984: 6–7). One group went west to the Bišbaliq region north of the Tianshan in present-day Xinjiang, crossed the mountains and occupied the

Turpan Basin where it established the Buddhist kingdom of Gaochang (850–1250), and expanded its influence to Qarašar[7] and Kucha. Subsequently, a number of Uyghurs continued on to Qäšqär on the southern edge of the Tarim Basin and joined members of the Turkish Qarluq tribe, their former allies on the Mongolian steppe (Geng, 1984: 8). The Uyghurs of Gaochang gradually gave up the nomadic lifestyle amid the relatively advanced settled culture of the area and fused with the indigenous Indo-Europeans, becoming farmers in a class society, fond of music, excursions and banquets (ibid.: 6). They are believed to be the direct cultural ancestors of Uyghurs today.

Although Chinese merchants had long been present in the region, which has been wholly or partially incorporated into the Chinese empire at several stages during its history, numbers of settled Chinese were small prior to the Qing invasion in the 1800s, and Xinjiang (meaning 'New Dominion' or 'New Border') became a formal province of China only in 1884. In comparison, the Turkic Uyghurs had been settled in the region in large numbers for almost a millennium before Han Chinese began to officially migrate to Xinjiang in 1821. This provides ample justification for a large number of present-day Uyghurs in describing themselves as a stateless minority in their own homeland. Since coming under Chinese political hegemony, the various ethnic groups in Xinjiang have to greater or lesser degrees aspired to self-determination, and the late nineteenth and first half of the twentieth century saw a number of secessionist movements flourish, if only briefly.[8]

Uyghur National Identity: A Recent Phenomenon

Notwithstanding the enduring attachment of the Uyghurs to the place they consider their homeland (see, for example, Gladney, 1990: 2–3), the concept of Uyghur national identity is a relatively new one.[9] Firstly, the ethnonym 'Uyghur' has suffered considerable discontinuity, having fallen into disuse in the 1500s as the last of the Buddhist Uyghurs in Turpan converted to Islam. Prior to the 1920s, the various Turkic Muslim groups dispersed across the region referred to themselves as *musulmanlar* [Muslims], suggesting an over-reaching Islamic identity, or employed the term *yärliklär* [locals] and used oasis-based ethnonyms such as *Ürümčilik* and *Kučaliq*, suggesting a series of atomized oasis identities (Saguchi, 1978: 62–3). The ethnonym 'Uyghur' was to reappear only in 1921, when emigrants from Xinjiang's Tarim Basin holding a conference on Turcology in Taškänt proposed that the name 'Uyghur' be used to designate all those previously known by oasis ethnonyms. The name was subsequently adopted by the Xinjiang provincial government in 1934, possibly at the suggestion of Soviet advisors who had recently completed the task of classifying their own minority groups (Gladney, 1990: 4). Secondly, the independent regimes established in Xinjiang during the second half of the nineteenth century and first half of the twentieth century cannot accurately be described as Uyghur nationalist movements for two reasons: on the one hand, the rebellions were rarely instigated by the Uyghurs (who tended rather to join others' movements) and, on the other hand, the rebels in each case favoured variations on the name 'Eastern Turkestan' and described themselves as 'Islamic' or 'Turkish-Islamic', suggesting a unification of Turkic Muslim groups in the region (and, in the case of the secular East Turkestan Republic, of Muslim and non-Muslim groups). This suggests that Uyghurs at that time did not wholly conceive of themselves as a separate ethnic and political entity.

From the early 1990s, however, the Uyghurs' sense of national identity began to strengthen. This phenomenon appeared partly as they defined themselves more and more in relation to the perceived religio-cultural and socio-economic threat posed by a rapidly increasing Han immigrant population (particularly in urban areas), and partly in response to certain influential domestic and international events: the reintroduction of conciliatory minority policies by Deng Xiaoping in 1980, the 1989 pro-democracy movement in China, the collapse of Eastern European Marxist–Leninist parties in 1989 and, most significantly, the disintegration of the USSR and subsequent formation of the Commonwealth of Independent States (CIS) in 1991. It was the last mentioned that definitively planted the notion of an independent state in Uyghur minds. Following the establishment across the border of five independent Central Asian republics (Kazakhstan, Uzbekistan, Kirghizstan, Turkmenistan and Tajikistan), the Uyghurs, the Tatars and the Salars became the only Central Asian Muslims in Xinjiang without an independent nation named after their ethnic group.[10] The vision of the CIS republics has since greatly encouraged Uyghur national identity, leading to the coining in 1995 of an alternative name – Uyghuristan – for a future independent state, and leading increasing numbers of Uyghurs to express resistance to Han rule in a variety of sub-political ways.[11]

The 'New Folk'

Along with the negative oral stereotyping of the Han, which occurred on a daily basis in urban Xinjiang in the mid-1990s, popular song proved more effective in uniting growing numbers of Uyghurs against the Han 'Other' than the 'poetry of resistance' of the 1920s and 1930s, more effective than competing regional attempts by intellectuals to project a new national consciousness (normally in print form), and more effective even than Islam.

For the purposes of this chapter, it will be useful first to outline a definition of the term 'popular music'. Grenier and Guilbault (1990: 390) characterize the theoretical debates surrounding the definition of popular music as quantitative (volume of sales and radio airplay), qualitative (focusing on the privileged relationships established through music), comparative (analyses of different genres) or political (the production and distribution of music by powerful institutions and the media). Of these, the first definition fits our context to a point, but carries with it certain limitations. The Uyghur songs I analyse here might certainly be described as popular in the sense that they enjoyed huge sales, but, as Richard Middleton (1990: 5–6) points out, sales figures are open to manipulation and distortion, and different musics sell at different rates over different time-spans. Further, none of these four definitions embraces the central notion of music becoming the vehicle for the expression of socio-political views. Kassabian's description (1999: 116–17) of the three main orientations of the term 'popular' in popular music and cultural studies is more helpful. The first – popular-as-folk – suggests a home-made, unmediated and often unpolished local form of music-making. The second – popular-as-mass – invokes contemporary forms of mass-produced and consumed music. She goes on to argue, however, that it is the third orientation – popular-as-populist – that has come to dominate, particularly in British cultural studies since the 1960s. This approach focuses on ways in which artists and audiences express social and political positions through music production and consumption. Over time, discourses on the term 'popular' have come to embrace the notion that audiences consciously engage with their popular culture, rather than the Frankfurt School position that they are passive victims of a 'false consciousness' imposed by music producers representative of dominant culture. In other words, the ways in which musical texts are used and interpreted are the 'ongoing product of people's attempt to represent their own experiences, and to speak in their own voices instead of hegemonic codes' (Manuel, 1993: 8). Music consumption thus constitutes 'a process of making meaning from, and contributing meaning to, popular culture' (Kassabian, 1999: 115).

The popular-as-populist model can be usefully applied to our context, with one modification to account for local political conditions. Whereas artists in democratic societies can be openly subversive and indeed gain subcultural capital from open rebellion, artists representing dominated ethnic groups in China cannot so readily flaunt social and political aims perceived to challenge the hegemony of a repressive state. Far from openly acknowledging their agency, Uyghur singers remain deliberately enigmatic when questioned about meanings and motives behind lyrical and musical texts for fear of political reprisal. After all, the Chinese empire itself is no stranger to the cynical use of music in nation-building projects, and has since earliest times mobilized music popular among the people in its goal to bring under one roof a staggering array of regional and ethnic diversities.[12]

Artists are usually attached to state-sponsored, professional song-and-dance troupes [*gewutuan*], paradoxically better known for the co-optation and control by the state of traditional art forms and minority representation. Since 1949, minority artists have been trained in these institutions, where they learn how to represent their ethnic identities in ways acceptable to the Chinese state (Baranovitch, 2001: 362–6). Correspondingly, the choice of works to be performed in official live or television performances is normally vetted by troupe leaders and by the local Cultural Bureau [*Wenhuaju*], responsible for monitoring the arts (Mackerras, 1985: 71–2). The latitude for personal interpretation, melodic subtlety and complex asymmetrical and syncopated rhythms traditionally enjoyed by the soloist or small Uyghur ensemble has been replaced in official troupes by a large folk orchestra of traditional and modernized instruments working from fixed music scores, leading to simplification, distortion and standardization. Lyrics contain messages of 'unity among nationalities' (that is, among the Han and China's 55 ethnic minority groups) and often promote government minority policies (Harris, 2004: Introduction).

From the early 1990s, Uyghur nationalist messages began to be conveyed through the medium of 'new folk', one form of commercially lucrative popular music in Xinjiang.[13] New folk music differs greatly from that performed by troupes in both performance style and lyrical content. It consists mainly of solo recordings of contemporary compositions, and enjoys a certain expressive freedom afforded by the octave-based modal structure (usually either heptatonic or pentatonic) which allows for interesting subtleties of tonal colour; the unique rhythms – characterized by extensive use of asymmetry and syncopation – associated with the traditional folk singing style and traditional stringed instruments such as the *dutar* (or two-stringed lute) also mark this musical tradition out as radically different from the musics performed by the troupes. Moreover, its song lyrics address prevalent social and political issues, borrowing or adapting lines by well-known and less well-known poets and writers.

Like some other professional minority musicians in China, new folk singers Ömärjan Alim, Abdurehim Heyit and Köräš Kösän began in the 1990s to try to subvert Beijing's control over the arts in the pursuit of alternative ethnic and national agendas.[14] In so doing, they attracted varying degrees of attention from the state censor, which has required artists and producers to submit new releases to the Cultural Bureau for political checks since 1995. Alim, Heyit and Kösän all had cassettes confiscated, and were often fined and/or forbidden to perform in public over the course of the decade.[15] When I met Abdurehim Heyit in the southern oasis town of Qäšqär in August 1996, he was having difficulties releasing his new cassette through Xinjiang-based producers who are subject to greater scrutiny by the censor than their counterparts elsewhere and was not permitted to tour.[16] Always careful to absolve himself of direct agency, he told me, smiling: 'They don't like my song words. *They say* I'm a nationalist!' (my emphasis). As a professional singer attached to a song-and-dance troupe, Heyit would normally be required to appear regularly in official state-controlled performances. Yet he told me he declined to appear in performances on Uyghur television, explaining: 'I don't want to play the songs the producers ask me to play … and they won't let me play the songs I want to play!' Perhaps the most famous of banned songs from this period is Ömärjan Alim's 'Mehman Bašlidim' ['I Brought Home a Guest'] from the cassette *Pärwayim Peläk* [Why Should I Care?]. The song employs an allegory in which the Han colonizer is depicted as 'the guest who never left' and the Uyghurs as slaves forced into the hostile desert.[17] However, censorship of popular music remained highly unsystematic, with some 'songs of nationalism' avoiding government attention.

Reproducing the Nation

One key to the success of popular music in conveying nationalist ideas is that it carries messages to the Uyghurs in their preferred cultural form. De Vos (1975: 9) lists aesthetic cultural forms such as food, dress, music and song as one of a number of markers of cultural difference that might be selected by group members in the definition of their group identity. Song and dance have been integral to Uyghur culture since ancient times and continue to be the mainstay and focal point of Uyghur social life, predominating at gatherings in the home, birthday parties, Uyghur dance restaurants, weddings, *mäšräp* [gatherings for feasting, storytelling, and music-making],[18] university dance halls and the bazaar, with its myriad cassette kiosks (Mackerras, 1985: 62–75; Smith, 1999: 231–3; Harris, 2002: 267–70). Significantly, a love of, and flair for, musical performance is also one criterion by which Uyghurs differentiate themselves from the Han whom they often dismiss as dull and introverted.[19]

Secondly, the orality of popular song also means that it is accessible to Uyghurs from all backgrounds, whether rural or urban. Although the late Uyghur novelist, poet and historian Abdurehim Ötkür was an undisputed symbol of Uyghur nationalist aspirations in the 1980s and 1990s, his media – poetry and the historical novel – were circulated predominantly in urban, often intellectual, spaces.[20] The extent to which his works reached the rural population – with its higher instance of illiteracy – must surely have been limited. Furthermore, the fact that the Uyghur language has undergone repeated script changes during the period of Chinese Communist rule means that Ötkür's work – published in the Arabic script ('Old Script') – is inaccessible to a generation of Uyghurs educated in the Latin script ('New Script') between 1960 and 1982.[21] In contrast, song words are communicated orally and can be received and understood by all. This is evidently why new folk singers have begun to borrow the poetry of Ötkür and other nationalist writers and use it – or adapt it for use – in their song lyrics. By so doing, they can transmit nationalist sentiments originally expressed in written or print form far beyond urban, intellectual circles and straight into the heart of the countryside.[22]

Thirdly, popular song can be rapidly disseminated via Xinjiang's low-budget and (partially) independent cassette industry. As Peter Manuel (1993: 2–4; 238) has shown in his study of mass-mediated cassette culture in North India, cassettes as one form of 'new media' are affordable, easy to produce, duplicate and pass on, and largely evasive of central control, making them the ideal vehicle for socio-political mobilization, even when banned by the censor. In Xinjiang, cassettes are transported from their place of production to large towns in the north and south. Uyghur merchants then buy the cassettes from urban distributors and take them home for sale in smaller, rural bazaars. In all of these centres, further 'pirate' copies pass from hand to hand. Moreover, as in other parts of China, there is a growing trend of young Uyghur men coming to urban centres from the countryside to look for work. During the 1990s, these migrant workers would gradually become familiar with popular 'us and them' – Uyghur vs Han – discourses, which were stronger in the city than in rural areas due to more intensive penetration by Han settlers, and with 'nationalist' songs heard at the bazaar. When they returned to the countryside, a copy of the cassette (or perhaps the memorized song lyrics, in a process of oral transmission) would accompany them. The cassette was then played (or the song performed) in the rural home before an audience of relatives, neighbours and friends, and the images and ideas within were reproduced in rural settings. With the advent of this performative dimension, Tuohy argues, popular song becomes 'an active means by which to experience the nation' (2001: 109).

This brings us to the fourth reason. The specific musical (sonic) texts created in new folk – the unique qualities of the traditional singing voice (predominantly a head voice but also articulated by nasal inflections) and sounds of the *dutar* – make it enormously affective. The traditional Uyghur singing style features subtle tone shifts of the melodic line, free melismatic ornamentation and, as with other Turkic musical traditions, a tendency to employ ululations (an inflection that draws on howls and/or cries to give the tone a 'lift'). With Alim's and Heyit's songs being sung almost exclusively within a minor (and modally heptatonic) tonal structure, this voice sometimes evokes fragility and a sense of mourning, and at other times quivering rage. It embodies a sense of mingled grief and frustration, which, combined with affective lyrical content, can give rise to very strong emotions. In this respect, Harris cites a Uyghur song composer as follows:

> A people who have suffered long oppression have soft hearts, they are easily shattered. There is much in their hearts that is unsaid. There is a special tragic note to their music. (2002: 273)

Forney, in an article for *Time Asia* (2002), similarly points to the tragedy in Heyit's music, characterizing him as the 'man of constant sorrow'. The *dutar*, meanwhile, contributes to new folk's appeal in two important ways. Like the Serbian one-stringed *gusle*, it may be said to assume an atavistic role as its sound 'travels across the dark centuries' (Thomas, 1999: 172–3), linking Uyghurs with ancestors who played the same instrument, and thus embodying continuity with Uyghur tradition. More significant still is the retention of traditional strumming patterns.

Finally, unlike co-opted Uyghur artists Kelimu and Bahai'erguli, who sing in the Chinese language, in effect becoming mouthpieces for China's all-inclusive national design ('singing collaborators'?), new folk singers sing in the Uyghur language. This ensures that messages reach rural Uyghurs who may know little or no Chinese, and it carries significant symbolic value. The Chinese state has frequently used vocal music as a vehicle for the dissemination of national standard speech (Mandarin) in the hope that local, regional and ethnic loyalties might be transformed into national (Chinese) ones (Tuohy, 2001: 117). Where minority languages have been retained in folk songs, the aim has been to represent the nation's ethnic diversity while simultaneously underscoring inter-ethnic harmony through the lyrics. At the same time, the state has all but institutionalized the (Han) Chinese language in minority areas in the spheres of education and employment. By favouring the Uyghur language, Xinjiang's new folk singers not only reject the assumed superiority of the Han language but also construct an alternative national (Uyghur) voice. For these reasons, new folk became the ideal vehicle through which not only to reflect prevalent social and political concerns in Xinjiang in the mid-1990s but also to construct and reproduce an alternative social, political and national consciousness.[23]

Five Songs by Ömärjan Alim

In the summer of 1996, one cassette in particular was blasted ceaselessly from cassette kiosks at bazaars in Ürümchi and oasis towns across Xinjiang. Wherever one went – Turpan, Kucha, Qäšqär, Xotän, Aqsu – Alim's voice rang out in private as well as in public, in rural as well as in urban, spaces, temporarily turning the cassette *Qaldi Iz* [Traces] into the Uyghur national soundtrack.[24] In an interview, Harris, a sound engineer involved in its recording, attributes its extraordinary success to Alim's ability to communicate with the peasants:

> He has a solid audience, he crosses boundaries of city and country, intellectual and peasant … Ömärjan has caught the heart of the Uyghur peasants, that's 90% of the population. He is popular because his words are direct, easily understood. He uses peasant language, proverbs. (2002: 278)

But plain language was clearly not the sole source of the cassette's popularity. Its overwhelming success derived also from its lyrical meanings. When asked what they liked about Ömärjan Alim's songs, the vast majority of respondents indicated the song-words, which they described as 'heavy with meaning' [*mänisi čong*], and which evidently articulated their situation *as they perceived it*. Including the gentle title track, 'Qaldi Iz' ['Traces'], which draws on a poem and novel by the late nationalist writer Abdurehim Ötkür, almost every song invites reflection on common grievances and is conceived within an implicitly or explicitly assumed framework of opposition to the Han.[25] For instance, 'Bulğanğan Sular' ['Dirtied Waters'] laments the environmental pollution believed by many Uyghurs to result from the (Han) economic development of the region;[26] 'Aldanma, Singlim' ['Don't Be Taken In, Sister'] is a didactic piece warning young Uyghur women not to mar their youth by frequenting discos and becoming a plaything for (often Han) men;[27] 'Tuğmas Toxu' ['Barren Chickens'] is a blackly humorous critique of Han colonization of the land and enforced birth control policy; in 'Bäzilär' ['Some People'], and 'Äwliya Dostum' ['My Immortal Friend'], Alim explores the thorny subject of the Uyghur puppet official (or 'collaborator'); 'Ränjimäyli Özgidin' ['Let's Not Blame Others'] and 'Häsrät' ['Sadness'] deal with perceived flaws in the Uyghur national character – that is, the tendency towards political passivity, infighting and collaboration with the (Han) oppressor; and, finally, in 'Därwaziwän' ['The Gatekeeper'], Alim is characterized as the 'illuminist', keeping a lonely watch over the fate of the Uyghur nation, determined to enlighten his people and steer them from repeating the mistakes of the past. Below, I analyse lyrical meanings in four of these songs – 'Tuğmas Toxu', 'Bäzilär', 'Äwliya Dostum' and 'Häsrät' – to show how social and political concerns prevalent among Uyghurs during this period of acute Uyghur–Han ethnic dichotomization were reflected and reproduced (in some cases with violent consequences) through the medium of popular song. Song analyses are supported by interview data gathered during a year of ethnographic fieldwork carried out in Xinjiang between 1995 and 1996, and during a six-week stay in Ürümchi in 2002.[28]

The Han Colonizer

'Tuğmas Toxu'	'Barren Chickens'[29]
{Tuğmas toxu yatidu	Barren chickens sit
Uwuluqni igälläp} (x2)	And occupy the roost
{Yürär särsan kočida	While they who'd lay twice as many eggs
Tuxum tuğqan hässiläp} (x2)	Roam the streets.
Tuğmas toxu katäktä	Barren chickens sit in the coop
Tallap esil dan yäydu	And eat the choice grain.
{Tuğmaydu ya katäkni	They lay no eggs yet won't give up
Tuğqanlarğa bärmäydu} (x2)	The coop to those who laid.
Oylap qaldim turmušta	I fell to thinking that in this Life
Barğu šundaq adämlär	Such individuals exist
Xuddi tuğmas toxudäk	Who, like barren chickens
Älni bizar ätkänlär	Invite the people's hatred
Yašisimu undaqlar	And though they live among us
Älgä bärmäs qilčä näp	Bring no benefit to the people
Xuddi tuğmas toxudäk	But like barren chickens
Ötär orun igälläp.	Occupy the best position.
Yašisimu undaqlar	Though they live among us
Älgä bärmäs qilčä näp	Bring no benefit to the people
{Xuddi tuğmas toxudäk	But like barren chickens
Ötär orun igälläp} (x2)	Occupy the best position.

The 'barren chickens' in 'Tuğmas Toxu' can be understood in at least three ways. According to one interpretation, they are the Han Chinese, depicted as the colonizer occupying the 'roost' or the beautiful land of Xinjiang. This colonizer, while adopting a birth control policy designed to control its own numbers, has imposed a slightly modified version of that policy on minority nationalities throughout China. For many Muslim Uyghurs – particularly those in rural areas and the deeply religious south – the concept of choosing not to bear children is preposterous and therefore humorous (another reason for the song's appeal). More significantly, the policy makes it practically impossible for the Uyghur population to stay abreast with the rapidly increasing Han immigrant population. Prior to the policy's introduction, many Uyghurs raised families of between 8 and 14 children, considering childbirth to be a blessing from *Xuda* [Allah], and the suggestion is that, had they been allowed to continue, Uyghurs could have fully occupied the land instead of being ousted from it by the Han ('they who'd lay twice as many eggs roam the streets'). Uyghur attachment to, and rightful ownership of, the land was often forcefully communicated by Uyghur respondents. Uyghur intellectuals Šöhrat and Räwiä maintained on separate occasions that Han Chinese have created a myth of origin regarding their history in Xinjiang and even that they stage archaeological tricks in order to 'prove' their presence in the region for hundreds of years. Less educated Uyghurs made equally indignant reference to this perceived rewriting of history, as when Batur, a migrant worker in Ürümchi, exclaimed: 'They [the Hans] say they were here first. They even say it in the books they write. They say they have always been here!' (Smith, 1999: 259–61).[30]

Based on a different reading, the 'barren chickens' are the Uyghur leaders, who make no attempt to gain rights and privileges for the Uyghur people, yet continue to eat finer foods (choice grain) and live in better houses (roost, coop) than those thought to have done more for the nationalist cause. This view of ethnic Uyghur officials as collaborators is not new. We know that, already under the late Qing, indigenous officials in Xinjiang retained from among local nobles conspired with Qing officials in the oppression of their fellow Uyghurs, although the Qing emperor forbade it. Along with Qing officials, they became popularly known as 'dogs with human faces' (Kim, 1986: 46). In 1995–96, amid an atmosphere of increased desire for self-determination, the Uyghur general public was once more extremely disillusioned with its indigenous representatives. Räwiä was one urban dweller who despaired that Uyghur leaders did not stand up to central government: 'Our leaders say nothing. I don't know if they don't care or if they are just too scared. *I* would speak up about things if I were a cadre' (respondent's emphasis). On another occasion, she argued that Uyghur leaders were 'in no danger of execution', and demanded to know why they went along with adverse policies proposed by Han officials. Similar views existed among rural Uyghurs, though usually aimed at local, lower-level officials. Tursun, a peasant in his 30s from Aqsu, remarked ironically that much of the tax he paid made up wages for Uyghur cadres and labelled them parasites. This popular view is also reflected in 'Tuǧmas Toxu', especially if we read the 'barren chickens' as a representation of the Uyghur leaders who enjoy many privileges while giving nothing back to their people.

A third interpretation casts white-collar Han immigrants as the 'barren chickens', reflecting the widespread Uyghur concern that Uyghurs are marginalized by default in the urban job market where Han-run state organs and private enterprises hire only fluent Chinese speakers.[31] Many educated Uyghurs complain that Han Chinese get jobs purely on the basis that their mother tongue is Chinese even though they may lack the necessary abilities. In this way, they potentially rob a more qualified Uyghur of the post. Söhrat explained how Han academics in Xinjiang were always assigned the best research projects simply because they were proficient in written Chinese. In fact, he argued, Uyghur researchers had just as much research potential – sometimes more – but were denied the same opportunities due to their lower level of Chinese proficiency.

With such a wide range of possible interpretations, it becomes difficult to identify who the 'barren chickens' – or those they represent – actually are, and this of course is one reason why new folk singers can sometimes avoid detection by the government censor. Even without the use of metaphor, it has been hard for the Chinese state to know how to interpret song lyrics. Tuohy (2001: 118) notes, for instance, that state leaders in the 1980s and 1990s were unable to reach agreement on whether rock singer Cui Jian's lyrics about the Chinese Communist Party's revolutionary heritage were patriotic or ironic. It can take some time for the authorities in Xinjiang to realize that a set of lyrics is politically problematic, partly due to the wide use of metaphor, allegory and allusion, and partly because songs are sung in the Uyghur language, indecipherable to all but a few Han Chinese. However, interview data suggest that the Cultural Bureau often does come to learn of political subterfuge, ironically through tip-offs by Uyghur 'collaborators' or spies. When a cassette is eventually banned, however, the censorship has the opposite effect to that intended: ordinary people suddenly become very interested in the product. In this respect, the Uyghurs might be said to resemble any other people in the world.[32] Harris (2002: 279–80) writes that Uyghur music producers and distributors in Xinjiang actually found ways to use censorship to commercial advantage. When a new tape was about to be released, they posted advertisements in shops urging customers to buy before the product was banned, thus stimulating public curiosity, boosting sales and ensuring still wider dissemination of the nationalist ideas within. While lyrical meanings in new folk remained ambiguous on the surface, the people could – and did – read what they liked into them, and those readings were invariably tempered by their perceptions of the social, political and economic climate – that is, their perceptions of their marginalized position in relation to Han immigrants and their continued oppression by the Chinese state.

The Uyghur 'Collaborator'

The second song, 'Bäzilär' ['Some People'], articulates popular Uyghur perceptions of the weakness and passivity of indigenous officials (and would-be officials) and of their unscrupulous pursuit of personal gain:

'Bäzilär'	'Some People'
{Älgä ämäs ämälgä xomar ikän bäzilär	Some are addicted not to the people but to power
Näpisi üčün jenidin kečär ikän bäzilär} (x2)	And sacrifice their own for the sake of greed
{Öz bäxtini özgining jäbirisidin izdišip	They seek their happiness in others' misery
Wijdanini görägä qoyar ikän bäzilär} (x2)	And pawn their consciences
Äl čongini äzäldin ällä süyüp saylaytti	In ancient times the people elected their leaders
Lekin älning közini boyar ikän bäzilär (x2)	Now some pull wool over the people's eyes
{Aläm degän barčiğa täng selinğan dastixan	The world is a table spread for all
Lekin uni uyalmay bular ikän bäzilär} (x2)	Yet some steal all without scruples
Yalaq yalap ögängän xuddi lalma itlardäk	Like stray dogs who've learned to lick at the dog bowl
Mötiwärlär aldida turar ikän bäzilär (x2)	Some stand before the powerful
{Mäydisigä urğanning hämmisila är ämäs	They beat their chests, but none are men
Sesip qalğan yağačdäk sunar ikän bäzilär}(x2)	Just split like rotten wood
Sesip qalğan yağačdäk sunar ikän	Just split like rotten wood. bäzilär.

Respondents interpreted *some people* as referring to Uyghur officials, puppet leaders chosen not by Uyghurs but by the Chinese government, accused of ignoring the misery of their people while themselves enjoying privileges extended by the Han.[33] One is reminded of the popular concept of the 'man of the people', summed up in the Uyghur proverb: 'A good man is in touch with the people; a bad man only with property' [Yaxši är älgä ortaq, yaman är malğa].[34] In addition to voicing keenly felt popular resentment, the song is apparently intended to prick the conscience of the officials themselves by accusing them of 'selling out' their ethnic group. Once again, it is worth noting that this perceived phenomenon of betraying the nation is not new. There are an unusually large number of words in the Uyghur language that express precisely this notion, for instance *milliy xa'in* [ethnic or national traitor], *milliy munapiq* [scum of the nation], *wätän satquč* or *satqin* [person who 'sells' the nation], *maqulči* [collaborator or 'Yes-man'].[35]

In the third verse, the metaphor of the dog, used during the Qing colonial period, resurfaces in the modern context. Though dogs in the wild exist in hierarchically ordered packs, living and hunting together as a team, the stray dog, once separated from the pack, becomes an opportunist and takes his chances. The domestic dog, meanwhile, may be characterized as parasitic, betraying his own kind to accept favours and an easy life under a dominant race. Contrast this with the other metaphor often used by Uyghurs to describe their national character, namely the 'sheep mentality'. Uyghurs often complain that they are too like the sheep that grace their dinner table (and joke that they should eat less mutton), the implication being that Uyghurs bow down too easily to leadership from without. This reflects their tendency throughout history to accept foreign hegemony, as well as their inability to produce a leader from among their ranks who is able to unite them. However, the sheep metaphor also suggests that Uyghurs tend to think and act as one, and this does not bear out current social realities. The 'stray dog' metaphor seems to reflect more accurately the perceived self-serving nature of the indigenous official, and can be linked to one of Alim's older themes: the idea that Uyghurs have been displaced from their homes by the Han 'boss' and forced into the hostile desert.[36] Once dispossessed, the temptation towards opportunism is too great, so that some of these exiled strays break away from the pack and sidle up to lick gratefully and obediently at the dog bowl proffered by the new master.[37]

In the final lines, Alim alludes to the perceived tendency of Uyghur officials to puff themselves up and make a big show of their status. Some people, he sings, pretend to be real men on the outside while inside they are broken and corrupt. The rotting wood metaphor evokes at once the notion of Uyghur leaders having no conscience and the sense that they are of no practical use – a house cannot be built with rotten wood. Again, we revisit the idea that a 'real man' is a man who thinks and acts for his people.

Social Climbers

The third song, 'Äwliya Dostum' ['My Immortal Friend'], was interpreted by respondents as dealing with low- and middle-level officials who are perceived to collaborate in order to advance their social status:

'Äwliya Dostum'	'My Immortal Friend'
{Äwliyadäk čaǧlaysän dostum özängni	You think yourself immortal, my friend
Bašqilarǧa sanjisän näštär sözingni} (x2)	Stinging others with your words
{Maxtay desäm azapliq dilim köyidu	Should I think to praise you, my heart burns
Maxtimaymän zadila tilim köyidu} (x2)	I can't praise you for my tongue burns
Way, way, way, way... hiligär dostum (x2)	O, o, o, o ... my sly friend
{Šir aldida tülkidäk qilisän süküt Ämma čüjä aldida bolisän bürküt} (x2)	Before the lion you fall silent as a fox Yet before the chick, you're an eagle

{Čiwin qonsa ğingšisän	You whine if a fly alights on you,
Kaltäk tägsä jim	But when struck by a stick say nothing
Šundaq xuydin bizlärni saqla Ilahim}	Allah, save us, from this character trait
(x2)	
Way, way, way, way … hiligär dostum	O, o, o, o … my sly friend
(x2)	
Way, way, way, way … äwliya dostum	O, o, o, o … my immortal friend
Way, way, way, way … älwida dostum	O, o, o, o … farewell my friend.
Älwida dostum.	Farewell my friend.

In the second verse, it is suggested that such individuals flaunt their status and act as though invincible before the 'chick' (the powerless Uyghur people) while, on the other hand, becoming servile before the 'lion' (the powerful Han and higher-ranking Uyghur leaders). The following lines 'You whine if a fly alights on you, / But when struck by a stick say nothing' can be read in at least two ways. One interpretation is that petty officials complain and offer excuses if an ordinary, powerless Uyghur approaches them for help, yet are silent and complicit when pressurized from above – that is, by the Han or higher-ranking indigenous officials.[38] A second interpretation suggests that the 'stick' is a thick wad of money, implying that such officials do favours only for those compatriots who can afford to bribe them. One respondent explained the ironic use of the word 'immortal' with reference to the saying 'Asman egiz, yär qattiq' [The sky is high, the ground is hard]. In other words, those who overreach themselves have further to fall and petty officials such as these will one day know that they are not immortal.

In interviews, Uyghur respondents frequently criticized individuals thought to be cooperating too closely with the Han authorities, for example Uyghur officials, Uyghur police and some religious personnel. Moreover, these criticisms often developed from the verbal level into direct action. According to Dilšat, who worked in tourism, a violent attack on an imam from the Idkah mosque in 1996 (one of his ears was cut off, and his arms slashed with meat cleavers) was intended as a warning to other religious figures not to collude with the Han hegemony.[39] According to him, the imam had 'helped the government in many ways' and was 'much hated'. This view was supported by Karim, a health professional from southern Xotän, who stated: 'The imam's links with the authorities were rather too close.' The violence did not always stop with a warning. Since the summer of 1993, a small number of militant Uyghur nationalists had begun to make assassination attempts on low- and middle-level Uyghur party cadres and officials where previously they had only targeted Han Chinese cadres, public security officials and military.[40] In 1995, a Hong Kong newspaper reported (slightly sensationally) that the Uyghur separatist movement was 'an organisation like the "Palestinian National Liberation Front", often conducting activities such as assassination with their spearhead pointed chiefly at local government officials, especially those in the public security departments'.[41]

The number of assassinations of Uyghur cadres, as well as attacks on Han police and soldiers, riots, and minor armed insurrections, increased significantly during the years 1995–97. One particularly horrific incident in 1996, which went unreported in the Chinese press, involved a multiple assassination of a Uyghur cadre and three of his relatives in his home in Kucha (significantly, victims' tongues were cut out before their throats were slashed) and was the first occasion on which the Chinese authorities encountered Uyghur suicide bombers (Smith, 1997). This background, then, provides the context for the closing lines of the song: 'Farewell my friend'. While one reading suggests that it is the bad character trait (that is, an inclination to prostitute oneself for power and material wealth) to which Uyghurs must say goodbye, a darker interpretation implies that it is Uyghur officials and social climbers – the 'immortal friends' – who must bid farewell to their lives. As one respondent put it, the song's closing line then assumes the meaning: 'You die!' [*Ölisän!*].

The Flawed National Character

The self-perception among many Uyghurs that they suffer from a flawed national character is developed in more depth in the final song, 'Häsrät' ['Sadness']:

'Häsrät'	'Sadness'
Bir anidin tuğulğan	Born of one mother
Qerindaštuq äsli biz	Once compatriots we
Qoydi bizni šu küngä	What's brought us to this day?
Osal päyli xuymiz.	Our bad character trait.
Miwä bärgän däräxni	Trees which bear fruit
Qurutmaqni oylaymiz	We leave to bleed dry
Kim qazansa nätijä	As we snap and gnaw
Šuni qišläp ğajaymiz.	At each others' success.
Dağdam yolğa patmaymiz	No room for us to tread one wide road
Tar kočidin qatraymiz	We hurry down our narrow lanes
Qiltaq qurup öz ara	Building traps for one another
Yeqitmaqni oylaymiz.	To cause each other's fall.

According to respondents, this song is the most emotive of the four. In the words of Šatgül, a middle-aged Uyghur woman in the service industry: 'When we hear Alim's songs, it does something to us … It gets us right in the chest [places hands on heart], makes us feel really agonized.' When I asked her whether this was a good or bad pain, she confirmed that it was a good sort of pain, suggesting that her experience of the song involved a strong element of catharsis. The sadness in 'Häsrät' derives from its preoccupation with notions of Uyghur national disunity (the narrow lanes as opposed to the wide road) and its perceived source: infighting and envy. This is a perception common among educated Uyghurs. For instance, two university graduates living in Ürümchi, Aliyä and Äziz described the difference between Uyghurs and Kazakhs thus: 'The Kazakhs are a much better people than us ... They are not jealous of one another. They fight big wars, we fight small ones.' They further cited a Uyghur saying, 'Paltining sepi yaɣač tur' [The axe-handle is ever made of wood], in which the axe blade symbolizes the Han hegemony, aided by the Uyghurs (the axe-handle) in its oppression of the Uyghur people (the wood).

In a 1996 interview, Dilšat told me that some Uyghurs were supplying information to the Chinese authorities in the hope of bettering their personal circumstances: 'People are really scared in Kashgar. And what they're most scared of is other Uyghurs ... spies.' These fears had multiplied by the time of my return to Xinjiang in 2002. Some said that the arrest of Räbiyä Qadir (popularly known as 'Xinjiang's millionaire businesswoman') in 1999 had been made on the basis of information leaked to the Chinese authorities by precisely such 'inside' spies. They deemed such behaviour widespread and attributed it to petty jealousy and a reluctance to see others achieve. Compare this view with the image in lines 7–8 of 'Häsrät', when once again the dog metaphor is evoked. This time we find the dogs fighting over the spoils. Hence Uyghurs listening to 'Häsrät' experience feelings of regret combined with emotional release or catharsis, in recognition of a painfully familiar social phenomenon.

Differing Views Towards Secession

The Uyghurs were undoubtedly more united as a nation (in the sense of being generally opposed to the Han presence) in the mid-1990s than at any other time previously, due to the domestic and international factors mentioned above.[42] However, there remained difficulties concerning ethno-political mobilization. Groups (and I present these as 'ideal types') that fully subscribed to separatist, ethno-political ideologies included young male intellectuals, young male petty entrepreneurs, and the unemployed, all hailing from urban settings. Groups who did not necessarily subscribe to such ideologies included the older generation, women and Uyghur peasants. In particular, views on secession – and the way to go about achieving this – differed significantly across generations, between rural and urban areas, and between genders. As Naby (1986: 245) had predicted a decade earlier, the attitudes of the young generation had become far more radicalized. The elders, however, were not given to impetuous acts, while both they and the middle-aged bore the scars of their persecution during the Cultural Revolution. Many women remarked to me that the Chinese state 'would never let go of Xinjiang', and preferred to focus on gaining equal rights and opportunities for Uyghurs within the current socio-political structure. Uyghur peasants had not at that time experienced competition from Han immigrants for education, work and resources on the scale experienced by urban Uyghurs, and so their grievances were fewer. Most protested about two issues in particular: the imposition by local cadres of adverse, over-centralized farming policies, and the vastly unpopular Han-enforced birth control policy. Few, it seemed, had begun to look beyond their immediate, everyday circumstances to consider the future of the Uyghur nation.

I would suggest, however, that the dissemination of nationalist discourse through the medium of popular song, together with negative oral stereotyping of the Han in the cities (and its eventual oral transmission to rural areas) played a significant role in the subsequent spread of separatist ideology to the countryside and to other social groups. While this is evidently difficult to measure, the year 1997 saw an increase in separatist violence such as bombings, armed attacks on Han Chinese police, mob attacks directed at Han police, military and civilians, and riots, including the largest in Xinjiang since 1949. On 5–6 February, young Uyghurs in the northern town of Ghulja attacked Han Chinese civilians indiscriminately on the streets, and burned the bodies of the dead. The riot was said to have been sparked by the execution of 30 young Uyghur separatists, the arrest of 100 Muslim students with pro-independence views and state suppression of so-called 'illegal religious activities'. These developments resulted in an intensified government crackdown in the political and religious spheres, and, eventually, in the cultural sphere.[43] Reports released by Amnesty International in January–April 1999 showed that Uyghurs recently detained on suspicion of 'ethnic splittism' [*fenliezhuyi* or 'attempting to split the motherland'] included secondary school teachers, peasants, merchants, a surgeon, a factory worker, 'millionaire businesswoman' Räbiyä Qadir and even a local Uyghur cadre (Amnesty International, 1999a, b).

Raising Awareness: Alim, the Gatekeeper

Confucius once said: 'In altering customs and changing habits, nothing is better than music.'[44] Like its historical predecessors, the modern Chinese state has made concerted efforts to commodify and disarm oppositional art (in the sense posited by the Frankfurt theorists of popular culture). In the mid-1990s, however, Uyghur artists began to resist these efforts, using new folk as a means to construct and disseminate representations of the Uyghur nation that contrasted sharply with the carefully packaged, exoticized images of 'happy', colourful, *passive* ethnic minorities produced by the Han regime (Gladney, 1994). These alternative representations, while not necessarily painting a nuanced picture of complex social conditions in the region, proved powerful reflections of popular socio-political perceptions and frustrations. They thus created an emotional resonance, derived from a sense of mutual validation, among Uyghurs of all walks of life. As Harris put it, 'The sense of the Uyghur community is being effectively redrawn through popular music' (2002: 280). Through the repetitive processes of performing, listening to (and unconsciously *hearing*) Alim's songs, the meanings, perceptions and assumptions contained therein were reproduced throughout urban society, and came to influence attitudes among a growing number of individuals in the countryside.[45] Alim's lamentations may therefore be said to possess an illuminative quality in the modern context, creating awareness of the need for ethnic unity in relation to the perceived religio-cultural and socio-economic threat posed by the Han. This role of 'illuminist' is explored in 'Därwaziwän' ['The Gatekeeper'], a fifth song taken from the cassette *Qaldi Iz*: 'There was a time when we lost everything to thieves; From now on, I shall be vigilant, for I am the gatekeeper.' Once more, the Han Chinese are portrayed as colonizer, this time as 'thieves' who have stolen the beautiful land of Xinjiang along with its natural resources. Meanwhile, Alim sings in the first person, apparently presenting himself as his people's lonely saviour.

Conclusion: Popular Music, Politics and Playing the Game

The events of the latter half of the 1990s show that, when taken too far by persons of a particular disposition, exhortations to ethnic loyalty can lead to violence both within and between ethnic groups, that songs of nationalism may – as in the former Yugoslavia – 'reaffirm hatreds between different peoples' (Hudson, 2000b: 168). It could for instance be argued that one extreme consequence of Alim's songs against so-called 'collaborators' (and perhaps one unforeseen by the singer himself) was to catalyse an increase in the number of assassinations and attempted assassinations on Uyghur cadres and personnel in the mid- to late 1990s. In other words, such events not only inspired Alim's songs, but may also have been *inspired by them*. This in turn begs the question: why have the Chinese authorities seemingly been so slow and unsystematic in their sanctioning of Uyghur songs of nationalism? To date, the only song to be censored on Alim's cassette *Qaldi Iz* is the title track, 'Traces'. This is a comparatively gentle song and arguably less likely to provoke ethnic tension than some others analysed here. Certainly, the language barrier created by publishing lyrics in Uyghur, added to the difficulties of interpreting meanings veiled in metaphor and allusion, may have partially hindered the monitoring process. *Qaldi Iz*, based as it is on a pre-existing nationalist poem known to the Han authorities, would come under suspicion much more rapidly than the original texts, and this is one possible explanation why this song was censored where others were not. However, it is my contention that just as colonial situations throughout history have produced individuals willing to cooperate with the colonizer, Uyghur nationalist song lyrics, along with other literary forms, will eventually be translated and made available to the Chinese state. Consider, for example, the fact that a nationalist poem, recited at a public gathering to celebrate Naw-ruz in Ürümchi in March 2002, was translated and passed to the authorities within just 24 hours, resulting in the arrest of the speaker.[46] Furthermore, it seems reasonable to assume that if uneducated Uyghur peasants are able to receive and understand the hidden messages in Alim's songs, educated Han officials, trained to identify political references in minority texts, might also be capable of the same.

One might suggest (though it is pure speculation) that, in this case, the Cultural Bureau weighed up the advantages and disadvantages of giving airplay to songs

that highlight disunity among the Uyghurs and decided that it was in the interests
of the state to let them circulate. After all, Alim's mix of lamentation of disunity
and exhortation to unity will affect different individuals in different ways. There
remains a strong likelihood that some Uyghurs, far from reacting positively and
vowing to build unity among their people, may instead end up internalizing
negative perceptions such as that of the 'bad character trait', resulting in low
ethnic self-esteem and gradual loss of hope. Conversely, if the authorities were to
ban the entire cassette or arrest its author, Alim would be heralded as an ethnic
hero and martyr and the opposite effect would be produced, that of encouraging
and fuelling ethnic pride and resistance.

Epilogue

By 2002, the environment surrounding music and politics in Xinjiang had
significantly changed and public opinion regarding Ömärjan Alim was split. Some
of those interviewed remained loyal to the singer, and continued to laud him as
the 'voice of the Uyghurs'. They circulated rumours of his arrest and censorship,
and claimed with evident pride that he had been warned by the government not
to sing 'songs that threaten the unity of the nationalities' [*minzu tuanjie*]. Others,
however, deemed him a hypocrite, claiming that he had 'sold out' in recent years.
The example given most frequently was the story of Alim reputedly opening a
dance hall in his northern hometown of Ghulja, to which Uyghur girls came to
drink, take drugs and socialize with men. This act was perceived to contravene
Alim's popular didactic piece 'Aldanma, Singlim' ['Don't Be Taken In, Sister']. In
an interview in 2002, relatives of the artist claimed that Alim had never been in
trouble with the state, insisting that he was 'unaware of the content of his songs'
since they were *written for him* by local poets and writers and he himself was
'entirely uneducated'. Clearly the family's standard line of defence, this argument
has apparently been – successfully – used to defend Alim against charges of 'ethnic
splittism' in court.[47] Alim's double release in 2002, *Häsät Qilma* [Don't Fall Prey
to Envy], appears to contain no comparably explicit reference to Uyghur–Han
relations, concentrating generally on intra-ethnic social themes. Such a shift would
certainly suffice to cause ardent Uyghur nationalists to deem him a sell-out, and
may be precisely the result the Chinese authorities had hoped for. Permitting (or
perhaps even encouraging?) Alim to continue in a diluted or castrated form allows
the state to orchestrate his public fall from nationalist glory and further promote
the sense of hopelessness already taking root among the Uyghur people.

  In the wake of the new cultural crackdown, triggered by the aforementioned
public recital of a nationalist poem in March 2002 and encouraged by partial
US endorsement of China's 'anti-terrorist' campaign, Xinjiang's new folk singers
were forced to search for alternative ways to voice popular discontent. In some
cases (and possibly Alim's), this meant stepping aside to allow as yet unknown
and undetected champions of the cause to emerge, for example Tašmämät Batur,

the name on many lips in 2002. For Alim's closest competitor, Abdurehim Heyit, it meant resorting to the power of music itself. The title track of his 2002 release, *Ömüt* [Hope], was a powerful instrumental, conveying passion, desperation and determination. In it, the *dutar* may be said to become a 'political instrument ... giving voice to the collective feelings of the group' (Cooke and Doornbas, 1982: 53). Friends of the singer told me that it was now simply too dangerous to use nationalist lyrics, adding that it would be 'a mistake to connect Heyit with Ömärjan Alim in any way'.

During the current period of maximum state control over the political, religious and cultural spheres in Xinjiang, we might expect to see Uyghurs develop new, symbolic means of expressing dissatisfaction with their situation. Indeed, symbolic acts of dissidence are already emerging in the sphere of religion. While numbers of Uyghurs entering the mosques in the regional capital Ürümchi were small in the mid-1990s, those same mosques had been pulled down and replaced by new ones twice their original size in 2001–2002. Like Heyit's instrumental response to increased controls on culture, some respondents indicated that the mass return to the mosque represents a symbolic act of resistance to the increased repression of religion since the mid-1990s. The Chinese state may be able to co-opt Uyghur imams or simply replace them with state-trained counterparts, but it remains to be seen whether it can replace the unifying force of Islam itself. Meanwhile, Heyit's response to the question of whether hope endures in Xinjiang suggests that the new 'silence' is temporary: 'Where there's life, there's hope' [*Hayat bar bolsa, ömüt bar*].

Notes

1   This chapter develops themes that appeared briefly in my thesis (Smith, 1999) and combines interview data and media analyses from it with new song translations and new interviews conducted in 2002. I am indebted to the Economic and Social Research Council for supporting initial fieldwork in 1995–96. Also, I would like to extend my thanks to co-panellists and members of the audience for their useful suggestions and comments at the Annual Meeting of the Association for Asian Studies in New York, 2003.
2   See Hoppe (1992) for an ethnic breakdown of Xinjiang's population.
3   Gardner Bovingdon (2003) has been engaged in fascinating research on the ways in which contemporary Uyghurs preserve and disseminate an alternative (and sometimes fanciful) vision of a distinct national past through the medium of oral histories.
4   For a detailed analysis of ethnic boundary maintenance in two towns in Xinjiang in the mid-1990s, see Bellér-Hann (2002) and Smith (2002). I refer to the Han Chinese as 'The Han' or 'The Han Chinese' throughout this chapter in recognition of the tendency of many Uyghurs in 1995–96 to portray the Han as an immovable, uniform 'Other' in everyday popular discourse. This in no way suggests that all Han settlers in Xinjiang are 'the same', simply that Uyghur perceptions were often voiced in uncompromising terms. Nor does my use of this blanket term suggest that all Uyghur views on the Han

are identical. In fact, Uyghurs from different age groups hold nuanced views with regard to Han immigrants with older Uyghurs distinguishing between first-generation Han settlers who were willing to respect local culture and newly arrived immigrants who are not (Smith, 2000).

5   I employ the term 'collaborator' throughout, although the closest equivalent to the original Uyghur term (*maqulči* or 'person who says "OK"') would be 'Yes-man'. Despite common Uyghur perceptions of their indigenous leaders, it is of course impossible to categorize all Uyghur officials in black and white terms as either a 'man of the people' or a 'collaborator'. Interviews carried out in 1996 suggested rather that individuals occupied different points on a scale between altruism and self-interest, and that these positions were far from static. See also Stan Toops's illuminating comparison (1992) of two recent Uyghur leaders, Tömür Dawamat and Ismail Amat, in which the former is characterized rather as a 'cipher' for state-generated rhetoric, while the latter is shown to pursue a viable political agenda that reflects the realities of the region.

6   I borrow this term from the Albanian *iluminist*, connoting a poet who gives his life to spreading a message of self-elevation to his fellow countrymen (Sugarman, 1999: 447).

7   These days, Qarašar forms part of the Bayingholin Mongol autonomous prefecture. While Uyghurs prefer the historical name, the Chinese have renamed the area Yanji Hui Autonomous County [*Yanji huizu zizhixian*].

8   For writings on the Yaqub Beg rebellion (1866–77), see Tsing (1961) and Kim (1986); on the Turkish–Islamic Republic of Eastern Turkestan (1933–34), see Forbes (1986); and on the East Turkestan Republic (1944–49), see Forbes (1986) and Benson (1990).

9   In my writings on Uyghur identity, I start from the assumption that human identities are relative and conjunctural: in other words, that they are formed in relation to an 'Other' and are fluid and changing, formed at particular moments in time in response to a specific set of social, economic and/or political circumstances (Clifford, 1988: 10–11; Gladney, 1996). For a discussion of the relative and fluid nature of ethnic boundaries, see Barth (1969) and Eriksen (1993: 10–12).

10   The Salars are said to have originated from a Turkmen tribe (Schwarz, 1984: 39–40), and therefore might be said to have their own country in Turkmenistan. The Tatars and the Salars in Xinjiang numbered only 4,821 and 3,660 persons respectively in 1990, compared with a Uyghur population of 7,194,675 (Hoppe, 1992).

11   Prior to the Chinese Communists taking power in 1949, Western travellers identified the region as 'East Turkestan', reflecting the dominant presence of Turkic groups. The words 'East Turkestan' also appeared in the names of the independent regimes of the 1930s and 1940s, and continue to be favoured by some contemporary separatist movements.

12   Tuohy (2001: 110–18) shows how the Chinese state has used popular music and song variously as a means to assess the attitudes of the empire's subjects, mobilize the nation against foreign invaders, and represent the nation in a way that stresses ethnic inclusiveness. See also Perris (1985: 93–122).

13   This term was coined by Harris (2002: 272) in her survey of the popular music industry in Xinjiang.

14   Baranovitch (2001) focuses on the increasing degree of agency displayed by minority artists in China in the creation of alternative representations of their ethnic identity. Among his 'new voices' is Inner Mongolian singer Teng Ge'er.

15 For details of Kösän's experiences, see Harris (2002: 265–6).

16 Heyit's 1994 trilogy *Mung-zar* [Sadness] was released through a studio in Xi'an, Sha'anxi province, far to the east of Xinjiang.

17 For a full translation in English, see Smith (1999: 176–7).

18 These days, women can take part equally with men in a non-religious form of *mäšräp*, intended to allow people to rejoice through the medium of the performing arts (Mackerras, 1985: 68). Up until the 1950s, however, participants were all male. The *mäšräp* functioned as a rite of passage into manhood, a vehicle for regulating moral, religious and social etiquette, and a means of forming male peer groups. In the mid- to late 1990s, this 'traditional' form of *mäšräp* was resurrected in the city of Ghulja, North Xinjiang, and among Uyghur communities in Almaty, Qazaqstan, with the modern aim of creating and maintaining Uyghur national culture (Roberts, 1998: 675). Such *mäšräp* quickly came under government suspicion in the People's Republic as popular arenas for the dissemination of separatist ideologies and literatures.

19 Mackerras (1985: 66) remarks that the spoken play [*huaju*] popular among Han Chinese has singularly failed to make an impression among the Uyghur because it lacks music, the ingredient so essential to their cultural identity.

20 Ötkür's novels were fictional accounts of events that occurred before the Chinese Communists came to power in 1949. In them, he expressed themes and ideas relevant to the present, escaping the censor by dressing these in analogous historical situations (Rudelson, 1997: 163–5).

21 See Bellér-Hann (1991: 72–5) on the history of script changes in Xinjiang.

22 See, for example, 'Čillang Xoruzum' ['Crow, My Rooster!'] by Abdurehim Heyit, from the tape *Mung-zar* [Sadness]. Harris (2002: 278) gives examples in Ömärjan Alim's work. There is an interesting comparison here with the Albanian nationalist movement during the period from the start of the Albanian War of Independence in 1898 through the declaration of an independent Albania in 1912 to its recognition by the Great Powers in 1918. Sugarman writes that villagers gained a 'deep-seated sense of themselves as being Albanian' only after nationalist poems were transformed into men's narrative songs (1999: 441–5). In this process, figures such as *çetë* [armed guerrilla unit] commander Sali Butka composed revolutionary poems that fused features of village song texts with nationalist themes in a form of folk poetry. Sugarman hypothesizes that *çetë* members, who were encouraged to become literate, began to sing the poems as songs, and that these were then taken up by fellow villagers when members returned home.

23 In presenting this phenomenon as a two-way process, I follow Tuohy, who models musical nationalism in China as a 'mutually transformative process of making music national and of realizing the nation musically' (2001: 108–9)' and Sugarman (1999: 421), who sees Albanian literary figures as simultaneously producing the nationalist discourses of the Albanian Rilindja ('rebirth') and being produced as national subjects by them.

24 Harris (2002: 270) notes that Xinjiang's bazaars function as an 'unofficial pop chart', where the number of shops and restaurants playing a certain cassette provide a reliable guide to the latest hit. See also Baranovitch who writes that Teng Ge'er's 1989 release 'The Mongol' was still frequently sung in rural areas of Inner Mongolia in the mid-1990s, 'suggesting that his alternative [ethnic] representation is accepted by a large portion of the people he claims to represent' (2001: 371).

25 An exception might be 'Wäsiyät' ['Testament'], which tackles the social problem of drug abuse and addiction among young Uyghurs, although many Uyghurs relate even this problem to their sense of political impotence, or to the unequal life chances afforded them under the Han hegemony. For an English translation of the poem 'Iz' ['Traces'], see Allworth and Pahta (1988). The song was subsequently banned from radio airplay and public performance.

26 Inner Mongolian singer Teng Ge'er similarly sang in 1994 of aggressive Han colonization and ecological destruction in his homeland in 'The Land of the Blue Wolf'. Baranovitch describes the song as 'simultaneously a tragic elegy, a cry of protest, and an effort to raise the consciousness of other Mongols' (2001: 369).

27 This song alludes to a small minority of young Uyghur women in Ürümchi and other urban areas who are said to have adopted 'bad modern ways' (where modernity is perceived to have been introduced by the Han and as running counter to Islamic social mores). These girls adopt a role comparable to that of the Japanese 'hostess', drinking, dancing and, in rare cases, sleeping with Han businessmen for money.

28 An anonymized list of respondents is available for reference in the appendix.

29 In recognition of the fact that 'content analysts are not innocent readers' (Frith, cited in Shepherd, 1999: 172) and in order to achieve inter-subjectivity, all song translations and their interpretations were prepared by the author in consultation with Uyghur respondents during the summer of 2002. For respondents' invaluable help, I extend my sincere gratitude. Elegance in the target language is partly sacrificed in favour of retaining as far as possible the original vocabulary, metaphors and cultural concepts in the source text.

30 See also Bovingdon's account (2002: 49–52) of a lively exchange between two women – one Uyghur and one Han – on the question of indigeneity to the region.

31 I deal with Uyghur perceptions of socio-economic inequalities in depth elsewhere (Smith, 1999: 242–68).

32 See Cloonan and Garofalo (2003) on the social and political aspects of popular music and censorship.

33 Uyghur leaders are hand picked by the Chinese government according to the appropriateness of their political attitudes. They must normally complete five years of political education at the Central University for Nationalities (formerly the Central Institute for Nationalities) in Beijing before assuming their posts. Mackerras observed that 'no Uyghur could rise to real power who espoused local nationalism' (1985: 77), and this remains the case today.

34 According to Ämät's annotation (2001: 399), the proverb implies that a man who thinks of his people and native place is pure while one who thinks only of the road to riches is selfish.

35 In her work on Albanian nationalism, Sugarman (1999: 425) hypothesizes that patriotic slogans such as 'Albania hates a traitor' appearing in songs included in nationalist intellectual Mitko's 1878 collection of folk songs had probably been added long after the songs' creation, in an attempt to awaken and unite the Albanian people.

36 See Alim's song 'Mehman Bašlidim' ['I Brought Home a Guest'].

37 Cf. the term *zougou* [literally 'running dog' or stooge] in Chinese, used to describe Chinese who collaborated with Western or Japanese imperialists. *Zougou* translates into Uyghur as *yalaqči* [literally 'person who licks'].

38 Cf. Uyghur rock singer Abdulla's song 'Šükür' ['Thanks'], which deals with Uyghur passivity (Harris, 2002: 276–7; Harris gives no discographic details as this was a live performance).

39 See Smith for a catalogue of ethnic disturbances in Xinjiang 1949–97 (1999: Appendix I).

40 Cf. shifting boundaries in South Africa with regard to 'internal' and 'external' Others. In the 1970s, Inkatha encouraged their members to defend the Zulu kingdom against 'outsiders' (at that time the government, whites, Indians and Xhosas). Yet in the 1980s, Zulus opposed to the Zulu kingdom were targeted as 'the enemy within' (Morris Szeftel, African Studies Seminar, Department of Politics, University of Leeds, 7/12/94).

41 *Lien ho pao*, Hong Kong, 27 February 1995 in Summary of World Broadcasts (Asia Pacific), 1 March 1995, FE/2240 G/4.

42 See Bovingdon (2002) for an engaging account of means of everyday resistance among ordinary Uyghurs in the latter half of the 1990s, and Smith (2000) for an analysis of the emergence of ethno-political ideologies among Uyghur youth.

43 For information about the repressive measures adopted by the Chinese state since 1995 and in the post-September 11 period, see Amnesty International (1997; 1998; 1999a, b; 2002), Human Rights Watch (2001) and Kellner (2002: 16–27).

44 Confucius, quoted by Kong Yingda, *Liji zhengyi* (cited in Tuohy 2001: 107).

45 The Chinese state has deliberately employed musical repetition in its goal to create a 'voice of the people', through daily broadcasts on television, radio and even public loudspeakers (Tuohy 2001: 117, 123). Alim's messages have been popularized on one level through a similar process of repetition, with Uyghur customers 'accidentally' hearing his songs as they browse the bazaar. I was fascinated during a stay in Kucha in 1996 to find a microcosm of competing musical nationalisms, with state-sanctioned, co-opted minority music blaring out of public loudspeakers in the predominantly Han-settled New Town, as independently produced Uyghur pop musics blared from cassette kiosks in the predominantly Uyghur-settled Old Town.

46 Naw-ruz means New Year's Day in Persian and is the beginning of the year for the people of Afghanistan, Azerbaijan, Iran and Tajikistan. Peoples in other Central Asian republics of the former Soviet Union, as well as some Uyghurs in Xinjiang, have also recently begun to hold Naw-ruz celebrations.

47 Personal communication with Rachel Harris, November 2002.

Discography

Alim, Ömärjan. *Pärwayim Peläk* [Why Should I Care?] (Censored: no publishing details).

Alim, Ömärjan. *Qaldi Iz* [Traces] (Ürümchi: Minzu chubanshe, CN-M06-95-0002-0, 1995).

Alim, Ömärjan. *Häsät Qilma* [Don't Fall Prey to Envy] Parts 1 and 2 (Ürümchi:Xinjiang yinxiang chubanshe, CN-H11-01-374-00/A, 2002).

Heyit, Abdurehim. *Mung-zar* [Sadness]. Parts 1, 2 and 3 (Ši'än: Ši'än kino studiyasi un-sin näšriyati, CN-H02-94-316-00/A, 1994).

Heyit, Abdurehim. *Ömüt* [Hope] (Beijing: Zhongguo minzu yinxiang chubanshe, CN-A25-02-0003-2/V, 2002).

Ge'er, Teng, 'The Land of the Blue Wolf', *Meng Sui Feng Piao* [Dreams Float with the Wind] (Baidai (EMI)/Zhonghua wenyi yinxiang lianhe chubanshe, CN-A49-94-348-00/A, 1994).

Ge'er, Teng, 'The Mongol', *Teng Ge'er: Hei Junma* [Teng Ge'er: Black Steed] (Xueyuan yinxiang chubanshe CN-A56-96-0001-0/A, 1996).

Appendix: List of Respondents

Key Informants

Abdurehim Heyit: summer 1996, Qäšqär, South Xinjiang and August–September 2002, Ürümchi city, North Xinjiang.

Notes: new folk singer, one of two artists popularly characterized as the 'voice of the Uyghurs', born in Qäšqär, performed with the Central Minorities Song and Dance Troupe in Beijing for two decades, now affiliated to the Xinjiang Uyghur Autonomous Region Song and Dance Troupe in Ürümchi city, practising Muslim, early 40s, male.

Aliyä: throughout 1995–96, Ürümchi city, North Xinjiang and Kucha, South Xinjiang; August–September 2002, Ürümchi city.

Notes: former postgraduate student, works in social sector, based in Ürümchi city, early–late 20s, female.

Äziz: throughout 1995–96, Ürümchi city, North Xinjiang and Kucha, South Xinjiang; August–September 2002, Ürümchi city.

Notes: university graduate, teacher, based in Ürümchi city, early–late 20s, male.

Dilšat: summer 1996, Qäšqär, South Xinjiang.
Notes: university graduate, works in tourist industry, based in Qäšqär, early 20s, male.

Räwiä: throughout 1995–96 and September 2002, Ürümchi city, North Xinjiang.

Notes: *minkaohan* (educated in Chinese rather than mother tongue), university graduate, employed in state work unit, based in Ürümchi city, late 30s–early 40s, female.

| Šatgül: | August–September 2002, Ürümchi city. |
| **Notes:** | secondary education only, works in tertiary industry, based in Ürümchi city, mid–late 40s, female. |

| Šöhrat: | throughout 1995–96, Ürümchi city, North Xinjiang; June 2002, Europe. |
| **Notes:** | university graduate, intellectual, based in Ürümchi city, late 20s–early 30s, male. |

| Tursun: | summer 1996, Aqsu, South Xinjiang. |
| **Notes:** | peasant and father of three, living with family in small rural community in Aqsu, semi-literate, early 30s, male. |

Occasional Informants

| Batur: | April 1996, Ürümchi city, North Xinjiang. |
| **Notes:** | secondary education only, migrant worker, based in Ürümchi city, mid-30s, male. |

| Karim: | summer 1996, Xotän, South Xinjiang. |
| **Notes:** | health professional, based in Xotän, practising Muslim, mid-50s, male. |

Relatives of Ömärjan Alim (new folk singer and the second of two artists popularly characterized as the 'voice of the Uyghurs'): September 2002, Ghulja, North Xinjiang.

| **Notes:** | all based in Ghulja, all female and representing all generations. |

Author's note: In order to protect the anonymity of informants, all names have been altered, birthplaces are omitted, and only broad descriptions of profession are given.

Chapter 7

The Singer and the Mask: Voices of Brazil in Antônio Nóbrega's *Madeira Que Cupim Não Rói*

Robin Warner and Regina Nascimento

For Brazilians the linked questions 'Who am I?', 'Who are we?' do not have easy answers. In general, in Latin America, there is a postcolonial tendency to seek a source of resistance to assimilation into the cultural sphere of the United States through being simultaneously linked to, and alienated from, Europe (Beardsell, 2000). Brazilian national identity is further complicated by the existence of historically well-established regional autonomies, as well as by the diversity of the ethno-cultural baggage carried by successive waves of intercontinental immigration (beginning with the transhipment of African labour in numbers that made Brazil the foremost recipient of slaves in the Western hemisphere and including, for much of the twentieth century, an influx of immigrants from Japan, the Middle East and Europe).

It has often been said, indeed, that it makes more sense to talk about 'Brazils' than Brazil. In modern times, moreover, the pattern of internal migration, from rural areas to zones of industrial growth, has uprooted and continues to uproot many millions of people from a relatively traditional rural environment and thrust them into an often precarious existence in or on the fringes of the megacities that now host three-quarters of the country's population (Chant, 1999: 244). Brazilians, then, have tended to experience a tension between centres and peripheries (within both national and global contexts) that has had problematic consequences for both individual and group self-definition. Moreover, in a country that is the eighth largest world economy and one of the world leaders in the introduction of new technology, late modern economic trends have had a strong impact on national life. The characteristic emphasis of neo-liberal policies on generating economic growth with little concern for more equitable distribution of wealth is very apparent, with high levels of unemployment and a quarter of the population living in poverty on incomes below $50 a month (Maxwell, 1999: 54). It is hardly surprising that the severe social problems associated with huge disparities in standards of living, and widespread economic deprivation, are a staple of concerned discussion in the serious media.

Brazil's popular music industry, especially in the last 40 years, has enjoyed considerable success abroad as well as domestically. Its capacity to reflect or give voice to widely shared social aspirations and concerns as well as to entertain is attested by the degree of control and censorship exercised by the military regime of the 1960s and 1970s, when many musicians and composers associated with the broad spectrum of styles and musicians generally known as MPB (Brazilian Popular Music) were subjected to censorship or even more stringent forms of official harassment. One of the core tendencies of MPB has been a search for musical innovation through the incorporation both of Brazilian regional folk music material and of styles and motifs drawn from a variety of non-domestic contemporary sources. The Tropicália movement initiated by Gilberto Gil and Caetano Veloso at the end of the 1960s, with its pastiche treatment of a 'broad array of old and new styles of national and international provenance such as rock, bossa nova, mambo, bolero and liturgical hymns' (Dunn, 2001: 93) and, more recently, the 'mangue beat' style of Chico Science and Nacão Zumbi, blending heavy metal and rap with 'maracatu' and other Bahian forms (Vianna, 1999: 105; Crook, 2001: 241) are instructive examples, in their different ways, of a highly effective combination of domestic influences with 'appropriations of the exogenous' (Perrone and Dunn, 2001: 2).

While much of the musical output of Antônio Nóbrega, the singer/performer with whom this chapter is concerned, might be considered as falling, in broad terms, within the genre of MPB,[1] his position is a little peripheral when compared with the more mainstream status of, say, the group Mestre Ambrósio (see J. Murphy, 2001) or the singer Alçeu Valença, who, like Nóbrega, draw inspiration from the traditional music of the rural north-east. While MPB often reconciles local, traditional elements with global musical styles, Nóbrega explicitly privileges the former, performing songs whose composition is inspired by folk traditions or which are closely based on folk originals, with a marked preference for traditional instruments, the deployment of traditional para-musical presentational skills and a conservative approach to technologies of sound reproduction.[2]

Nóbrega's approach is not simply a matter of exercising preference between musical styles or instruments. There is a well-established current of thought in Brazil, the origins of which can be traced at least back to the writings in the 1920s of the cultural anthropologist Gilberto Freyre and other influential intellectuals of his generation, that prizes elements of traditional regional folk culture both as embodiments of authentic national identity (Vianna, 1999: 58–62) and as important resources in a broad national educational project, a view particularly favoured by the Popular Culture Movement of the early 1960s (Schwarz, 1992: 133–5). Broadly in line with such perspectives, Nóbrega seems to regard the reaffirmation and renewal of folk art traditions and techniques as a process that operates both on the musical material itself and on the socio-cultural awareness of the audiences for whom it is performed. Sometimes obliquely, sometimes openly, he engages with a number of issues that have long provoked and continue to provoke debate in Brazil: race and class and culture, tradition and modernization, and their role in national self-definition. Our aim here is to consider what Nóbrega's approach to musical performance contributes to these debates and to the problematic question of national identity.

Nóbrega was born in 1952 in Recife in Brazil's north-east and received his musical training (violin and voice) there. It is worth bearing in mind that the north-east was the earliest region of Brazil to be intensively colonized by Portugal, and it enjoyed a certain economic pre-eminence, based on slave-labour, up to the beginning of the nineteenth century. As a consequence of extensive ethnic intermixing between Portuguese, Africans and Amerindians, the existence of subregions with very distinct geographic characteristics and the persistence up to relatively recent times of different types of traditional rural economies, the north-east possesses a particularly rich and varied heritage of traditional popular culture, and is widely regarded as 'a treasure chest of folk music gems' (Schreiner, 1993: 236). Nóbrega's interest, as a university student, in local folk music soon led him into the orbit of the Armorial Movement, a grouping of writers, musicians and artists under the mentorship of the poet and dramatist Ariano Suassuna, dedicated to the re-evaluation of north-eastern folk art. Especially since moving to São Paulo in 1983, Nóbrega has broadened his creative practice to include other popular entertainment forms such as dance, mime and circus arts, devising stage shows combining various traditional performance skills; this is exemplified in many of his performances including (with year of first performance) *Mateus Precepeiro* [Mateus the Nativity Player] 1985; *Figural* [Configurations] 1990; *Brincante* [Entertainer] 1992; *Segundas Estorias* [Further Tales] 1994; *Na Pancada do Ganzá* [To the Beat of the Ganzá] 1995; *Madeira Que Cupim Não Rói* [Wood that Termites Don't Gnaw] 1997; *Pernambuco Falando para o Mundo* [Radio Pernambuco Calling] 1998; *O Marco do Meio-Dia* [The Mark of Noon] 2000; and *Lunário Perpétuo* [Lunar Almanac] 2002. The shows themselves sometimes undergo further development and adaptation, often with the inclusion of items from other productions; an updated version of *Figural*, for instance, was performed in London in 2000.

History as Folk Performance in *Madeira Que Cupim Não Rói*

Each of Nóbrega's albums is made up of musical material originally composed and developed for a theatrical production. *Madeira Que Cupim Não Rói* (1997), the album with which we are concerned here, is no exception, since it is not simply a collection of songs, but retains much of the narrative and thematic coherence of the stage show from which it derives. It begins with 'Abrição de Portas' ['Opening of Doors'], a traditional summons to households to provide refreshments for the street performers of a *reisado* (a popular pageant based on the arrival of the Magi) and ends with a farewell to the audience, 'Vou-me embora' [I'm leaving], and many of the intervening items are concerned with motifs and figures of

Brazilian history salient in the popular imagination and filtered through the medium of folk art.

The album also reflects the highly stylized mode of performance of the stage show, including the evocation – the impersonation, with masks and costumes – of a range of characters. It is particularly worth noting, in this respect, that one of the folk performance traditions appropriated by Nóbrega is that of the *brincante*, an itinerant popular entertainer who combines the roles of jester, clown, acrobat and dancer with those of balladeer, singer and musician. Two earlier stage shows, *Brincante* (1992) and *Segundas Estórias* (1994) constituted a 'jester's epic', the story of a (fictional) traditional performer – Tonheta – whose life and art is narrated and mimetically portrayed, through a mixture of dance, stage dramatization, music, mime, circus skills and even ventriloquism, by a pair of travelling entertainers, Mestre Siduca and Rosalina (played by Nóbrega and his wife Rosane). This complex layering of the performance situation seems intended both as a projection of Nóbrega's own multi-faceted artistic personality and as a means of achieving greater expressive resonance by mapping personal experience on to more broadly recognizable cultural models. The description provided by Nóbrega in the programme notes for the stage version of *Madeira Que Cupim Não Rói* certainly hints strongly that the figure of Tonheta is a vehicle for just such an expressive synthesis of the private and the public, of inner feeling and outward stylization:

> Visto de fora … um misto de pícaro, bufão, palhaço, arlequim, vagabundo … Sentida por dentro é uma colcha de retalhos desses tipos populares que povoam as ruas e praças do meu país, que me tocam profundamente, e me deixam num estado de desordem interior, en que os contrários dor e alegria se confraternizam misteriosamente. (Nóbrega, 1997)

> [Looked at from the outside … a mixture of rogue, buffoon, clown, harlequin, tramp … Felt from within, he is the sort of patchwork quilt of traditional confection that abounds in the streets and squares of my country, which touches me deeply and leaves me in a state of inner confusion in which the opposites 'happiness' and 'sadness' mysteriously mingle.]

It is as an indication of overall artistic strategy, perhaps, that we should understand Nóbrega's insistence that, while the content of *Madeira* reflects an evolution of his work towards more specifically musical modes of expression, the figure of Tonheta continues to be an important presence.

Madeira is by no means unique in Nóbrega's output in its concern to bring musical and other performing traditions to wider attention. The preceding album, *Na Pancada do Ganzá* (1996), is largely inspired by anonymous folk songs of the north-east collected 70 years earlier by the poet and musicologist Mário de Andrade. *O Marco do Meio-Dia* (2001) similarly evokes historical individuals and communities that live on in folk memory, as well as musical elements associated with traditional festivals and rituals. *Madeira* itself offers a particularly rich sample of traditional forms. Besides anonymous folk songs, musical tributes to musicians of the past, and songs linked to traditional pieces of street-theatre (including a comic number traditionally performed by an acrobat wearing a monkey costume), the collection includes evocations of figures with a powerful hold on popular imagination, such as bandits and messianic preachers of the north-eastern backlands. Our analysis will concentrate on the title-song of the collection and on a triptych Nóbrega terms 'cantigas do Descobrimento' [songs of the Discovery], since they provide instructively clear examples of the strategies by which Nóbrega brings to the fore the question of Brazil's cultural identity, especially his view of the interweaving of Ibero-Mediterranean and Afro-Indigenous elements. The album appeared during the preparations for official celebrations of the quincentenary of the 'discovery' of Brazil, and these songs in particular seem designed to challenge some key assumptions underlying the official view.

The title 'Madeira Que Cupim Não Rói' translates literally as 'wood that termites don't gnaw', a description linked, in the song itself, to the term 'madeira de lei' [top-grade wood], in use since the eighteenth century, when official quality controls were put in place for the trade in hardwoods. The lyrics, those of a *marcha-de-bloco* [carnival procession number] composed by the legendary Pernambuco musician Capiba for the Recife Carnival in 1963, utilize the allusion to high-quality hardwood as a metaphor for artistic–expressive and general moral qualities of innate soundness and long-lasting resistance to adversity and corruption possessed by the *bloco*, drawn from a neighbourhood association in the Recife district of Rosarinho. The song's importance for Nóbrega, and particularly that of the phrase that supplies the title of the album, seems to lie in its articulation of pride in the enduring worth of the skills and virtues of ordinary people and its scornful disregard for official, and possibly suspect, values and standards. With a brash show of confidence (competitive rivalry with other *blocos* is a not uncommon theme of the lyrics of carnival parade songs),[3] the people of the locality announce that they have come to claim the championship, 'queiram ou não queiram os juízes' – that is, whether the official judges award them the title or not. The closing lines of the refrain clearly identify the communicative function of the song: to perform it is to demonstrate the performers' maintenance of traditional artistic standards of excellence and protest against the injustice of denying them the recognition they deserve:

E se aqui estamos, cantando essa canção,/viemos defender a nossa tradição,/e dizer bem alto que a injustiça dói;/nós somos madeira de lei que cupim não rói.

[And if we are here, singing this song,/we have come to stand up for our tradition/and cry out loud that injustice hurts;/we are top-grade wood that termites don't gnaw.]

These lyrics vigorously assert group identity centred on the traditional skills of ordinary people. They also provide a very clear illustration of patterns and strategies – found, in one guise or another, in many songs of the collection

– that serve to foreground both the importance of continuity with the past for a community's sense of cultural identity and the way individual experience of selfhood is inextricably bound up with what Pierre Bourdieu has described as 'that being-perceived which exists fundamentally by recognition through other people' (1992: 224). In general, expression through singing, especially in groups on ritualized occasions, will tend to highlight and strengthen the relationship between individual and collective activity. The somatic origin of the individual voice to which the 'sonorous, bodily element of the vocal utterance' calls attention (Dunn and Jones, 1994: 2)[4] is subsumed in a collaborative production of sound and meaning. In this particular song, such effects are themselves highlighted by the way the discursive subject of the lyrics (which are first delivered by an individual singer, then repeated by a number of voices) switches from third-person self-reference (as in 'Madeira ... is coming to town') to assertions made by a communal 'we'. Indeed, the explicit appearance in the final line of the pronoun *nós* [we], a subject previously indicated only by verb inflections, carries a strongly contrastive emphasis – 'we, on the other hand', as it were – stressing the exclusion of outsiders and the cohesion of the group.[5]

Nóbrega's treatment of this earlier musical material is clearly designed to suggest he has not altered it to suit contemporary tastes, but rather made it possible for it to be heard here and now on its own terms. The opening section of the track deliberately gives the impression of a scratchy 'historic' recording, with characteristically muffled vocal and instrumental sound, before moving on to an acoustically clean version free of analogue 'grain'. The effect is to emphasize that this is a creative actualization – a re-presenting, as it were – of a performance that took place many decades ago, with an added element of conscious tribute to a 'past master' in a musical genre linked to cultural traditions that are still very much alive. The song thus constitutes a particularly apt example of the way the creative artistry of voice (and instrument) connects generations (Holloway, 1994: 197).

Most of the songs in this collection, in fact, raise questions of identity through exploiting inherent ambivalences and paradoxes of the performance situation. Not only are there frequent shifts from one persona – one mask, one voice, one perspective – to another; there is also full exploitation of the switches in focus between individual performer and collaborative realization made possible by the singer/vocal backing and voice/instrument contrastive format of this type of musical performance. This strategy is evident in the triptych on the 'discovery' of Brazil: 'Chegança' ['Landfall'], 'Quinto Império' ['Fifth Empire'] and 'Olodumaré' (the name of the principal Yoruba deity). While the three songs (the lyrics of which were written in collaboration with the Recife poet Wilson Freire) are concerned respectively with the Amerindian, Portuguese and African contributions to the historical forming of a people and a culture, it is worth noting that there is no neat separation of ethnic or racial contexts and motifs. 'Chegança' makes it clear that it was the Amerindians who originally discovered and occupied 'a new world beyond the horizon' while the details of their lifestyle that are mentioned are taken from (and thus incorporate the perspective of) Portuguese eye-witness accounts of the first contacts. The song's title, moreover, while based on the verb *chegar* (to arrive), actually denotes a traditional festival entertainment. One version commonly performed in Brazil's north-east is an adaptation of the traditional Iberian enactments of battles between 'Christians and Moors', ending in the defeat of the latter and their conversion to Christianity – an evangelizing theme that marked, of course, the early contacts between the Portuguese and Amerindians. A similar sort of conflation is suggested by the characterization of the Portuguese sailors in 'Quinto Império' as a mixture of North-African and Lusitanian stock, and the nostalgia for what has been left behind that underlies the outlook of the mariners is explicitly echoed by the enslaved African of 'Olodumaré'. Again, while the title 'Quinto Império' alludes, in the first instance, to a form of millennialism current in the epoch of Iberian maritime expansion, the term *quinto* (fifth) was also applied to the ships carrying convicted criminals from Portugal to forced labour in Brazil, hinting at an analogy with the experience of slavery recounted in 'Olodumaré'.

On the other hand, the three songs are clearly differentiated in musical style as well as in what could be termed the psychological profile of the personae that are presented. For instance, in 'Chegança', in which Amerindian musical culture is suggested by the prominence of 'flutes' and 'whistles' (instruments specifically identified in early Portuguese descriptions of Amerindian music), the refrain consists entirely of repeated statements of 'sou' [I am], followed by a series of names of indigenous peoples – Pataxó, Xavante, Cariri, Ianomami, Guarani and so on. In the verses, the Indian singer describes a hospitable natural environment of fertile natural resources and harmonious human coexistence, but the ominous arrival of goal-driven Europeans signals the end of an Edenic existence and the birth of a nation that was to evolve through a long process of often-violent ethnic and social conflict.

> E assustado/dei um pulo na rede, /pressenti a fome, a sede,/eu pensei 'vão me acabar'./ Me levantei/de borduna na mão. /Ai, senti no coração/o Brasil vai começar.

> [And startled/I leapt out of my hammock,/I foresaw hunger and thirst,/I thought, 'they'll be the end of me'./I arose/with a club in my hand./Alas, I sensed in my heart/ Brazil is about to begin.]

The attribution to past witnesses of a knowledge that could only be informed by current insights into Brazil's history features in all three songs. 'Quinto Império' evokes the navigational skills, tenacity and driven mentality of the Portuguese maritime explorers, and celebrates their achievement in pushing back the frontiers of the unknown – 'I tore open the legends of the Fearful Ocean, for the King, the Glorious One, there is no longer any darkness on the sea' the singer claims. The singer's conviction that it is his destiny to leave his homeland behind and sail to the ends of the earth is further suggested through the plaintive high-pitched accompaniment and sonorous melodic line reminiscent of a Portuguese fado in the refrain 'Ai mundo velho/novo mundo hei- achar!' [Alas, old world/a new world I shall find]. We should remember here that fado, traditionally considered, in Portugal, as an expression of the sense of separation and homesickness of a maritime nation, literally means 'fate'. The lyrics of 'Chegança' allude more than once to a mystique of historical destiny often attached to the Portuguese voyages of maritime discovery, and the treatment of the Fifth Empire theme itself (belief in the predestined protagonism of Portugal and her maritime territories in the fulfilment of Old Testament prophecies of the Second Coming) is reminiscent of the poem of the same title in *Mensagem*, the most widely read work of the Portuguese post-symbolist poet Fernando Pessoa (1950: 76–7). The emphasis in the Pessoa piece is on a compelling vision that drives people to abandon their homes and settled lives for a spiritual quest. Two stanzas scorning those who bide complacently at home, never experiencing the force of the dream whose wings could lift them out of their humdrum existence, are followed by a ringing exhortation: 'Ser descontente é ser homem!/Que as forças cegas se domem/pela visão que a alma tem! [To be discontented is to be human!/May the blind forces be tamed/by the vision that the soul holds!], and the poet confidently affirms that 'a terra será teatro do dia claro que … noite começou' [the world that began as night will be a theatre of clear day], a motif that, as we have seen, is echoed by Nóbrega's singer.

Although the lyrics sung in the first person are clearly meant to evoke a specifically European–Portuguese perspective, to the extent of using the archaic form (and an archaic spelling in the printed version) for 'El-Rey' [the King] in referring to 'El-Rey, o Glorioso' [the glorious king or the King of Glory], matters are not so straightforward where the refrain sung in chorus is concerned. It is addressed to Our Lady in Afro-Brazilian guise, 'Iaiá', thus suggesting the presence (historically perfectly feasible) of Portuguese-Africans among the crews of the caravels in 1500. In any case, even the fado-like elements in the song can be interpreted as traditionally Brazilian, since it is probable that the genre (dating from the early nineteenth century) was, at the very least, heavily influenced by musical forms imported from Brazil (Vernon, 1998: 6–7). The choral refrain, moreover, matches a steady rhythm to natural word-stress in a way that suggests an aid to coordination of rowing. In conjunction with the allusions in the lyrics to various Portuguese voyages of discovery, the overall effect is to emphasize that what is being presented is a consolidation of many experiences rather than a single one:

Iaiá, me dá teu remo,/teu remo pra eu remar,/meu remo caiu, quebrou-se,/Iaiá, lá no alto mar.

[Lady, give me your oar,/your oar so I can row,/my oar fell and was broken,/Lady, out on the high seas.]

The enslaved African of 'Olodumaré', on the other hand, sees the future as unknown and uncertain, just as his nostalgia goes hand in hand with the bitter resentment felt by those who suffer enforced exodus as opposed to the soulful longings, heard in 'Quinto Império', of those whose determination to go beyond the known takes them far from home. There is a marked contrast in this song between the gentle mood of the nostalgic refrain and the angry energy of the verses that speak of capture, transhipment in inhuman conditions and hard labour in the plantations and mines of the new country. There is a note of pride, however, as it is precisely through his people's strength, stamina and capacity to resist hardship that a new country has been built:

> E mesmo escravo,/nas caldeiras das usinas,/nas senzalas e nas minas,/nova raça fiz brotar./Hoje, essa terra/tem meu cheiro, minha cor,/o meu sangue, meu tambor,/minha saga pra lembrar.

> [And even as a slave,/among the boilers of the sugar mills,/in plantation blockhouses and mines,/I made a new race spring forth./Today that land/has my smell, my colour,/my blood, my drum,/my saga to remember.]

Although the scope of our commentary has necessarily been limited it has probably sufficed to give some idea of the way *Madeira* consistently touches on a set of interlinked motifs: the mix of races, each with important historical contributions to both national consciousness and the country's cultural heritage, the social value of traditional culture, and the important role of musical elements in the traditional festivals and performance genres in which a communal sense of identity finds expression. It seems clear that Nóbrega's stage performances and albums are not merely intended as showcases for unjustly neglected musical material, but also designed to challenge condescending attitudes to traditional popular culture in general.

Tradition, Renovation and Identity in a Globalized World

At this point it might be useful to introduce a broader theoretical background against which to consider song performance as social communication and some of the effects that processes of modernization and globalization can have on cultural traditions and notions of social and cultural identity. Intellectual opinion in Brazil, as in other countries of Latin America, is marked by contradictory tendencies with regard to cultural influences from abroad. Positive attitudes to the incorporation of global innovation have often alternated with a pessimistic suspicion that the maintenance of distinctive local cultural identity may be incompatible with projects of modernization associated with Europe and the United States. The sense of a threat to cultural difference posed by the spread of Western mass culture has in many ways been sharpened by the economic and political trends of the last decade and 'the impact of thousands of banal cultural artefacts coming from the Anglo-Saxon world' (Larrain, 1999: 196). On the other hand, Brazil's numerous and varied traditional festivals and rites and the wide cross-class participation in them are often regarded as healthy manifestations of popular democracy. Stressing the inherently egalitarian and anti-authoritarian qualities of such celebrations – and confirming Bakhtin's view of the carnival spirit as a suspension of hierarchical rank and privileges and the dismantling of barriers of caste, property and profession (1994 [1965]) – progressive Brazilian opinion tends to value them as 'manifestations of the diversity of social identities … instances of cultural synthesis in which we are all actors … sites of resistance to the crisis of identity stemming from a globalized world' (Tolaba, 2000).[6]

Nóbrega's expressed aim of fostering collective cultural self-awareness as a means of enhancing social cohesion continues the approach of many Brazilian artists and writers in recent times who, in the words of the cultural sociologist Alfredo Bosi (1994: 344), have made the effort to cross the ideological and psychological barriers that separate them from both the day-to-day and the imaginative life of the people. Indeed, Nóbrega's approach to performance art seems to share Bosi's view of the aesthetics of social communication in that he explores the possibility of using stage presence, voice, gesture and strategies of audience involvement to produce a form of art capable of transcending social divisions. Nóbrega is also keenly aware of the particular problems posed by the current world economic order. In an interview given in London in August 2000 he insists that traditional popular culture, when effectively presented, is a useful riposte to cultural elitism and an important resource, for a country such as Brazil, in the struggle to resist global trends towards homogenization and maintain the distinctive integrity-in-diversity of its culture:

> Somos um país com uma riqueza cultural enorme, temos um país múltiplo com uma unidade de língua … Mas o Brasil é ainda um país desconhecido por nós mesmos; um país cuja alma começa a despertar mas que tem que lutar contra a pressão que sofremos no sentido de nos dispersarnos, que é muito grande, principalmente pelo poder econômico, político da grande indústria cultural que toma conta do mundo, capitaneada pelas Estados Unidos. Isso faz com que realmente a gente corra o risco de perder o que a gente guarda de mais importante. (Lou, 2000: 25)

> [We are a country with an enormous wealth of culture; we are a pluralistic country with a single language … But Brazil is still a country we ourselves are unfamiliar with; a country whose soul is starting to awaken, but which has to fight against the pressure on us to move apart from each other, which is very strong, mainly because of the economic and political power of the great cultural industry that is controlling the world, led by the United States. And the result is we run the risk of losing the most important things we have.]

The globalization of culture, as described in a pessimistic essay on 'McDonaldization' (Münch, 1999), refers to the way cultural products are less and less attached to a specific place of production, presentation and appropriation. This process has paradoxically resulted in an increase in the number and diversity of the cultural products available to the individual consumer, while favouring the predominance of entertainment culture over other forms (such as regional or folk culture) and encouraging a high level of standardization. The overall result is that, as Münch puts it:

> Behind the many and diverse cultural events on the global market hide a small number of similar recipes for success ... If culture is nothing more than a gigantic selection of wares then the paths to an understanding with others are blocked [and] we lose our common self-determination in the sense of deciding together on how to live. (Münch, 1999: 138, 144 and 145).

The point about the blocking of communicatively-reached consensus is an important one here, since Nóbrega, as we have seen, is particularly concerned with performance as communication, and often foregrounds his function as a re-animator of meanings and experiences emanating from elsewhere and other times.

Before commenting in more detail on this strategy, it would be as well to outline some basic features of the type of performance situation he creates. One useful starting-point is the insight of Lucy Green that musical performances comprise an element of display, defined as 'something akin to wearing a mask'. This presentational strategy is, at the same time, a relationship constructed interactively by displayer and onlooker, and is closely related to what Green (1997: 5–7, 21–31) terms the delineation of musical performance – that is, its socially and culturally contextualized meanings. In addition to the strategic configuration of performance-as-mask, however, we should also keep in mind the practical function of the various masks, headgear, costumes and ventriloquist's dummies that Nóbrega makes use of on stage (listeners to the albums have to make do with the drawings and photographs that appear next to the printed lyrics of each song). Not only do such stage artefacts enable the same performer to appear in several different roles, but they also serve to block the audience's attention to facial expression and divert it to gesture, mime, dance-movement and voice-quality. The type of mask used by Nóbrega tends to be of the traditional sort that, in Peter Brook's view, has a particularly powerful effect in performance precisely because to wear it is, for the actor, 'to be liberated from one's own subjectivity' (Brook, 1987: 219). Nóbrega's traditional masks and costumes (whether associated with African or Amerindian rituals or whether in the form of the heavily stylized face paint and apparel of a traditional European clown) and the emphasis they place on bodily modes of expression enable him to create the impression of being not so much an individual artist as the current animator of ritualized patterns of performance inherited from a long line of similar folk performers.

Following the interactional approach pioneered by Erving Goffman, we take the view that the division between the stage performer and her 'scripted' role as persona or staged character corresponds to a difference between the theatregoer (who pays for the ticket and generally 'has untheatrical activity to sustain') and the onlooker 'who collaborates in the unreality onstage' (Goffman, 1986: 129). Where the capacity of performance to influence socio-cultural attitudes is concerned, the distinction between the two spectator roles is as important as that between the two performing roles. The theatrical frame of imaginative collaboration between persona and onlooker can also function as a setting for discourse oriented to reaching consensus between two members of society at large. In the case of Nóbrega's performances, we could say that the professional performer and entertainment-arts teacher/researcher takes the opportunity to engage rhetorically with the beliefs and attitudes of the theatregoer (or CD purchaser).

One broad intellectual framework for analysing Nóbrega's songs and performances as social communication is provided by Jürgen Habermas's theory of communicative action, an analysis of the potential for social cohesion embodied in language use in a shared culture (Habermas, 1984, 1989, 1996, 1998). The central notion of action oriented to reaching understanding is connected to questions of identity, since, 'in coming to an understanding about something in the world, actors are at the same time taking part in interactions through which they develop, confirm and renew their membership in social groups and their own identities' (1989: 139). Two areas in particular to which Habermas devotes attention are of direct relevance to features of Nóbrega's performances with which we are concerned.

1   While, for Habermas, reaching agreement on coordinating action principally depends on the possibility of unconstrained and rationally based argumentation realized through utterances that carry implicit claims to validity as factual truth or normative rightness, the types of communication that express inner experiences are not treated as exempt from interlocutors' prerogative of testing (and, potentially, of rejecting) their validity. Habermas insists that even aesthetically stylized forms of subjective expression carry a claim of sincerity that is often evaluated by recourse to notions of 'artistic truth, aesthetic harmony, exemplary validity, innovative power and authenticity' (1998: 396). These contested terms, moreover, are commonly used as criteria for evaluating 'artistic expression'. It is worth noting that when Habermas comes to discuss, among current paradigms of social action, the model of dramaturgical action originally developed by Erving Goffman, he stresses the problematic nature of sincerity in stylized self-presentations, in which 'false' performers and 'honest' performers alike are completely governed by the need for expressive consistency (Goffman, 1971: 72).

2   The importance accorded by Habermas to cultural traditions is relevant here, both as elements of the background of uncontroversial knowledge against which new agreements are negotiated and as central examples of the general problem of interpreting texts and forms inherited from the past – the challenge, that is, to 'set in motion once again the disturbed communication between the

author, his contemporaries and us' (1984: 133). Nóbrega is consciously engaged in recontextualizing musical and lyrical traditions of the past and his oeuvre lends itself to a Habermasian analysis for this reason.[7] The interpreter's aim should not be to provide access to a preserved object as if it were a museum piece, but to engage with the original context of communication as a virtual participant in a dialogic correspondence (Habermas, 1984: 136). Where the broader social meanings of Nóbrega's reproductions are concerned, it is also worth noting that, for Habermas, the task of hermeneutics is not merely one of establishing the current relevance of traditions: their transmission must also be guided by a process of critical monitoring (1996: 98).

Our comments on the theory of communicative action are by no means intended as a reductionist view of Nóbrega's artistic and social project, and still less is it implied that his objectives are routinely achievable. Anthony Giddens, a social theorist who, like Habermas, assigns a central importance to language-use as the medium of social practice, sees the increased reflexivity and the diminution of trust and ontological security typical of late modernity as tending to undermine the project of the self and confuse the parameters of group identity (Giddens, 1991). The reworking of traditional cultural forms mentioned by Nóbrega, together with the dismantling of previously strong links between place and identity, exemplifies the disembedding and destabilizing tendencies of postmodern society. While old-style 'exclusive' nationalism, predicated on control of delimited territory and cultural common denominators, may no longer be a viable focus of collective identity, a firm sense of national identity can, nevertheless, be a benign influence if it is based on the idea of nation as ethical community, owing special rather than exclusive obligations to its members and tolerant of multiple affiliation and cultural pluralism (Giddens, 1998: 130). Such a model may be something of an ideal, but it is not impossible to realize, at least in Nóbrega's belief, and a thorough re-assimilation of traditional popular culture can certainly contribute to this end.

Our theoretical overview, it is hoped, helps to clarify the concept – or project – of a socially cohesive cultural identity that informs Antônio Nóbrega's re-animations. His skilful manipulation of what Goffman terms 'footing' (1981: 124–49), the communicative relations between performer and audience, seems designed to create a conscious awareness of the conventions and mechanisms of performance. The impression of a stable underlying 'artistic personality' (Green, 1997: 36, 45) is deliberately weakened by the ambivalent status of the lyrical subject as between stereotype and individual, as well as by switches of mask and voice and the overt exploitation of a range of stylized effects of vocal characterization to convey switches of mood or viewpoint within a song. Such effects, moreover, are presented as belonging to the performance repertoire of the *brincante* figure whose role Nóbrega is playing, sometimes including a display of the folk entertainer's traditional para-musical vocalizations, such as trills, yodels, exaggerated laughter and cries of encouragement to other performers. The effect is to draw attention not to the personality of the individual artist, but to the overall coherence of what is performed, its artistic 'authenticity' to use Habermas's term, and the accumulated variety of human experience and expertise that has gone into the performance. In Nóbrega's songs the identity of the performing persona vacillates between the subjective voice of an individual 'I' and the collective, generalized expression of a 'we' constituted in social space, in historical experience and in performance traditions and conventions. The overall effect is to raise questions in the audience's mind as to a range of assumptions to do with personal and group identity and open them up for possible redefinition.

Where Nóbrega's revival of songs and styles inherited from the past is concerned, a critical perspective, as outlined in Habermas's hermeneutics, enables us to recognize something more than mere reduplication in technologically enhanced form. The hermeneutic, in fact, is a double one in that, as interpreter, Nóbrega consciously re-creates performances that were themselves recontextualizations of earlier traditions and experiences. A number of the songs of *Madeira* are based on traditional Brazilian adaptations of old world originals. The 'public domain' (that is, traditional and anonymous) Brazilian lyrics of 'Abrição de Portas', for example, are actually derived from a medieval Peninsular text, while those of the similarly anonymous 'Quando as Glórias que Gozei' [When the Bliss that Once Was Mine] are first delivered in a declamatory style and at a relatively slow tempo, then repeated to a relatively upbeat dance tempo with a fuller instrumental accompaniment. In thematizing in such ways the process of reproduction of cultural heritage, Nóbrega is effectively inviting reflection on the elements of the past that represent a 'desired continuity' (Williams, 1981: 187). The critical appropriation of traditions can thus play its part in broadening agreement on what could constitute 'a non-alienated, solidary social life' (Habermas 1996: 98).

Conclusions

It seems preferable to raise some further broad issues here rather than attempt to reach a neat closure. Following a line of questioning, adopted by Floya Anthias (1999) as to the analytical scope of ethnic approaches to difference and identity, it is perhaps worth asking whether Nóbrega's celebration of difference in coexisting cultural traditions and deployment of a notion of ethnicity based, at least in part, on point of 'origin' runs the risk of overlooking problematic political issues such as those of gender and class. Firstly, it should be noted that what Nóbrega emphasizes is not the coexistence of different cultures in itself, but their process of integration, and especially the potential collective self-awareness this fusion can generate. *Madeira* might thus be said to challenge static notions of ethnicity and culture by celebrating not just the formation, but also the ongoing contact and merging of ethnic group identities. It is true, on the other hand, that the role of women in the forging of the nation is largely passed over. Women's voices are heard in the chorus sections of Nóbrega's songs, but they tend to be members of a collectivity, with no specific gender orientation. The three historical experiences presented in the Triptych of the Discoveries are voiced by male Brazilians (in 'Chegança' even the choral refrain is sung entirely by male voices), and the presentation of women as addressees, or in narrations and descriptions, stays, for the most part, within the conventions of the type of song concerned. We should bear in mind, however, that the social or political protagonism of women is rarely a feature of the folk ethos and musical material of the traditional rural societies that Nóbrega aims to re-animate. A similar consideration of absence from the folk canon possibly applies to the apparent failure to acknowledge contributions to national culture made by descendants of twentieth-century immigrants from Europe, the Middle East and Japan.[8] However, the links between class and ethnicity in Brazil may be involved here.

The groups in question, relatively recently established, constitute economically advantaged sectors of Brazilian society in comparison with the majority of non-white Brazilians.[9] There is a consistently implied class perspective in *Madeira* in that the songs present Brazilian identity as a synthesis of the traditions and life-experiences of ordinary people, and what is positive in present-day Brazil as something achieved through the collective endeavours – and sacrifices – of the exploited and disadvantaged, rather than the privileged and the powerful. A persistent influence of the Armorial Movement should perhaps not be discounted here (and, indeed, Capiba, the composer of the title song of *Madeira*, was an active septuagenarian member of the group). The movement's activities in the 1970s were to some extent a resumption (with a necessarily more aesthetic slant) of the more overtly class-conscious projects of the Department of Cultural Extension of the University of Pernambuco (of which the radical educationalist Paulo Freire was the first director) which had been subject to censorship and finally closed after the military coup of 1964.[10] In the recent opinion of another ex-Armorialist musician, Antônio José Madureira (whose Balé Popular de Recife [Recife Popular Ballet] deploys traditional performance skills in a similar way to Nóbrega's Teatro Brincante), one important achievement of the Armorial Movement was to 'transfer an authentic culture from the poor rural classes to the urban middle-classes', thus preparing the ground for the marked growth in prestige of north-eastern folk music over the last decade (Calvacanti, 2000).

While racially or politically motivated violence has been by no means absent, it is worth making the point that the consolidation of democracy in Brazil in the last decade or so of the twentieth century (and even including transition to a Workers' Party presidency at the start of the twenty-first) has not been marked by racist tensions and ethnic conflicts on the scale that followed the end of repressive political systems in parts of Europe. For that matter, the incidence of racially instigated violence in Brazil compares well with periods of transition to less repressive systems in parts of the American continent where the prevailing notion of national identity similarly rests on assumptions as to successful assimilation of immigrants and racial mixing. The historical process of racial integration in

Brazil has been a long and sometimes troubled one, but, with the glaring exception of the repressive violence practised on native Amazonians and their culture, it is one that, to superficial appearances, has been carried through. Nevertheless, and despite the complex intertwining and blurred definitions of class, colour and race in modern Brazil that have allowed democratic and authoritarian regimes alike to defend a mythology of harmonious racial integration, research over the last decade has tended to point unambiguously to 'the great discrepancy between the idealization and the reality, in terms of discrimination and racial prejudice, for the black population in Brazilian society' (Hasenbalg and do Valle Silva, 1999: 154). Discrimination and inequality in Brazil affect not only statistically verifiable areas such as jobs, health and education but, equally, less quantifiable zones of the everyday lives of many non-whites, such as socialization, self-esteem and self-identity (Hanchard, 1999: 13–14). Awareness of race/class issues as a national problem started to grow, in any case, from the mid-1970s, with the appearance of black political organizations, such as the Unified Black Movement, that strongly reject notions of mixed-race 'harmony', while promoting awareness of distinct Afro-Brazilian identity, and mounting campaigns both against discrimination in general and on flagrant specific issues such as the murder of street-children. (Winant, 1999: 104, 109). The culturo-musical counterparts of these movements include the emergence of culturally-oriented forms of black consciousness, for example the establishment of groups such as Olodum, engaged both in performance and social activism (Armstrong, 2001: 180), and more commodified Afro fashions (Dunn, 2001: 178–9). These movements have certainly served to counteract the myth of Brazil's special immunity to the social problems afflicting other former slave-owning nations. Nevertheless, a survey conducted by Hasenbalg and do Valle Silva suggests that more widespread awareness does not currently translate into support for confrontational action by the discriminated group against the discriminating group, but rather into support for 'a wide-ranging movement with an interracial and interethnic character' (1999: 174). This is not altogether surprising, since the political stability and relative prosperity of the last decade has seen large numbers of people moving up from the bottom ranks of society into the middle class (Maxwell, 1999: 54). The expansion of educational opportunities, the resurgence of political parties and the emergence of grassroots movements and municipal activism in general have all combined to create a deeper political engagement on the part of Brazilians at large, and with it the possibility of establishing a broad consensus in favour of redistributive modernization.

Against this background, the view that encouraging wider awareness of a shared traditional folk culture can play a part in promoting Habermas's notion of 'solidary social relations' is not an unduly idealized one. While Nóbrega's approach is not markedly radical, in campaigning for an increased awareness and appreciation of a cultural heritage that is valuable precisely because it has been created by a symbiosis of diverse ethnic traditions in ordinary communities, he is aligning himself with many other politically-conscious Brazilians who are insisting that constructing a fair, tolerant and fully participatory society and sustaining a distinctive national identity and culture are goals that must not be incompatible with continued modernization and economic progress.

Notes

1 The scope of broad designations such as MPB is, of necessity, somewhat indeterminate. The term is currently used to denote popular music in general, but can also serve to differentiate one overall style from another. For example, where the music industry's annual awards are concerned, MPB is often treated as one of the subcategories of popular music in Brazil (others include pop-rock, regional and samba).

2 Unlike some Armorialists, especially Suassuna himself, Nóbrega docs not overtly criticize the mixing of traditional styles with global innovations. Indeed, the title-song of the album we consider here is dedicated to the memory of Chico Science.

3 The first words of the song deliberately differentiate members of Madeira from a rival local *bloco*, Inocentes do Rosarinho. The mock-intimidating display involved in ritual boasting between contestants is not necessarily as rare as is suggested by Green (1997: 21–6) in her remarks on display as an element of musical performance. It is often found in advertisements, for instance, as noted by Cook (1992).

4 Although discussing ritualized grieving rather than celebratory display (as is the case with carnival processionals) Elizabeth Tolbert similarly notes that 'the quality of voice itself is crucial to the negotiation between the personal and the collective' (1994: 192).

5 The pronoun *nós* is further marked in that its inclusion is at the expense of the regularity of the lyric's scansion. We should also bear in mind that reference to self-plus-addressee(s) is often realized in colloquial Brazilian Portuguese by *a gente* ['people', 'folk']; the choice of the first-person plural pronoun *nós* can thus serve in itself to direct attention to matters of an exclusive group identity.

6 The author of these formulations, the artistic coordinator of a São Paulo theatre, is commenting here on the millennium celebrations of the Festa Juninha, a traditional St John's Eve festive event.

7 Nóbrega's project can be considered in the light of the theoretical hermeneutics of G.H. Gadamer, on whose theories Habermas draws explicitly here.

8 However, the song 'Mestiçagem' ['Racial Mixing'] of *O Marco do Meio-Dia* envisages the sexual union of Japanese, Syrio-Lebanese and Germans with partners of more traditional racial mix, as part of the process of creating a society 'more and more mixed, more and more authentic, more and more Brazilian'.

9 There is a contrast here with the USA, where relatively recent immigrants, such as Latinos of various provenances, tend to be economically disadvantaged groups, often competing for Welfare with urban Afro-Americans. See Hanchard (1999: 12) and Winant (1999: 107–8).

10 See Sampaio (1998), commenting on the re-establishment of the Department of Cultural Extension.

Discography

Nóbrega, Antônio, *Na Pancada do Ganzá* (Brincante, BR0001, 1996).
Nóbrega, Antônio, *Madeira Que Cupim Não Rói* (Brincante/Eldorado, BR0002, 1997).
Nóbrega, Antônio, *Pernambuco Falando para o Mundo* (Brincante, BR0003, 1998).
Nóbrega, Antônio, *O Marco do Meio-Dia* (Brincante/Eldorado, BR 0004, 2001).
Nóbrega, Antônio, *Lunário Perpétuo* (Brincante BR0005, 2002).

Chapter 8

Popular Music, Tradition and Serbian Nationalism[1]

Robert Hudson

Ne slušaj narodnjake
Umri prirodnom smrcu!
[Don't listen to folk music
Die a natural death!]
Graffiti in Belgrade – Summer 1998

As an ideological resource, culture has served as a source for, or even an accelerant of, conflict. Indeed, it is a truism that culture is never far removed from politics, but in Serbia the relationship between the two is particularly intense. On the relationship between politics and folklore, the Serbian ethnologist Ivan Čolović commented that Serbian politics is saturated with folklore and that, from the late 1980s, every political leader, every political programme and every political battle in Serbia has made reference to folkloric texts that resort to traditional clichés (Čolović, 1994: 37). The main vehicle for carrying the imagery, values and antagonisms of these mythical tales has been the *pesma*, which may be translated as either 'poem' or 'song' since the meanings, in Serbian, are interchangeable. Indeed, the concept of song as embodying tradition is embedded in Serbian cultural identity, and this has served as a powerful cultural resource for Serbian nationalism since the nineteenth century. In the 1990s the stimulation of nationalism by popular and traditional Serbian songs involved a process of ethnification – a cult of the folkloric – in which popular music contributed to the estrangement, alienation and distancing of the Other. This is a process with roots long buried in the past, but one that continues to flourish at the dawn of the twenty-first century.

Songs, Church and People

Anthony Smith argues that, 'a national identity is fundamentally multi-dimensional: it can never be reduced to a single means' (1991: 14). In the Serbian case, one of the key vehicles in the creation of Serbian national identity and the project of a Greater Serbia is the interdependence of *pesme, crkva i narod* [songs, church and people]. This is a relationship founded upon a myth of community and common culture as expressed in those poems and songs that articulate the historical memories, legends, symbols and traditions of the people, which are framed by the Orthodox faith. These concepts and themes are often expressed in the same elevated imagery, usually highly symbolic, that is found in early tribal songs,[2] epic folk poetry and varieties of popular music. In the Serbian case, there are two sources in particular: the traditional liturgical literature of the clergy, and the peasant traditions of folk singing, together with the oral recitation of narratives in verse by illiterate and sometimes blind singers [*guslari*] (Holton and Mihailovich, 1998: xxviii).[3] Whereas the former tradition was eventually secularized for a historically self-conscious bourgeoisie, it was the *guslari* who were to become the composers and keepers of the people's history. These two roots became intertwined in complex ways.

The Serbian traditional music canon is made up of liturgical settings, national epics and peasant folk songs accompanied by the *gusle*, a one-stringed bowed instrument. There are two seemingly contradictory themes in the Serbian self-representation of historical identity. On the one hand, Serbia understands itself as alone, hated and misunderstood by non-Serbs; the Serbs are a victimized people, defeated in battle, often forced into exile and abandoned by God. On the other hand, the Serbs are depicted as a valiant, warrior folk who often fight alone (as in the 'brave little Serbia' imagery of the First World War), and who, above all, in this context, are God's 'chosen people'.

Often, elements of these two interpretations are interwoven. Accordingly, Serbs might make reference to the myth surrounding the battle of Kosovo or to the frequent migrations from Ottoman oppression, most noticeably those of 1690–91, 1705 and 1737, while simultaneously describing themselves as God's chosen, heavenly, people. The battle of Kosovo, fought on 28 June 1389, is an event which, through popular tradition, legend and mythology, has become the touchstone of Serb national identity. This epic battle has been described as 'the foundation of a people's historical consciousness and awareness of its ethnic identity' (Judah, 1997: 36), and the common myths and historical memories of the Serbian people have centred on the Kosovo legend (Smith, 1991: 14). In particular, the music, ballads and folk songs about the battle of Kosovo were constructed in the nineteenth century by 'national awakeners', such as the philologist Vuk Karadžić or the prince-bishop and poet Petar Petrović Njegoš. Later, these works would serve the needs of a common public culture (Hudson, 2000b: 168).

In addition, biblical themes abound in the Serbian literary canon that feeds traditional Serbian music. The evening meal before the battle of Kosovo is depicted as the Serbian 'Last Supper', overshadowed by betrayal and internecine strife, while the migrations of 1690–91 and 1705, which led to the settlement of Serbs in Vojvodina and the Slavonijas, are treated almost like the Babylonian captivity, describing a people in bondage and slavery, forced out of necessity to fight or work for alien powers. This theme has been explored in the literature of Miloš Crnjanski, with his 1929 work *Seobe* [Migrations] or more recently in Stefan Petrović's 1994 film of the same name, and the imagery of 'leading people out of captivity' recurs in relation to the retreat of the Serbian army, under the command of Vojvoda [Marshal] Mišić, from the Bulgarian and Austro-Hungarian forces in 1915.

From a contemporary perspective, the nature of the imbrication of songs, church and people is well illustrated by a video clip of a girls' choir singing the old First World War song 'Tamo daleko' ['Over There, Far Away'] in one of the Olympic sports halls in Pale, the former capital of Republika Srpska, in 1992.[4] The audience listens to the choir of little girls, conducted by an Orthodox priest, before the president, Radovan Karadžić, addresses the Serbian people who are gathered there to celebrate their identity and the first year of the existence of the Republika Srpska as an independent state. Although I will return to this song again, at this stage it is worth noting that these celebrations in the sports hall in Pale enable us to reflect upon Anthony Smith's musings on the nature of a culture community whose members were united, if not made homogenous, by the appeal to 'common historical memories, myths, symbols and traditions' (1991: 11).[5]

The Balkan Wars and the First World War: Stimulating National Identity

Texts have contexts and nations are themselves narrations (Bhabha, 1990), so let us look at some earlier examples of the role of popular music in stimulating the articulation of national identity, during the period of the Balkan Wars and the First World War. The popular music of that period gave voice to an ethnic identity characterized by a sense of uniqueness and a collective solipsism tinged with triumphalism. Patriotic songs celebrating Serbia's trials, tribulations and victories experienced in these wars have taken on an almost sacred aura. These songs embody the putative Serbian qualities of heroism, pride, aggression, stubbornness, the conviction that they have been victimized and a belief in their ultimate victory.

Some of these songs, which were discouraged at least in the years of Tito's leadership (1945–80), gained popularity in the 1960s when they were stripped of any nationalist message, rebranded as *narodna muzika* [folk music] and produced by Belgrade record companies such as Yugoton, Radio-Televizija Beograd, Beograd Disk and Diskos. Serbian military songs from the First World War, along with proscribed Second World War Četnik songs, with their nationalist sentiment fully reinstated, became extremely popular on the eve of the break-up of the Socialist Federative Republic of Yugoslavia, and could be bought in cassette and CD formats in markets in all the towns throughout the Former Republic of Yugoslavia and the Republika Srpska. Examples would include compilation tapes with general titles, such as *Srpske: sa verom u Bogu i Srbiju* [Serbian (Songs): With Faith in God and Serbia], purchased in Novi Sad in July 1995, *Kolo*, purchased in Belgrade in September 1998, or *Samo Sloga Srbina Spasava* [Only Unity Will Save the Serbs] and *Srpske Narodne Pesme* [Serbian National Songs], both purchased in Trebinje, Republika Srpska, in November 2000. These are the very songs that could be heard once more over loudspeakers during clashes between Serbs and Kosovar Albanians at Kosovska Mitrovica in March 2000. The public performance of these songs served as a spur to Serb demonstrators, inciting them to express their identity and collective wounded pride.

When the First World War broke out, the Serbs had been initially successful in fighting against the vastly superior forces of the Austro-Hungarian Empire. Although the Serbs lost their capital Belgrade in December 1914, they nevertheless continued to harry the Austro-Hungarian army deep inside Serbian territory, as the Serb army retreated from Belgrade. Eventually the two armies confronted each other at the Kolubara River that same month and the Serbs won a major victory under the leadership of Vojvoda Mišić.[6] The Austro-Hungarians were driven back to the river Sava and out of Serbia. Belgrade was liberated in due course. It is within this context that songs such as 'Marš na Drinu' ['March to the Drina'] were composed and first sung.

The Drina is symbolically very significant to Serb national identity, as it is the Drina that serves as the river frontier between Serbia and Bosnia, which had been held by Austria-Hungary since 1878. The idea of crossing the Drina in 1914 and 1915 stimulated an irredentist desire that would resurface in the 1990s, among Serb nationalists, led by paramilitaries such as the late Arkan (Željko Ražnjatović) and Dr Vojislav Šešelj. 'Marš na Drinu' has come to symbolize the pride of the national dream of uniting Serbs in Bosnia with those in the Kingdom of Serbia.

> Putem ide četa momačka
> Vedra čela, srca junačka
> Rano moja, hej
> A pred četom Mile komandira,
> 'Hej, trubačik, "Marš na Drinu"'
> Nek se sada
>
> Chorus of a kolo
>
> Svirajte mi Marš na Drinu,
> To je pesma stara.
> Kad je čujem zapeva mi
> Srca iz nedara.
> Tri su cara pobedili.
> Ratinici i seljaci
> Pevali su Marš na Drinu
> Za cele junake.
>
> [Along the road march a company of lads
> Cheerful faces, heroes' hearts
> And from the front of the company,
> Mile commands,
> 'Hey, trumpeter,

Play me the "March to the Drina"'

Chorus of a kolo

Play me the 'March to the Drina',
It's an old song.
Whenever I hear it my heart sings out with joy.
Three emperors have been victorious.
Warriors and peasants
Sang the 'March to the Drina'
And all the heroes.][7]

'Marš na Drinu' was composed in 1915 by Stanislav Binički. In four-time, in a major key, in the form of a Serbian kolo, or round dance, it has become extremely popular and many recorded versions of this song are now available. The title 'Marš na Drinu', which had been representative of Serbian ambition and, in the First World War, of pushing back the enemy, crossing into Austro-Hungarian Bosnia and freeing kindred populations, had, by the 1990s, been transmogrified into the dream of building a greater Serbia, by marching across the Drina into Bosnia-Hercegovina. That 'ratnici i seljaci' [warriors and peasants] and 'cele junake' [all the heroes] in the final lines of the chorus should be united symbolizes the common purpose of the whole nation in a bid to build a greater Serbia.

By October 1915, the whole of Serbia had been occupied by the combined forces of Germany, Bulgaria and Austria-Hungary. The Serbian army retreated through Kosovo and Montenegro into Albania. They were harried by Kosovar Albanians along the route, who resented the reincorporation of Kosovo into Serbia after the 1912 Balkan War. The Serbs reached the Adriatic coast and were evacuated to Corfu by the French, where they stayed until 1916, when they joined their French and British allies on the Salonika front. This event fits in well with the migration discourse of the Serbs, with references to 1690–91 and 1705, to say nothing of the retreat from the Krajina in 1995. The theme is fully developed by Miloš Crnjanski, in his epic novel *Seobe* [Migrations], in the poetry of Zaharia Orfelin (Holton and Mihailovich, 1998: 63) and Paja Jovanović's oil painting *Seoba (Srpskog naroda)* [The Migration of the Serbian People, 1690] (1896), in which the whole nation, represented by soldiers, knights, peasants, priests and womenfolk, are united in their flight from Kosovo, the 'cradle' of the Serbian nation.[8]

The song that commemorated the epic migration of 1915 was 'Tamo daleko' ['Over There, Far Away'], a song composed in 1916 about loss and yearning for the homeland. 'Tamo daleko' is played in triple time. It starts off in a minor key, on a sombre note, followed by a section in the relative major of the dominant key on the third line of the first verse, symbolizing hope, and in turn followed by a fall back into the tonic minor key. It is exile on the island of Corfu that provides the background to 'Tamo daleko'.[9] A sense of primordial identity, linked to family and nation, is embedded in this song, with father and son giving up their lives for the nation:

> Tamo daleko,
> Daleko od mora,
> Tamo je selo moje,
> Tamo je Srbija ...

> ... Bez otadžbine na Krfu živelih ja,
> Ali sam s ponosom klic' o,
> Živela Srbija.

> [Over there and far away,
> Far from the sea,
> There is my village,
> There is Serbia ...

> ... Without a fatherland, I would live in Corfu,
> But alone in my pride, I would shout out for joy,
> Long live Serbia.]

Other lines in the song contrast Corfu with Serbia: 'Over there, far away, where the lemon flowers blossom [Corfu] / There was the only road for the Serbian army' and 'over there, far away, where the white tulips are in flower [Serbia] / There a son and his father, both give up there lives together'. 'Tamo daleko' was to become a potent symbol of Serbian cultural and national identity; the melancholy of the loss of homeland would, through victory at the end of the First World War, be transformed into a great sense of national self-pride.

I have already mentioned the impact of the video clip of the singing of 'Tamo daleko' in the sports hall in Pale. There was something millenarian about this event, with President Karadžić's claims that the Republika Srpska would last for a thousand years. Furthermore, bearing in mind the function of song, church and people as the foundations of Serbian national identity, there is, with reference to Ernest Gellner (1995: 4), a Caesaro-Papist element to this scene, vis-à-vis the support of the state by the church, a theme that runs throughout the Serbian historical meta-narrative. The Serbian state and the Serbian autocephalous church were founded by the brothers Stefan Nemanja (1168–96) and Sveti [Saint] Sava (1175–1236) respectively in the twelfth century, and state and church have remained closely interlinked and interdependent.

A similar example was provided by a clip from Radio Televizija Srbija on 25 January 1995, when it transmitted a music festival from the Red Star Belgrade Stadium featuring some of Serbia's leading popular musicians and stars. The event was brought to a close when a girl, aged about 12, came onto the stage, took up the microphone and broke into 'Tamo daleko'. The audience in the stadium, mostly made up of youngsters and young adults, was euphoric in its accompaniment to the young singer. The focus here was on youth, the implications being a reverence for a semi-mythologized past with which the future survival of the nation might be forged.

From *Gusle* to Guitar

A 'primordialist' approach to ethnic identity, as rooted in 'blood and soil', continues to dominate, as is demonstrated by the populist writer Momor Kopor, who, writing from the town of Trebinje, part of the Republika Srpska, in southern Hercegovina in 1992, commented that:

> When I think back over the last year and its most important events I will put in first place hearing the voice of that young fighter, the sound of whose *gusle* travels across the dark centuries uniting him with his ancestors who played on the same instruments, and the defiant bursts of gunfire into the sky which accompanied that sound.[10]

The theme of the *guslar* had been explored at a much earlier date by the American journalist John Reed in his account of his exploits in the Balkans and in Russia during the First World War:

> Every regiment has two or three gypsies, who march with the troops, playing the Serbian fiddle or the bagpipes, and accompany the songs that are composed incessantly by the soldiers – love songs, celebrations of victory, epic chants. And all through Serbia they are the musicians of the people, travelling from one country festa [*sic*] to another, playing for dancing and singing. (Reed, 1994 [1916]: 12)

He goes on to add that this music was 'transmitted from generation to generation through the far mountain valley the ancient national epics and ballads'. Similarly, Crnjanski in *Seobe* also recounts the role of the *guslar* in time of war, in a scene in which the war-weary Vuk Isaković, a colonel of Serbian origin serving in the Austrian army, reflects on his unrequited love for the wife of Prince Karl Alexander of Würtenberg:

> Although he, like his fellow officers, had had to learn to dance, and was indeed a fine dancer, she never chose him as a partner; so when the sweet viols began to play, he was obliged to bow to some old crone in her entourage – they all adored him. After these soirées he and his friends would carouse till dawn, singing to the *gusle* at the top of their lungs and bursting with eloquence and vitality. ([Tsernianski] Crnjanski, 1994: 93)

This is one of the many passages in *Seobe* which contrast the seemingly high cultural values of Western Europe with those earthier values of the Balkans. Indeed, throughout his novel, the sound of the *gusle* serves as a leitmotiv for Serbian identity, rendered more poignant for these Serbian exiles who were serving foreign masters in alien lands.

More recently, a documentary for the British TV Channel 4, *The Ethnic Cleansers and the Cleansed: The Unforgiving* (1992), depicts a scene in which a company of soldiers of the Bosnian Serb Army of the Republika Srpska is situated at the top of Mount Trebević, overlooking the town of Sarajevo which stretches along the banks of the River Miljaćka. They are drinking *šljivovica*, raw plum brandy, from a bottle that is being passed from man to man. Among them, a *guslar* strikes up his *gusle* and bows its single string, as his voice drones in accompaniment. The others take up the chorus, launching into epic song. This incident took place in the summer of 1992, yet there was a peculiar relationship between past and present, between ancient and modern: singing songs about a mediaeval past, to the accompaniment of a traditional folk instrument, against such a contemporary military setting, with its armoured vehicles, mortars and heavy machine guns. It was this particular scene, with my own personal memories of the countryside around Mount Trebević, from a much happier time at the end of the 1970s, which prompted me to investigate further the link between popular music and the stimulus it provided in whipping up nationalist sentiments.

Yet, culture is not fixed. It is constantly evolving, and this may be expressed by both the different mechanical and material forms that are employed, as well as the lyrics and images that are produced. For example, the *gusle* is still played today, although, often in the 1990s, musicians resorted to the traditional instrumental ensemble accompaniment of accordion, double bass and clarinet. This kind of arrangement provides the basis of the *narodna muzika* [traditional/national music] that, since the 1990s, has been more commonly referred to as *izvorna muzika* [authentic music]. Simultaneous with the playing of *izvorna muzika* has been the development of *novokomponovana narodna muzika* [newly-composed folk music], a contemporary, neotraditional variant of *narodna/izvorna* that is currently played on television and heard in nightclubs throughout Serbia.[11]

From the beginning of the 1990s, *narodna muzika*, *izvorna muzika* and *novokomponovana muzika* were broadcast on radio and television throughout the day and night. Indeed, in November 1991, in Belgrade, RTS established a new radio station called Poselo 202 (meaning 'folk party') which broadcast different varieties of folk music 24 hours a day. In 1992, the aptly named Ponos Radio [Radio Pride] also began to broadcast 24 hours a day with an emphasis on folk music with political, militaristic and/or patriotic overtones (Barber-Kersovan, 2001: 78). With this came new national political songs, settings of the *nova narodna patriotsko-politička poezija* [new national patriotic–political poesia], which located the current military conflicts in the patriotic rhetoric and mythology of the past for a new generation. One such example is quoted in Čolović (1994: 101).

Hvala tebi, Karadžiću Vuče,
Naša deca tvoja slova uče.
Srpski narod pamti tvoje lice
Ti si otac srpske ćirilice.

[Thank you, Vuk Karadžić,
Our children are learning your words.
The Serbian people remember your face
You are the father of Serbian Cyrillic.]

The song is a reference to the nineteenth-century language reformer and national awakener Vuk Karadžić, and to the role and impact of education in teaching children an alphabet (Cyrillic) that distinguishes them as Serbs and culturally excludes other South Slavs – by implication, the Croats.

Kim Burton (1999: 273) draws an interesting comparison between *novokompanovana narodna muzika*, with its accordion and clarinet or violin and steel guitar accompaniment and the country and western music that is to be found in the United States, seeing in this development a music from the village that has been transformed into a music that answers the needs of working-class life. The instrumental ensemble of accordion, double bass and clarinet has, in more recent times, often given way to electric guitars and keyboard. Furthermore, whereas the imagery in the lyrics previously reflected earlier standards, with reference to a raft of poetical and mythical images taken from the canon of nationalist literature, there have been many examples more recently of *guslari* singing songs that are based on the death of promising young footballers, the progress of the war or the careers of notorious Belgrade gangsters (Burton, 1999: 273). Yet, whatever the lyrics, *guslari* probably found a wider audience in the 1990s than at any other time since the end of the Second World War. Radio stations in Belgrade, during the first half of the 1990s, broadcast traditional nationalist songs, alongside new interpretations of Četnik songs from the Second World War and contemporary songs from the then current wars that celebrated new heroes, such as the late Arkan or Kapetan Dragan, who accompanied himself with the guitar rather than the *gusle* of the more traditional singers (Čolović, 1994: 61–70). The case of Kapetan Dragan is particularly interesting within this context. Čolović has described him as 'one of the first heroes of the Serb-Croat war', who first appeared on Serbian television screens and in newspapers in the spring of 1991. He became a media sensation as a commentator on the conflict. Čolović has said that his tales of the war and the media showcasing of his work transformed him into a 'mitski arhetip' [mythical archetype], the face of folklore, or the 'epski junak' [epic hero] of the war.

The Use of Cultural Tradition in Expressing National Chauvinism

One of the questions that needs to be addressed is why it is that in the contemporary period there has been a return to traditional elements in the expression of national chauvinism. To answer this, firstly, we need to address the role of culture in the nationalist discourse. Ernest Gellner, in his *Nations and Nationalism* (1983: 58–62) recounts the tale of national awakeners at work in a mythical rural Ruritania, seeking to empower their national identity in cultural opposition to the Empire of Megalomania. In this passage Gellner portrays what he describes as 'a characteristic scenario of the evolution of a nationalism', namely the process of gathering together and interpreting demotic culture, such as folk music and dance, folk costume and oral literature, in a bid to formalize a nascent national culture. Similarly, Anthony Smith comments on the mobilization of the 'people' by intellectuals and professionals in popular ethnic communities and fully develops this in his chapter on 'nationalism and cultural identity' (1991: ix and 84–96). This process of ethnification has been common throughout Eastern and Central Europe since the 1820s; in the case of Serbia, there is the gathering of tales by Vuk Karadžić – *Najstarije pjesme junačke* [The Oldest Heroic Songs] (1841) and his *Srpske narodne pripovijetke* [Serbian Folktales] (1821) – as well as Jovan Sterija Popović's *Boj na Kosovo* [The Battle at Kosovo] (1828), to name but two 'national awakeners' working in the field.

Because of their exclusion from the European mainstream the Serbs have forged their identity out of a return to forms of cultural traditionalism in a process that is common to most postcolonial societies. With the break-up of Yugoslavia and the growing sense of isolation, first in one conflict and then in another, with all the attendant horrors of ethnicized identity politics, Serbia was banished from the so-called European mainstream. Popular music became important in furthering the cause of Serbian national identity, and as something to hold on to for a community that had lost its once privileged position both within Yugoslavia and in the international community. A projected Serbness [*Srpstvo*] was found in some of the cultural elements of the past that were considered to be purely Serbian, as opposed to Southern Slav or Balkan – in other words, the cult of an essentialized folkloric.

Here is one example of the application of the Kosovo myth to contemporary nationalist folk music in the track 'Srpkinjica jedna mala', from a cassette of nationalist songs, purchased in Belgrade, at a street market, in 1995:

Srpinjica jedna mala
Na Kosovu cveće brala.
Od tri boje venac vila
Pa se njome zakitila.

Crvena je krvca bila
Na Kosovu što se vila
Zato crven boju nosim
I sa njom se ja ponosim.

Plavo nebo k'o sloboda
Ideal je srpskog roda
Zato plavu boju nosim
I sa njom se ja ponosim.

Belo mleko majka pila
I mene je zadojila
Zato belu boju nosim
I sa njom se ja ponosim.

Jedan venac tri su boje
Trobojnica srpska to je
Crveno, plavo i belo
S njom se diči Srpstvo celo.

[A little Serbian girl
Was picking flowers in Kosovo.
From three colours she wove a wreath
With which to adorn herself.

Red was the blood
That was shed at Kosovo
Thus red is the colour that I wear
Of which I am very proud.

Blue sky – like freedom
The ideal of the Serbian people[12]
Thus blue is the colour that I wear
Of which I am very proud.

Mother drinks white milk
And she passes it to me
Thus I wear the white colour
Of which I am very proud.

One wreath, three colours
This is the Serbian tricolour
Red, blue and white
With which all Serbs unite.]

This is a lively 'pop-kolo', common to Serbia, played by a village band in four-time with an accent from a double bass on every first and third beat. An accordion leads and the song is sung by a male soloist. The lyrics denote the weaving together of the colours of the Serbian tricolour flag into a wreath of flowers that have been gathered by a young Serbian maiden from the field of the Battle of Kosovo. These colours, red, blue and white, are worn proudly by both the maiden and the singer. They are highly charged with nationalist symbolism: red for the blood spilled by Serbian warriors on the battlefield; white for the milk given to her children by the Serbian mother-nation; and blue for the skies, the symbol of Serbian freedom, and, indeed, of heavenly Serbia. Do these sacred national symbols, gathered by the Serbian maiden, represent the desire for a united greater Serbia, made up of the Krajina Serbian territories, centred on Knin and the Republika Srpska based in Banja Luka and in Pale in the first half of the 1990s? Certainly, this is borne out by the last line, 'S njom se diči Srpstvo celo' [With which all Serbs unite]. On a deeper level of signification, this song depicts the figure of the Kosovo Girl, an iconic symbol of Serb identity who appears in the ballad of the 'Kosovska devojka' and other songs from the epic Kosovo song cycle, and who, according to the myth, gave succour to the wounded warriors in the first morning after battle.

Indeed, two key figures running through the mythology of Serbian identity are 'the warrior hero' and the 'mother/sister'. The role of the 'warrior hero' can be traced back to the Kosovo epics – with Prince Lazar, Miloš Obilić and the fallen heroes on the field of Kosovo – through to the myths and tales of Marko Kraljević. The theme is taken up with the brave soldiers of Vojvoda Mišić in their retreat through Serbia in the First World War, the Četniks of the Second World War and, so the Serbian nationalist discourse would logically conclude, the paramilitaries of Arkan and Vojislav Šešelj in the so-called wars of Yugoslav secession. The theme of *majka/sestra* [mother/sister] is also a dominant one in the poetry and literature of Serbia, and has resurfaced many times in the patriotic nationalist songs that emerged into the popular culture domain during the 1990s: for example, in the song 'Srbija naša majka mila' ['Serbia our Darling Mother'], reference is made in the refrain to the Serbian mother-nation giving succour to her children, a common trope in nationalist discourses:

Ima jedna zemlja stara
Što na nebu ima cara.
Ima Cara,
Oj Lazara
Što sa suncem razgovara.

Srbija, naša majka mila,
Srbija sve nas je rodila,
Živela, živela, živela Srbija.

[There is a country of old
Which has a tsar in the heavens.
She has a tsar,
Oh, Lazar
Who speaks with the sun.

Serbia, our dear mother,
Serbia you bore all of us,
Long live, long live, long live Serbia.]

So, veneration of this mother/sister figure – who either gives birth to the nation, through her sons who become future soldiers defending the national community, or, as the sister-figure, gives succour to the wounded warrior hero – is a potent image in Serbian nationalist discourse, while common to many other European discourses.[13]

Turbo Folk

Apart from the revival of older, traditional forms of popular music in a bid to stimulate Serb nationalism in the declining years of the Socialist Federative Republic of Yugoslavia, new songs and styles were also created in the early 1990s, such as *novakoponovana narodna muzika*, mentioned above. Of all the new styles, the most notorious was turbo folk, described by one non-nationalist Serbian acquaintance as 'the music of the Devil'. Much has been written about turbo folk by both journalists and academics in the West.[14] For example, journalist Peter Morgan described turbo folk as 'the music of isolation' (1997: 58), while another, Robert Black, described the singers of turbo folk as the 'balladeers of Ethnic Cleansing' (1994). Black added that turbo folk represented 'the sound of the war and everything that the war has brought to this country'.

> Turbo is a music in which harmony always overcomes all difference and no space is left for doubt – in yourself, your lover or your nation. It is not just high-octane 'party' music, but music perfect for paramilitaries in need of both nationalist kitsch and high-adrenaline music forms ... This form fuses love songs and older folk tunes that are either implicitly or explicitly ethnically Serbian, with contemporary dance music. (Monroe, 2000)

Turbo folk is a fusion of Western rock, oriental Turkish rhythms and *sevdah* or *sevdalenke* [love songs]; the irony being that the latter are a Bosnian form. The popularity of turbo folk in Serbia in the 1990s was demonstrated by the fact that most discotheques throughout Serbia were transformed into 'folkothèques' where turbo folk was played exclusively, to say nothing of the 24-hour coverage on Belgrade radio and television stations.

In an Internet article, the Belgrade-based playwright Biljana Srbljanović commented on the phenomenon of turbo folk, as seen on the Serbian television channel TV Pink in 'programme after programme':

> The singers, mostly women who usually wear as little as is decently possible work hard to evoke the whirling atmosphere of a roadside haunt of long-distance lorry drivers. This type of woman, predominantly a bleached blonde, her lips and breasts swollen with silicone injections, is being deliberately built up as an ideal to be emulated. (Srbljanović, 2000)

Such a description may be applied to singers such as Lepa Brena (Fahreta Jahić), Vesna Zmijana and Simonida Stanković, whose songs celebrated the deeds of Arkan's paramilitary Tigers in Bosnia-Hercegovina. Even Sonja Karadžić, daughter of the former president of the Republika Srpska, Radovan Karadžić, tried, and failed, to exploit this musical form. These, then, are the siren voices of Serb nationalism, singing their songs of seduction in a time of conflict and crisis. Svetlana Veličković (aka Ceca), the 'Queen of turbo folk' and widow of Željko Ražnatović (Arkan), would appear in battle fatigues near the front line in the fighting against Croatia. However, there was nothing particularly exceptional in this act, since singers on all sides were dispatched to the various fronts to raise morale amongst the troops.

Turbo folk may be characterized as 'brash glamour, uninhibited hedonism and an "exotic" eastern chic' (Thomas, 1999: 72). Nonetheless, these Balkan balladeers provide a link between song and politics as did their *guslar* forebears. Rather than being explicit in the lyrics, the nationalist discourse is often implicit in the music and kitsch of turbo folk, particularly in the atmosphere that surrounds the performances. For example, the rallies held during the 1993 elections for Arkan's Stranka Srpskog Jedinstva [Serbian Unity Party] – then supported by President Slobodan Milošević – were a mixture of populist political propaganda and rock concerts. Ultimately, it is not just lyrics that convey a nationalist message in popular music, but also the culture that surrounds the lives and activities of singers and fans and how the music is used – consider, for example, Ceca's concert against NATO during the bombing of Yugoslavia in the spring and summer of 1999. In a similar vein, one should consider the recourse to popular folk music and folk dancing on the bridges over the river Danube in Belgrade and Novi Sad in the spring of 1999, at the height of the NATO conflict with Yugoslavia, in a bid to celebrate the Serbian nation's defiance of the international community. Performances were given by turbo folk singers such as Ceca and Lepa Brena, as well as by Yugoslav pop-rock stars such as Zdravko Čolić.[15]

Such attempts to raise the people's morale in a time of national crisis were used by the Milošević regime, when pragmatically convenient, as a reinforcement of national–patriotic values, further promoting the perceived superiority and unity of Serbian identity as something rooted in a common culture and founded upon a sense of shared historical identity that reached back to mythologized perceptions of a 'glorious' Serbian past. This was a return to the kind of political rallies that had taken place in the late 1980s, but now supported by a wide range of turbo folk singers, including Ceca, singing: 'You can be as happy as me – just join the Serbian Unity Party' (Thomas, 1999: 172). Ceca's role as 'Queen of turbo folk' is also an example of the mother/sister or Kosovo Girl paradigm, just as her late husband, Arkan, was an example of the warrior/hero or Kosovo warrior figure from populist nationalist discourse.[16] Indeed, the marriage between them came to symbolize an act of union between music and national 'heroism', a union that has played a key role in the forging of Serb ethnic identity throughout the last two centuries.

By contrast, songs popular in a war – that add something to the colour and content of the social life and provide amusement – can have lyrics located far from the political arena: for example, Bajaga's 'Moji drugovi' ['My Mates'], from Miloš Radivojević's 1994 film *Ni na nebu ni na zemlji* (released with the English title

'Between Heaven and Earth'), a song which became highly popular with soldiers of the Bosnian Serb Army during the wars in Bosnia-Hercegovina. This became the song of the war in the Republika Srpska, and yet there is no reference in it to fighting but rather only to male comradeship and the perennial Serb theme of migration. This is a song of diaspora:

Moji su drugovi biseri rasuti po celom svetu
I ja sam selica pa ih ponekad sretnem u letu.
Da l' je to sudbina ili ko zna šta li je,
Kad god se sretnemo uvek se zalije
Uvek se završi s nekom od naših pesama.

Moji su drugovi žestoki momci velikog srca
I kad se pije, kad se ljubi kad se puca
Gore od Aljaske do Australije
Kad god se sretnemo uvek se zalije
Uvek se završi s nekom od naših pesama.

Da smo živi i zdravi još godina sto
Da je pesme i vina i da nas čuva Bog
Da su najbolje žene uvijek pored nas
Jer ovaj život je kratak I prozurji za čas.

(Hajdemo...)

Za moje drugove ja molim vetrove za puna jedra
Puteve sigurne a noći zvezdane i jutra vedra.

Da li to sudbina...?[17]

[My friends are scattered like pearls throughout the whole world
And I am a migratory bird who sometimes meets them in flight.
It is destiny, who knows what it is,
But whenever we meet up we always have a great booze up
And finish with some of our songs.

My mates are hard lads with big hearts
And when there is drinking, when there is kissing and when there's any shooting
Whether up there in Alaska or down in Australia
And always, when we meet up we drink and finish up with some of our songs.

Let's live and drink a toast to another year
Full of songs and wine and God's protection
That the best women are always around us
Because life is too short and it is running out.

(Let's go...)

For my friends, I pray for good winds and full sails,
Safe voyages, starry nights and clear mornings

Is it destiny...?]

This is a *vojnička pesma*, a soldiers' song, which, despite the differing lyrics, theme, subject matter and instrumentation, is similar in function to the Kosovo ballad, as sung by Bosnian Serb Četniks to the accompaniment of the *gusle* above the hills of Sarajevo. Is this not the contemporary war's equivalent of 'Marš na Drinu', in a Serbian context, or, by comparison, of 'It's a Long Way to Tipperary' or 'Pack up Your Troubles' in a First World War British context? Yet, although this *vojnička pesma* does not explicitly celebrate the war, in terms of performance it is inextricably linked to it. Furthermore, in the post-Dayton peace, it has become a key signifier of Serb identity, as was witnessed in June 2001 when the song served as the theme tune for the Yugoslav national team playing at the International Water Polo competition in Budapest.

Conclusions

The songs outlined in this chapter demonstrate how the musical materials, lyrics, iconography and performative contexts of popular song can form a highly charged symbolic economy in which populist politics merges with essentializing discourses of cultural tradition in the articulation of ethnicized concepts of the nation, national identity and nationalism. Brutal contemporary conflict and the horrors of ethnic cleansing are recast through appeals to historical legitimacy, paradoxically based on an almost timeless mythologized heroic past. The cult of the folkloric in Serbia, in both its nativist and modernized variants, is testimony to a wider contemporary phenomenon: the dramatic increase in culturally based, often ethnicized, political movements rooted in 'new traditionalism' and 'primordial loyalties' (Friedman, 1994: 78, 86).

Notes

1   An earlier version of this chapter was originally published in the June 2003 edition of *Patterns of Prejudice* (http://www.tandf.co.uk/journals). The author is indebted to Dr Barbara Rosenbaum, editor of *Patterns of Prejudice*, for her invaluable help and advice.
2   'Tribal songs' were collected and preserved in the nineteenth century, by Johann Wolfgang von Goethe and Vuk Karadžić amongst others. The label 'tribal songs' was used to distinguish them from the Kosovo Ballads and the songs of Marko Kraljević; the music referred to here comes from much earlier folk roots. South Slav 'tribal'

societies migrated into south-eastern Europe from late fifth and sixth centuries AD, although I am not suggesting that the music is that old. Examples of these songs may be found in Holton and Mihailovich (1998).

3   Church choral music serves a patriotic, national ideal in the nineteenth century. In creating this music, composers such as Borislav Stanković, Ilija Stojanović and Steven Mokranjac travelled around collecting folk songs – like Béla Bartók and Zoltá Kodály did in Hungary – and transformed them into a more urbanized form. See Pejović (1995).

4   This clip was part of the documentary film *The Ethnic Cleansers and the Cleansed: The Unforgiving*, a Barraclough Carey production for the UK TV Channel 4. The term 'Republika Srpska' should be distinguished from Serbia proper or the Republic of Serbia, which alongside the Republic of Montenegro is one of the two remaining constituent republics of the Federal Republic of Yugoslavia – renamed the State of Serbia and Montenegro in March 2003. The Republika Srpska, by contrast, refers to the Serbian entity in Bosnia and Hercegovina. During the war (1992–95) its capital was Pale, situated about 20 kilometres south-east of Sarajevo. Since the Dayton peace agreement of November 1995, its capital has been Banja Luka.

5   The theme of the song 'Tamo daleko' was one of Serbia's greatest ordeals during the First World War, when the Serbian army and its dependants were forced to retreat through Serbia and Albania, crossing the Adriatic to safety in Corfu, before returning to Serbia and eventual victory, via the Salonika front.

6   The battles of Kolubara, Cer and Suvobar were the three great Serb victories of the First World War.

7   All the translations of songs in this chapter are by the author. However, I would like to thank Dr Francis Jones of the Newcastle University for his advice on my translation of this particular song.

8   This currently hangs in the Natonal Museum at Pančevo.

9   An alternative interpretation of this event might be that it symbolized the end of the old Serbia, given that it was from Corfu that Crown Prince Alexander and Nikola Pašić planned the future Kingdom of the Serbs, Croats and Slovenes (that would be re-named Yugoslavia in 1929).

10 Momor Kopor's article, entitled 'Predeo spružen mrženjom' [A Region Burning with Hatred], was published in *Pogledi*, on 17 January 1992, quoted here from the translation in Thomas (1999: 172–3). In the article Kopor recounts his travels through the Hercegovinian mountains in the south-eastern part of the Republika Srpska.

11 The paradoxical focus on 'newness' in the *novokomponovana narodna muzika* and the *nova narodna patriotsko-politička poezija* should not obscure the 'retrograde orientation' of their appeal to a mythologized past (Barber-Kersovan, 2001: 77).

12 The word *rod* has a stronger meaning than 'folk' or 'people', suggesting a family or clan.

13 Compare Marianne for the French or Britannia for an older – and now discredited in some circles – sense of British identity. In the Serbian example of the mother/sister theme, there is also something of the sacred, with a *soupçon* of the Marian image of the *Pietà* or indeed the nativity.

14 See the documentary by Hawker (1994) broadcast on Channel 4 (United Kingdom) in 1994.

15 As Barber-Kersovan (2001: 82, 85) notes, it is one of the paradoxcs of the war that rock music – associated with 'American' or 'Eurocentric' attitudes and given wide

coverage by the Western media – should feature so heavily in the concerts organized by the Serbian authorities.

16 Of particular interest here is Eleanor Pritchard's reference to a passage in the Yugoslav magazine *Duga* (21 January 1995: 75): 'The connection between Ceca and Arkan is far greater than the love of two mortals. It isn't a connection between the president of a party, and the premier Yugoslav folk singer. The connection originates in a myth, the roots of which are in Kosovo! The connection between Ceca and Arkan is the connection between the Kosovo girl and the Kosovo hero ... The war has ended and the Kosovo girl has healed the wounded hero and made him her beloved' (translated and quoted in Pritchard, 1999: 147).

17 Lyrics taken from *Rok lira: tekstovi i akordi, vodič kroz ovdašnjji rok n roll* (Belgrade, undated and no publisher given).

Discography

Due to the particular situation of Serbia, most tracks come from compilation cassettes purchased in street markets which are in all likelihood pirated copies. Hence no production/artist details are available. Instead dates of purchase are given.

Bajaga, 'Moji drugovi' featured in Radivojević (1994). See filmography for details.
'Srpkinjica jedna mala' (1995) from a pirated collection with no title sent from a friend in Republika Srpska.
Various Artists, *Srpske: sa verom u Bogu i Srbiju* [Serbian (Songs): With Faith in God and Serbia] (1995). Includes tracks 'Marš na Drinu', 'Srbija naša majka mila' and 'Tamo daleko'.
Various Artists, *Kolo* (Atlandida, 1998).
Various Artists, *Samo Sloga Srbina Spasava* [Only Unity Will Save the Serbs] (RTB, 2000).
Various Artists, *Srpske Narodne Pesme* [Serbian National Songs] (RTB, 2000).

Television documentaries

Hawker, Mark (1994), *Zombie Town*, broadcast on Channel 4 (United Kingdom) in 1994.
The Ethnic Cleansers and the Cleansed: The Unforgiving, a Barraclough Carey production for Channel 4 (Princeton: Films in the Humanities and Science, 1994).

Filmography

Petrović, Stefan (1994), *Seobe* [Migrations].
Radivojević, Miloš (1994), *Ni na nebu ni na zemlji* [Between Heaven and Earth].

Chapter 9

Those Norwegians: Deconstructing the Nation-State in Europe through Fixity and Indifference in Norwegian Club Music[1]

Stan Hawkins

That music informs us of a sense of identity within the context of national boundaries is of symbolic importance and has far-reaching implications for music studies. Indeed, the signification of this is complex, as cultural, political, and social circumstances of genres demand very distinct ideologies for deriving pleasure. As sociologists have pointed out, musical practices within very close local contexts often bear little resemblance to one another. This assertion can be borne out by the varied responses one finds to dance culture, where styles and trends in club culture function cross-culturally. In fact, the likelihood of, say, a Norwegian dance track being enjoyed, comprehended and danced to in the locality in which it is produced is the same as it being received in a remote town on the other side of the planet. In other words, music is not only culture- and generation-specific, but also pan-national. One of the central aims of this chapter is to identify a number of features that relate to constructions of Norwegianism within a stylistic category of music that is broad-based and predominantly European. Clearly, any study of dance music can usefully take on board the relationships that exist between music and national identity. This can be overwhelmingly dense, but this should not deter us from at least attempting to think about why this is the case and considering how we might proceed with understanding the nature of the relationships that exist between music and nationality.

In earlier studies, I have suggested that analysing musical pleasure might be undertaken through a decentred approach, which insists that the text in question is always negotiable (Hawkins, 1999, 2001, 2002, 2003). People always make choices as to how they want to be positioned in relation to music consumption, as much as to musical interpretation. Indeed, one of the merits of a decentred approach to understanding how national stereotypes are constructed through musical expression is the exposure of the dualisms that traditionally relate to constructs of identity as constituted in asymmetrical oppositions. In recent years musicological studies have gradually realigned themselves to a critical stance that examines ideologies of difference, with a move towards a reconceptualization of identity categories (Solie, 1993; Middleton, 2000). One of the goals of this chapter is to build on this approach and attempt to conceptualize how the negotiation of music's 'fixity' depends on configurations that are organized around cultural similarities and differences.[2] With reference to a dance track, 'Da Kingue D'Mazda' by a Norwegian group called, quite aptly and not without a touch of playfulness, Those Norwegians, I will provide a reading that foregrounds the question of local identity and how it can be brought into a dialogue with music criticism.

Defining the Cultural and Social Context

Geographically, where musicians and bands come from represents a potential for understanding how political power structures and dominant cultural expectations function at national level. Within Norway, an industrialized and prosperous European nation-state, music is produced and managed as cultural capital. Certainly, music is about power and can evoke internal states that occur dialogically between our external social and political environments. Discursively constituted, music functions in a way that situates us symbolically and thus mediates an individual and collective cultural awareness. In a Norwegian context, the pull and appeal of commercial music, and its associations with national, regional, collective and/or individual identity, draws on a large pool of national and international codes, which remind people of their connections to, as much as their detachment from, others. In effect, this raises a range of interesting questions concerning categories in music and the problematics of difference within identity.

Let us begin with the idea that constructions of identity are always negotiable through musical expression as we enter biographically into the familiar and the unknown. As Shepherd and Wicke have argued, because the 'meaning of music originates *ultimately* with the individual' (1997: 177), music is constructed through relations of difference. This becomes evident when we observe how pleasures empower people through popular music and fulfil certain political roles as the individual becomes immersed in the experience of music. Shepherd and Wicke have argued that, at every moment, music is fixed in its articulation. Yet it is the 'negotiability of this fixity' that demonstrates a continuous dialectic in process between body, space and place. Inextricably linked to this process is the issue of geographical location, which offers a useful way to consider relationships between music and identities. For some time sociologists and cultural theorists have employed the term 'local' to conceptualize the relationship between music and physical space. Conceptually, the term functions as an index for national and regional identities or scenes linked to particular cityscapes, and can indeed be employed to denote consumption and production practices within an urban or rural setting. Arguing this point, Andy Bennett has defined the local as a 'highly contested territory that is crossed by different forms of collective life and the competing sensibilities that the latter bring to bear on the interpretation and social realization of a particular place' (2000: 53). From this, we could say that it is through the local that music helps steer the formation of individual and collective identity. Functioning as a soundtrack for identity, music secures notions of self-definition in real or virtual time (Ruud, 1997: 38). Furthermore, music profiles people's engagement with their biographies, their cultures and their societies in a manner that is profoundly symbolic.

In considering the wider implications of musical fixity, I want to explore further the role of national identity and the development of industrial capitalism in Norway and the impact this has on social and cultural processes in the everyday lives of people. To date, a fair amount has been written about the process of Norwegianization [in Norwegian, *Norskifisering*] from various perspectives. It is important to bear in mind that Norway is a relatively young country with a small population of just over 4.5 million. With its constitution formed in 1814, the country is still in the midst of an ideological struggle to define itself for itself.[3] Investigating the implications of this in relation to popular music, media scholar Kate Augestad (1997), has noted how a sense of 'nostalgic utopia' is propagated through sets of traditions that are primarily intent on constructing romantic nationalism. Particularly prevalent in this construction is the connection between nature and nation, a seemingly integral component in the mythic discourses of national identity (Berkaak, 1996). In her critical analysis of Norwegian nationality, Augestad (1997: 142) emphasizes the ideological flavour of the west coast of Norway, *Vestland*, an area that strives to represent itself as part of a perfect and innocent nation eager to accommodate its inhabitants. Importantly, her critique reminds us that cultural diversity in this region far exceeds the homogeneous notion of national identity The implications of this are far-reaching. Pursuing this same question in relation to the musical preferences of Norwegians and the construction of national identity, cultural critic Anders Johansen has insisted that: 'The Norwegian people's music, the music we would rather play and listen to, is international pop and rock' (1995: 24). With reference to traditional folk music [*slåttemusikken*] and the problematics of national authenticity, Johansen rejects any significance of this in today's climate. In his approach there is a deep scepticism for the politics of 'national culture' [*Kulturpolitikk*] as promoted by the state and the hegemonic position it attempts to sustain within Norway, especially in the promotion of the *ekte norsk* [genuine Norwegian].[4] In many ways, Johansen's polemic has resonances in the more modernist tendencies of the sociologist Dag Østerberg, whose views on mass identity I will return to later.

The northernmost Norwegian university city of Tromsø has contributed significantly to the production of a wide breadth of Norwegian popular music, not least within the genres of commercial pop and dance. Emanating from Tromsø, Those Norwegians – the only musicians from Norway to be listed in *House: The Rough Guide* by Sean Bidder (1999) – provide a compelling case-study for questioning notions of identity. The track I have selected from the album *Kaminzky Park* (1997) fulfils two aims in this chapter: firstly, to consider how music can be read locally and, secondly, to explore the question of national identity against a shifting plane of global and local categories. In a general sense, my assertion is that Norwegian dance music is transnational and aligned to similar musical expressions found in localities all over Europe. The DJs and clubbers I have consulted verify that the dance scene in Norway mirrors the developments taking place in other European and North American countries. This is further substantiated by the fragmentation of dance music into myriad different styles in Norway. The club scene in Oslo alone in 1999 revealed a bewildering array of trends. Describing the 'genre-chaos' of the dance scene in Oslo, one national paper identified 16 new styles: beats, big beat, cheese, deep house, downtempo/chillout, drill'n'bass, eklektisk, jump up, Miami bass, minimalist techno, Netherlands trance, Norwegian house, nu skool, poptrance, psychedelic trance and tech-house (*Dagbladet*, 1999). Notably, each style was accompanied by a concise description of what the music signified. For example, Norwegian House, the style best that typifies the example we are looking at in this chapter, was depicted as 'buldrende, funky, episk og tidvis skranglete og stadig mer populært i utlandet' [booming, funky, epic and occasionally rickety and gradually more popular abroad].

'Da Kingue D'Mazda': Questions of Musical Expression and Social Commentary

Let us now turn to the track 'Da Kingue D'Mazda' by Those Norwegians. What kind of musical features characterize this dance track? What are the social signifiers that emerge from the house style Norwegian? And how might the mechanisms of identification in the musical processes set up a trajectory of desire that can be understood as inter-subjective in their representation?

Layers of guitar riffs wash over a bouncy, booming bass line to add depth to the intensity of the repetitive four-on-the-floor kick beats. Throughout this five-minute track, a dash of shuffle-brushes on scraping hi-hats are worked into the polished programming of cyclical grooves. Repetition is organized through the sequencing of grooves into the mix, which demarcates the textural directionality and quirkiness linked to compositional experimentation. Indeed, the inventive use of sounds capture a retro, deep house style through analogue-type samples, filtering effects and 'dry' reverb. As with most club tracks, there is a coolness in the slick production that instantly conjures up fun on the dance floor. To a large extent, the retro flavour of the technological tricks expose a simulation of what one might consider an authentic ideal. Mostly, this is borne out by the cheesy synth solo in the middle part of the song, which emulates one of the early analogue synths from the late 1970s. In my reading of this track, the coolness in musical expression seeps through the gestural drive of the drum patterns and their metric organization as the groove articulates a wealth of musical ideas. More specifically, the rhythmic phrasing is organized by a central kit riff that consists of a shuffle-type feel with four-on-the-floor kick drum beats coupled with snares and handclaps on the second and fourth beats. Added to this are shakers, triggered always on the offbeat, which are spiced up with closed hi-hats on the second and fourth offbeats. As the groove is processed, so the aesthetic of the mix becomes more discernible.[5]

In 'Da Kingue D'Mazda' the level of socio-political commentary provides a link to understanding the sounds themselves as the recording spells out the absence of the artist through the sampled voice. Self-parody is grounded in the thick Norwegian accent of the recurring vocal sample (I'm da king d'mazda). Here it is the patterns of notes, syllables and gestures in this hook that provide a crucial point of identification especially at the end of phrases where the backing cuts out as the words enter. I would suggest the deliberate slip to the 'da' instead of 'the' embodies a potent self-parody which the majority of Norwegian youth, who are fairly fluent in English (their second language), will pick up on and interpret as being either incompetent or just downright silly. As in the other Nordic countries, emphasis is placed on the way young people speak English, which can denote both coolness in attitude and humorous intent. As the track's title and hook line suggest, the reference to being 'da king of Mazda' subsumes a satirical subtext that has to do with not being able to articulate the voiced, dental fricative 'th' sound. Satire is further exploited in the written form of the title, with the use of the French genitive form, d'Mazda, 'of Mazda'. Here the reference to another 'da' form further heightens an ironic recourse to self-deprecation through the use of put-on broken English. Similarly, the spelling of king as 'kingue' on the album cover highlights the playfulness and deliberate pretentiousness of the clever title.[6]

Notably, the sampled phrase 'I'm da king d'mazda' is the only lyrical reference in the track. For this reason, the words are memorable and worthy of further consideration. Aware that my suggestion that this vocal sample has a humorous quality raises a number of questions linked to personal interpretation, I am keen to further explore how musical meanings are produced inter-subjectively. Consider an intentional put-on English accent by a Norwegian and the idea that this might be received as funny. By whom and in what kind of context might this evoke a distinctly humorous response? And to what extent does humour operate at a local and national level? Identifying nuances in the voice, its inflections and accent in a foreign (albeit a second) language as quirky clearly raises a number of issues. The challenge of appreciating or responding to humour is that 'you have to be there' and conversant with the idiolect being represented. It is worth considering the obtuse, irregular and often disconcerting conditions for humour if and when they cross national boundaries especially through musical expression. Furthermore, in considering what makes a musical gesture or vocal utterance seem amusing, we might ask what are the conditions that produce humour in any given context? Again we are back to the question of dialects of representation, musical style and inter-subjectivity. Whenever I have played this track to classes of Norwegian students, there has been an instant reaction of amusement when the vocal sample enters. Conversely, in England, at both conferences and seminars, when I presented this track, responses were noticeably indifferent until the humorous intent was explained. From this, it became evident that there are any number of reasons connected to a national, as well as a local, context as to why we find something humorous or not.

On the matter of humour, that it results from a *release of tension* is a well-worn assertion that has been addressed more or less rigorously in Freud's seminal discourse on joking and its connection to the unconscious (1976 [1905]). Freud's concept deals with the psychological restraints linked to cultural and social phenomena and how these often make it impossible to express oneself freely or easily. It is well known that pent-up mental conditions often find their outlet in jokes, ridicule and laughter, which confront the very things our instincts are inhibited by. Not surprisingly, issues dealing with nationalistic traits are one of the main topics of jokes. How these filter through musical expression is what concerns me most here. In 'Da Kingue D'Mazda', humorous intent raises a number of issues that should not go amiss. For instance, coded humour and joking might be considered as polysemic when it comes to understanding how pleasure is disseminated through this track. As for the deliberate silliness of the title and the poking-fun, put-on Norwegian–English accent in the vocal sample, we might consider this in itself a form of submission, insofar as it releases oneself from the normal strictures of grammatical correctness. In a sense, such an act signifies a loosening up as Those Norwegians draw on their own unique brand of expression: a mockery of the linguistic, political and global constraints that impinge on their everyday lives. At any rate, the repetitive vocal sample bespeaks an idiolect that is exclusive, signifying to the insider a pronounced caricaturization. Indeed, one of the most important ways in which we experience popular music is through sympathetic responses to artists and bands. In this complicated process, the recognition of playfulness determines how empathy in the listener functions. For one thing, sensing humour in music is an imaginative activity, and this is based on the role of identification and the manner by which we engage in styles, trends, idioms and, most importantly, cultural hierarchies.

Commodities of Mass Production

The mood evoked in this track is, I believe, not one of triumph, but more of resignation through a sense of regional indifference in the face of globalization. One might ponder the purpose of the references to Mazdas, and how this subject matter contributes to the overall sense of meaning. The term Mazda, at least within the context of this track, throws up a number of issues directly relating humour to identity. To start with, the tensions between consumerism and materialism speak directly to Norwegian youth, as much as in any other affluent Western national context. In terms of its social function, the Mazda car has been used to symbolize a specific binary positioning of *us* and *them*, 'us' referring to those who are deemed more politically and environmentally correct through non-ownership of a car. I want to characterize the binarism of us and them in order to highlight the exclusive role of humorous intent in the stereotyping of the Other. Conjoined with the codes of musical address are the references to mass production in the car industry that underwrite the intention of purpose in 'Da Kingue D'Mazda'. It is as if Those Norwegians' polemic redraws the boundaries of a capitalist ideology to include their own more fragmented mediation in terms of style and aesthetic. In this regard, the style employed in 'Da Kingue D'Mazda' can be read openly as some general response to the consumer durables of Norway's economic boom. The car, like all consumables, denotes a lot more than a referent to recent urbanization patterns: the Mazda symbolizes cheapness, functionality and, not least, the era of the private motorist.[7] For sociologist Dag Østerberg, the brand Mazda alone provides a striking metaphor for the sprawling effect of Greater Oslo's expansion over a radius of 100 km. Significantly, Østerberg (1998: 41) employs the term 'Mazdaism' not only to identify the plight of the private motorist, but also to distinguish the mass from the elite. In no uncertain terms, his critique attacks the growth of materialism and new capitalist liberalism in Norway's capital city. The essence of this perspective is indisputably modernist as Østerberg conceptualizes Mazdaism in order to position Norwegian identity at the heart of capitalist trends and global change. In actual fact, Mazdaism becomes an ideological tool for mourning the downfall of the nation-state through a Marxist-oriented narrative that links class to social status:

> Den mazdaistiske fortetning er dels et avtrykk av, og dels bestyrker den, lønnstakernes oppsplitting. Dermed får samfunnsklassenes skiller og motsetninger ikke noe tydelig avtrykk i det sosio-materielle feltet. (Østerberg, 1998: 39)

> [The phenomenon of Mazdaistic condensation is in part an effect, and in part a reinforcement of the splitting of the working class. In this manner the divisions and contradictions between the social classes have no clear imprint in the socio-material field.][8]

This observation of social decline through the Mazdaistic effect on the masses signifies a defining moment for Østerberg, as all the negative implications of consumerism are assembled within a cultural framework of Marxist alignment to Western modernity. This constitutes a space where the subscription to social fragmentation through materialism is considered problematic (Berkaak, 1996).

There is an interesting slippage between Østerberg's and Those Norwegians' perspective on Mazdas. In the case of the latter, one might sense a parodic reaction to an affluent working class through the stylistic codes of the music which, in turn, elicits a reaction of indifference to the Japanese car industry. At the same time, the uncoolness of this, which Norwegians refer to as being *harry*,[9] suggests a ludic display of irony that projects a progressive, self-reflective and industrialized Norway. Full evidence of this construction is discernible in the recording of 'Da Kingue D'Mazda', where live samples of nature are expertly mixed with traffic noise to sex up the effects of industrialization and prosperity. Notably, the components within the musical text are interchangeable with nonmusical references to industrialization. The point I am arriving at is that in such sonic experience, an employment of wry commentary becomes contingent on the opening up of a dialogic space where meaning is disseminated on many levels that deal with national identity, not least through the compositional regulation of crazed samples and catchy grooves. Musically, there is always this sense that a critical dialectic is established in this track for the individual. Indeed, all the sounds we experience are based on signification and communication no matter how they are grasped within various cultural contexts. This dialectic occurs through the full ramifications of the technological processing – slickness in control, choice of sounds and timbres, editing of samples – where an intentional play on a materialistic aesthetic discloses a number of elements relating to identity. In a sense, the production behind dance tracks can be understood in relation to modes of consumption: dance trends operate to position the body through socially encoded qualities that confirm a specific locality. Indeed, the site of this practice engages a consciousness that is all about an awareness of difference, and often this is played out by attitudes of indifference. Intertextually, technology meshes the local with the transnational as patterns are invented and squeezed into a musical arrangement that forms part of a cultural matrix. Within Northern Europe, dance trends have much to do with the development of the discursive constitution of the popular and its influence on the everyday lives of young Europeans. And, as an outgrowth of industrialized societies, the *popular* in music extracts, at the same time as it absorbs, the very social material that impacts on our daily lives. Thus, music is an ideological matter that is bound up in environments and social processes which determine what our identities most signify for us.

So far, my assumption presumes a constructive function whereby sound asserts a difference in the form of a double-take on dance music. As I see it, 'Da Kingue D'Mazda' is self-positioning in its relationship to a mobile locality where the regional, the national, effortlessly becomes the transnational. The nonchalant rhetoric of the musical representation signals a kind of indifference that works to destabilize through satire. Stylistically, we might consider dance music as a theatre of appropriation where structuration dramatizes musical borrowing, in the form of pastiche, by the construction of new liminal spaces. This is most evident in the musical processing of repetition where one cliché blends with another to critique the idealist goals and glaring paradoxes of an aspiring egalitarian society. It is as if Those Norwegians' construction of cyclic loops and mechanical riffs into compelling grooves through technological polish is intended to remind us that their landscape, in Tromsø, also belongs to the era of the jet plane, the Mazda car and the satellite dish. They fully recognize that 'Utkantnorge' (the Norwegian periphery) is scarcely that picturesque, slightly anachronistic kind of place which tourist brochures try to depict it as' (Eriksen 1993), and, in the case of Tromsø, we see an industrialized locality that is as much part of the globalized nation-state in its economic and cultural mission as the capital, Oslo.

National Identity and Indifference

The point I am arriving at here is that constructions of the local can be represented within a style that is characterized by a slick recording and production techniques that ultimately activate and encode matters of identity. In such moments of reception there exists a pleasure that belongs to identifying those qualities of identity that lie deep within oneself. From this perspective, however, there is little that is immanent when it comes to understanding the construction of one national identity over the other in the domain of Euro-dance music. Such sentiments are borne out knowingly by the voice sample, 'I'm da king d'mazda', the function of which is diegetic in its transporting of the narrative structure of identification. Of all the musical codes, the spoken voice is the consistent signifier of identity – it captures a playfulness that draws us into the popular. At any rate, the accents on the word 'King' and 'Mazda' blatantly evoke a silliness that parodies the materialistic show-off. This is underwritten by the bouncy groove, a central code within the track that produces a trajectory of fun through sarcasm. It is from this position, then, that the track becomes not only accessible but self-reflexive, and comprehensible to the listener/participant. Above all, the voice with its foreign English accent, and its location in the mix, denotes a context where the meeting of traditions and innovation takes place through a cunning interplay of difference.

All this returns us to the question of how one defines and negotiates constructs of national identity and (in)difference. That Those Norwegians might assume that we-know-that-they-know-that-we-know they are from the small remote town of Tromsø in Norway does not seem that important in the end. Within a European perspective, the boundaries of dance music are fluid and interchangeable and this might explain why dance trends easily cross over national boundaries. Indeed, the effect of Those Norwegians' musical production is to unmask the same authentic (or inauthentic) preferences that other musical genres aspire to. In dance music, clearing the local space frequently means accessing musical styles without lyrics and all the baggage that comes with language. What we hear in the solitary sample phrase 'I'm da king d'mazda' is a constructedness that is inter-subjective. Importantly though, the musical markers of parody, with all their attendant pleasures, need not be read cynically; on the contrary, they might be considered as mediating a self-assurance in the reinscription of the local. As if to labour this point, Those Norwegians feign their idiomatic control of English through a series of musical codes that deconstruct the cultural tunnel between Norway and the Anglo-American music industry. In fact, the track 'Da Kingue D'Mazda' makes explicit the trappings of national stereotypes that might just take themselves too seriously at a local level. In this way, the frivolity and mockery in constructing oneself (in opposition to the Other) locally can reveal a more serious clue to the questions surrounding global romanticism (Kvifte, 2001). Moreover, the idea of Norwegian identity within a Scandinavian context cannot be overlooked, not least when national sovereignty is fiercely defended in the wake of the fairly recent dissolution of Sweden's control over Norway (1905). Indeed, what seems to underwrite the existence of a Scandinavian identity is a pressing need for cultural exchange between common language groups, political policy and economic cooperation. In this respect, it is a salient fact that the three Scandinavian countries of Denmark, Sweden and Norway have always measured their collective identity against the cultural imperialism of large nation-states and the intensely monolingual voice of English within a European and global context.

Finally, in reflecting on the Mazda, with all its supposed irritating markers of taste and ridicule, I would conclude that Those Norwegians promote a postmodern version of the contested marketplace. Features such as collage and textural heterogeneity through technological manipulation typify the aesthetic associated with dance music. At the same time, a type of light-heartedness in the style signals a playfulness that I read as a flaunting of artifice, an artifice that is captured by crazed samples and a fresh approach to drum programming that forces disco into house. In the end, the track seems to state 'although we are Norwegians we are not that different from you'. And, it is through the discursive constitution of their musical expression and indifference that we can begin to interpret the power of music as a unique carrier of social and cultural knowledge. In sum, then, by emphasizing the stylistic indicators of attitude, technological virtuosity and (in)difference, Those Norwegians reveal a translucency of intention that acknowledges the complexity of the nation state's conceptual parking lot and all the idiosyncrasies that we associate with the pull in four-wheel drives.

Notes

1	Acknowledgements to colleagues and students at the Department of Musicology, University of Oslo, whose opinions on Norwegian identity and popular music have provided many provocative and important ideas during the preparation of this chapter. I would also thank my groups of Norwegian master degree students who have offered helpful insights into conceptualizing the problematics of identity in a local and national landscape.

2	I have borrowed the term 'fixity' from Shepherd and Wicke (1997) to refer to the semiotic critique on musical signification. The position I hold on this is that music is void of meaning until meaning is ascribed to it through language. Reconciling the tensions between the arbitrary and the immanent signification of music has been a problem in musicology. A way forward is to consider the organization of culturally imposed differences of musical meaning at local level. When we experience dance music as joyous, escapist, fun and erotic, this is the result of personal interpretation within the boundaries of a cultural system rather than the 'immanent' fixing of musical coding within the message.

3	Following the Napoleonic wars, a Union of Crowns under the Treaty of Kiel handed Norway over to Sweden. Understandably resentful of this, the Norwegians convened a meeting at Eidsvoll Verk in April 1814, where a new Norwegian king was elected.

On 17 May 1814 a new constitution was completed. Yet, the new king, Christian Frederick, was not recognized by Sweden, which insisted that the Swedish king, Karl Johan, be instated. War was narrowly averted by an agreement for devolved power on Sweden's part. By 1905, Norway's international standing had improved through trade, especially in fishing and whale products. In this year, a constitutional referendum indicated virtually no support for the union with Sweden, and the Swedes were forced to recognize Norwegian sovereignty. Now with Haakon VII on the throne, a Norwegian constitutional monarchy was established, and Oslo was declared the capital of the new Kingdom of Norway.

4   Johansen draws our attention to the 800 state-funded cultural–historical museums, with a new one opening every second day, where the main agenda is to strengthen national identity. Johansen's central and most critical prognosis (1995: 12–13) is that the person who believes that 'culture' has long roots and traditions which can be described as 'ours', transporting with it forms and expressions that generations before us have given their thoughts and dreams to, is nothing short of a national romantic with (troublesome) leanings towards fundamentalism.

5   One type of sequencing I am referring to is cumulative where shorter riffs give way to longer ones through transformation. Throughout dance tracks such as the one under study here, the metric divisions of 4/4 are continuously transformed during their repetition by subtle repositionings of the 'beat' through syncopation and inflection. Gesturally, the rhythm is pulled around to the extent that we never actually encounter the same material twice. Unlike the forms of sequencing inherent in popular song, the linearity of club music depends on the continuous flow of material which hints at an open-ended repetition. For a more detailed discussion of this compositional process with reference to the example 'Da Kingue D'Mazda', see my earlier work (Hawkins, 1999, 2001).

6   With the title of this track, and especially the 'da' word, one cannot escape a number of other references within a Norwegian context. For example, another Norwegian group from the mid-1990s employed the 'da' in their name, Flava to da Bone, with all the inflections of humour one might expect.

7   The private motorist is taxed more in Norway than anywhere else in Europe, and, for many, owning a car symbolizes the epitome of selfishness. Collective transport is considered politically (and environmentally) correct.

8   Thanks for the translation into English by my colleagues Erling Guldbrandsen and Hallgjerd Aksnes.

9   This is a Norwegian reference to a person who lacks style and modesty and walks round with a big grin on their face trying to be smart. The term refers to someone who confidently flaunts their perceived economic status and shows off without any sensibility for style or irony.

Discography

Those Norwegians, 'Da Kingue D'Mazda', *Kaminzky Park* (Paper Records/Pagan USA, PAPCD00IX, 1997).

Afterword

Richard Middleton

Like the editors of this volume, I am writing from the vantage-point of a university that recently introduced a degree course in 'folk and traditional music'. The core focus of the course is on 'the traditions of these islands' (the title of one of the modules). But immediately questions arise. First of all, questions of political nomenclature. How should we describe 'these islands'? Do they include a 'United Kingdom' (it has been notably less united since Scotland and Wales were granted a certain level of autonomy), 'Britain' or 'Great Britain' (the latter suggesting an uncomfortable hangover of imperial pretension), or even the 'British Isles' (but why are they 'British?')? Where does this leave 'Ireland', and should we speak of 'Northern Ireland' or 'the North of Ireland'? A second group of questions has more to do with the actual music cultures. For such has been the degree of cross-influence, historically, between 'English', 'Scottish', 'Welsh' and 'Irish' traditional musics, so important have been the broader links, for example into Continental Europe or now involving the net of 'Celtic Connections' (including Brittany and Galicia) or the diasporas (the Irish in the USA, the Scots in Canada), and, more recently, so radical has been the impact of newer styles with less specific geographical identities (rock music, dance beats, jazz, and – broadest of all – 'world music'), that it proves all but impossible to distinguish and delimit separate traditions of these islands, and to tie them to national or quasi-national homes. Both sets of issues come together in the 'Northumbria question'. Since the course is located at Newcastle upon Tyne, it is natural that the strongest focus of all should be on the traditions of the north-east of England – an area still named in many contexts as 'Northumbria'. It is many centuries since Northumbria was a kingdom, stretching from the Humber to the Clyde, from the North Sea to the Irish Sea (its power was at its peak in the seventh century AD), yet this historical background suggests why its music is both specific and irreducibly hybrid. Recently, the British government offered the people of the north-east a regional assembly with a rather small amount of autonomy. The offer was decisively rejected – even though, on the cultural level, the rise of the 'Geordie Nation'[1] (accompanied now by the policy aim, familiar in declining industrial areas, of pursuing economic regeneration through cultural regionalism) has been inexorable.

Newcastle University is also the lead partner in a regional consortium whose music programmes have been awarded the status of Centre of Excellence in Teaching and Learning. The Centre's title (and its agenda) is 'Music and Inclusivity'. The concept of inclusivity points towards many of the buzzwords – pluralism, hybridity, multiculturalism – that are thematized in the discourse of globalization, together with its dialogical partner of localism. And on this level it would seem hard to take exception to it. Yet one wonders how far it is from the Blairite 'Big Tent', a favoured image offered by a cynical power strategy that can be all things to all men (and occasionally women) only because it is not very much to any of them. If everybody and everything are inside, what is left outside? Is there anything – any music, any musical politics – to which we would want to object? At a moment when the multiple articulations of political identity, mediated by a host of other factors (most obviously religion), have become particularly pressing, and in some contexts have taken on such murderous forms, it seems less than adequate to offer a simple hymn to the virtues either of the global or of the local.

I start with these two examples of local perspective not in order to advertise Newcastle to the world, but to make the point that the book itself emerges from particular locations, with all that implies. As an intervention, it is itself inscribed in the processes it documents. At the same time, those locations are also multiple and complex – as a glance at the contributors' biographies will confirm. It is the single most striking achievement of the book, I think, that it exposes so richly that complexity, as it affects the processes of musical production, dissemination and consumption. To retrieve the language of the editors' introduction, if 'nation' (and its cognates, substitutes and close relatives) had taken on the status of a 'vanishing mediator', how strongly it has re-emerged into view! And in what a multiplicity of forms! Since Freud, we know that the repressed will always return – and, often, in unforeseen or, perhaps, uncomfortable guises. Slavoj Žižek often points out that affiliations to identities such as 'nation' are rational only up to a point. What really makes them stick is something extra, a surplus in the subject – an obscene if often surreptitious enjoyment that comes with acceding to the call of a master (here, race, blood, language, leader; or even, could it be, just 'tradition'?). This is at its most obvious under totalitarian systems (the case of Serbia in the Yugoslav wars is a good example),[2] but is by no means confined to them. While it is certainly imperative that we work to make visible what seemed to vanish, it does not follow, then, that the outcome will always be politically welcome. Still, what is clear is that, whether we think synchronically (so that 'nation' features as the middle term between 'local' and 'global') or diachronically (in which case the nation-state marks the passage between the pre- and late-modern), no simple three-moment schema can measure up to the complexity of actually existing world society.

It is useful at this point to return to Žižek's discussion of the 'vanishing mediator' in *For They Know Not What They Do* (Žižek, 2002: 179–97). In dialectics, he suggests here (with support from Hegel), we need to count not to three – as is conventionally assumed – but to *four*! How so? The argument is that between the first moment (the first 'immediacy' or 'positivity') and the second (the 'absolute' or 'external' negation of the first) comes a prior moment of negation. This 'inner negation' of the first moment emerges when we think about its conditions of existence – the internal antagonisms or 'lack' that alone make it possible. Having emerged, and having provoked the mediation represented by the second (external) negation, this first negation then 'vanishes' – it is the 'vanishing mediator' – but in the process it has pushed the dialectical movement to a four-step shape. Another way of looking at this, Žižek suggests, is to grasp that the first negation emerges *retroactively*: the effect of the second negation is to change our understanding of the very first moment because the inner contradictions that enabled that moment have now come into view – thus, as 'national' appears, the meaning of the moment that precedes it shifts: it becomes, precisely, 'pre-national'. Perhaps we could push the argument even further. If the middle term in the conventional triad relates to the first by double negation, maybe a similar relation holds between the second and third; negation doubled then squared. (This would fit with Hegel's view of totality – at least in Žižek's reading (2002: 99) – as always 'squared totalization': a system actually built out of a series of *failed* totalizations, each one leading 'logically' – that is, through its failure, to the next.) What is more, if retroactivity – a concept that Žižek takes from psychoanalysis – were to be fully realized, the always reversible relationship between 'origin' and 'effect' (as in the relationship between 'fantasy' and 'reality') might provoke us to speculate on the possibility of dialectical movement in *both* directions. This is not to imagine that we can 'go back' historically (which would amount to a symptom of 'vulgar nostalgia'), but rather that looking back along the chain of 'failures' might make them available for reinscription in new mediations. This, as I see it, would be to pursue to its fullest extent Žižek's frequent injunction to 'tarry with the negative'.

The question now becomes: where is the point of leverage (in other terms, the location of *agency*)? In an alternative reading of the second of his four moments, Žižek argues that it can also function as the moment of *event*, of maximum 'openness' – hence, as a moment of heightened subjectivity, when contingent choices become (what would subsequently come to seem) necessary (and the subject vanishes again). The issue is whether negativity is to be regarded as merely intermediary, a movement between two 'normalities', or as radical refusal. It is noteworthy that Žižek also translates this system into the form of a 'Greimasian semiotic square' (see Greimas, 1987). The idea of such squares is to lay out synchronically a particular semantic field in such a way that the full range of modes of difference is represented. Thus in Figure 1 the S1/S2 relationship represents an opposition or contrary, but another level – -S1/-S2, the level of contradiction or negation – is always implied as well, even if it is less overt, lying 'below' the level of the first. In terms of Žižek's dialectic, then, the movement would be from S1 through its internal contradiction to its contrary or antithesis (S2) and finally to the 'negation of the negation' (-S2). Figure 2 shows one of Žižek's examples.

For Žižek, as already pointed out, the critical movement – the most 'open' moment – is the second (marked X for this reason; the moment of the 'vanishing mediator', representing – if we put it in Lacanian terms – the subject's encounter with the Real). In Fredric Jameson's adaptation of Greimas (1972: 162–8; 1987: xvi), however, the key position – the one that typically takes longest to fill out and is therefore the most open – is the fourth, the negation of the negation. This may be the difference between a pre- and a post-psychoanalytic teleology. Nevertheless, it is worth noting that elsewhere in Žižek's account (2002: 117–37), when he discusses Hegel's 'modes of judgement', it is the *fourth* mode that, in completing

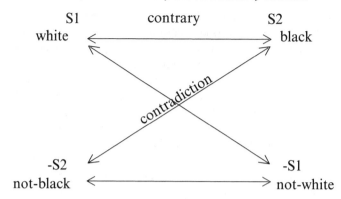

Figure 1   The Greimasian semiotic square

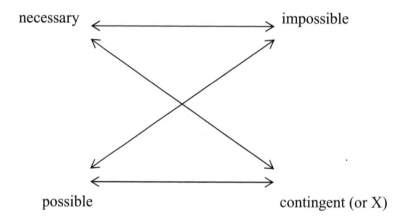

Figure 2   Žižek's Greimasian square

the dialectic, does so by positing contingency (retroactively) as necessity. This is the 'judgement of the Notion'– that is, how and under what circumstances an object measures up to its Notion – and it corresponds to the Hegelian proposition that the dialectic must take the form not only of Substance (necessity as self-movement) but also of Subject (contingency reformulated as necessity, the effect of particularizing subjectivity as it arises at the point of a gap in Substance, where Substance is inadequate to itself). Here is how Žižek puts it:

> 'Dialectics' is ultimately a teaching on how necessity arises out of contingency: on how a contingent *bricolage* produces a result which 'transcodes' its initial conditions into internal necessary moments of its self-reproduction. It is therefore Necessity itself which depends on contingency: the very gesture which changes necessity into contingency is radically contingent. (2002: 129)

The critical question now becomes which Subject will occupy this position. Far less significant is the arithmetical issue (second or fourth?); indeed, the confusion here might be taken as a symptom of the possibility already raised, that in principle *we can start at any point and move in any direction*. Is this how the famous 'negative dialectics' of Adorno can be sparked back into life?

Figures 3 and 4 – leaving all interpretation for readers to pursue – are two attempts to adapt the system to the subject matter of this book. (Here 'national' is a movable *actant* which might take different guises in different positions.)[3]

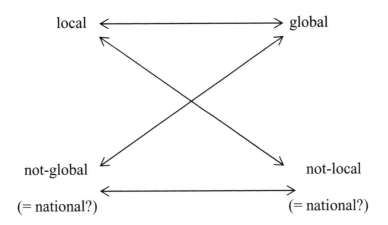

Figure 3   Local/global as a Greimasian square

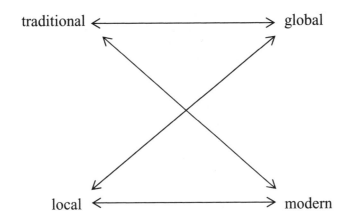

Figure 4   A second elaboration of the local/global as a Greimasian square

Although both Jameson and Žižck, in their different ways, translate the device of the 'semiotic square' into a form capable of representing dialectical movement (into 'squared totalization' one might say), there remains, of course, a danger with all such structuralist models that they pull thought towards synchronic closure: there is no visible 'outside'. Strangely, much the same comment might be made of this model's apparent intellectual opposite – what I will term, very crudely, 'positivism', including such tendencies as the 'transcendental empiricism' of Deleuze. Here too, albeit from a different direction, is an image of a One, an absolute totality, populated by a multitude of laterally related forces, and again there is no beyond. This is the world inhabited by two much discussed books on the politics of globalization by Michael Hardt and Antonio Negri, *Empire* (2000) and *Multitude* (2004). For Hardt and Negri, in the state of 'Empire' into which the world is moving, the nation-state (even the USA) loses its leading role, becoming at most a constituent in a multi-levelled network of powers, including also transnational corporations and global institutions such as the World Bank and International Monetary Fund, which together manage the global capitalist system. Increasingly, the registers of the political, economic, social and cultural coincide under the emergent hegemonic mode of 'immaterial' (that is, information- and affect-related) production; the product, then, is social life itself, the authority one of 'bio-power'. But resistance ('bio-political' resistance) also fills the social space. No longer located purely in any single class, or any other social group, still less in the 'people', this is identified with the 'multitude' – 'singularities that act in common' (Hardt and Negri, 2004: 105),[4] whose home is indeed 'the common': democracy moving beyond the structures of representation towards 'absolute democracy', the rule of everybody by everybody.

In his review of *Multitude*, Tom Nairn (2005a) takes Hardt and Negri to task – rightly, in my view – for their apocalyptic tone, in which careful political analysis is subordinated to a quasi-religious, indeed millenarian rapture; the sense of a utopian 'last time', grounded in a Spinozan absolutism, runs strangely parallel, Nairn points out, to the fundamentalist fantasies of those they oppose – the 'end of history' fanatics in Washington DC, both religious and secular.[5] Žižek's critique of *Empire* (Žižek, 2004: 195–202) also focuses on this absolutism. Democracy cannot be absolute, he argues, because any democratic articulation of a specific position performs itself out in preference to those it excludes; by contrast, true 'absolute democracy' could actualize itself only through terror. Similarly, Žižek goes on, 'multitude' can function only *as* resistance – that is, as countervailing movements on a stage laid out by a contextualizing authority (here, global capital); for the multitude to take power would inevitably produce the need for a substitute Master-Signifier (most likely, a totalitarian leader). Although Hardt and Negri are militantly anti-transcendentalist, their ontology of immanentist vitalism (which has a philosophical lineage running from Spinoza to Deleuze, both of whom they reference frequently) relies on an essence (what is common) that is treated as logically preceding (rather than taking account of) any of the social antagonism they describe. In Hegelian language, they are all Substance, and no Subject; and yet, just as their text is actually full of subjects that do not declare themselves ('we can and must intervene': Hardt and Negri, 2004: 263), so their concept of a multitudinous essence turns in effect into some kind of (surely transcendental) subject: 'the multitude is itself an active subject' and its task is nothing less than to bring into being 'a new race or, rather, a new humanity' (2004: 339, 356). Can we see here the 'millennial mysticism', identified in many 'world music' discourses by Martin Stokes (2003), pumped up to a particularly melodramatic point?

Despite the importance of these criticisms, however, we should credit Hardt and Negri not only with many telling arguments in both their books, but also with a thesis possessing an expansive and imaginative reach that, unlike many other globalization theories, at least attempts to measure up to the scale of the shift we are living through. Moreover, one of their key insights is pertinent to my own discussion here. This is the idea that, as the 'imperial' system approaches fulfilment – that is, as it fills the world – all sense of an *outside* – of an excluded Other – of the type which has sustained the identity of all previous social and political identities tends to be dismantled. We are not there yet. But we can see the moment rushing towards us when, on the one hand the world economy is, so to speak, *full* – that is, the supply of consumption capacity and of labour is insufficient to meet the demands of continuing expansion – and, on the other hand, the resources of natural capital (energy, water, minerals, soil productivity) come up to their limits against a backdrop of declining biodiversity and climatic efficacy. At that moment, sooner or later, 'there is no more outside' (Hardt and Negri, 2000: 186).[6] An awareness of this, usually unacknowledged or disavowed, is what now constitutes our political unconscious.[7] Characteristically, Hardt and Negri push their argument too far, suggesting that: 'In Empire, no subjectivity is outside, and all places have been subsumed in a general "non-place"' (2000: 353). On the contrary, the implications for subjectivity, and for the network of social, cultural and political affiliations on which it depends, are better understood in terms of a rebound mechanism: what used to be outside must be projected, in new ways or with new intensities, back inside. We can think of this as a new twist on the Lacanian deployment of the Möbius strip. Lacan uses this topological figure to point out the fuzziness of the boundary between 'inside' and 'outside': in traversing the strip (a rectangle twisted once, its ends joined up), we seem to cross from one face to the other but there is only one surface and only one edge – and we end up where we started. Lacan's concept of *extimité* marks the fact that the outside is always already inside the subject. While the psychoanalytic advance had thus already got to this idea – and indeed first enabled us to think it – Hardt and Negri give us a way to politicize it: by siting the idea itself directly on the social stage, they reveal its own *extimité*, for the outside was inside the body politic all the time. In a sense the Lacanian identity mechanism of the mirror phase is ratcheted up a gear, socialization doubled (as it were) producing the context for reflection squared: a sort of mirror dialectic, in which meaning can bounce, anamorphically, in many directions (and again one wonders if this is how the 'negative dialectic' might be forced back into movement).

It is in this context that the figure of the 'nation' must be rethought, not least for musical practice. It is important for the subject – musical or cultural no less than individual – that mechanisms of distinction and identification, including relationships with a Master-Signifier (a Big Other) continue to subsist; otherwise the result may be psychosis. But under hyper-*extimité*, identifications are 'scrambled'; as Others are internalized socially, borders are problematized. This, it seems to me, describes the situation that many if not all the 'world', 'national' and 'local' musics explored in this book inhabit. It is certainly the home for the many hybrid musics of the New Europeanness, as Philip Bohlman (2004: 276–331) calls it; since 1989, musical expressions of nationalism and other ethnic identities have undoubtedly been resurgent in Europe, but, as he points out, in new, mutable, multivalent and often inchoate forms. Consider the case of 'Irish music' as discussed by John O'Flynn (I mean the music labelled as such, not simply music produced in Ireland). At first positioned as subaltern – as the music of a self-consciously postcolonial state – this has moved to a hegemonic position within the symbolic economy of musical nationalism, functioning as the dominant fraction of the 'Celtic connection' and as a widely admired model for 'post-traditional' musical politics. This move clearly maps the shift of the Irish state itself from 'developing' status into a 'Celtic Tiger' incorporated within the core of the transnational economy (and, indeed, the music works as a brand within this economy as much as Guinness does). But at a deeper level what has happened here, surely, is that the music found that its previous Other had vanished, or at least had been transmuted into the shapeless flows of imperial capital; it was thus forced to fold back on itself (with a Möbius twist), assuming a position strangely *outside itself*. Or think of rap music. In the 1980s and early 1990s, this seemed clearly to be the voice of an internal colony in the USA, a 'hip-hop nation'; yet, since then American rap has become the dominant within a global rap coalition (willing or unwilling – the irony is, of course, particularly piquant in the case of France, as comes out in reading Brian George's chapter). Once again, an external limit has been reached and the music has folded back on itself, a slave becoming *at the same time* a master. Perhaps much the same applies to the case of Hispanic popular musics, both at the level of specific genres (for instance, the *flamencos jóvenes* discussed by the editors in their introduction, or the technobanda of the Los Angeles *barrios* discussed by Helena Simonett) and at the level of the musical 'latin' as a whole, as this has traversed the continents, internally and externally.

It is noticeable that all these music cultures are diasporic.[8] So, too, is Jewish music, unmentioned in this book but prominent in Bohlman's (2004) book, and another instructive example. Here is a culture that, of traumatic necessity, ended up filling the world, as it were, but then rebounding to a singular point – to Palestine/Israel, where a nationalist struggle, which is at once a symptom of a transglobal network of power, has conjured up a musical field riven by multiple ruptures (Euro/Yiddish/American/'Oriental') but at the same time with unmistakable global resonances: what had been expelled returns to the centre. Dana International's winning 1998 Eurovision Song Contest song, 'Diva', offers a striking focus. With an 'international' musical style out of Eurodisco, tricked out with orientalist gestures returning to haunt the metropolis that spawned them, the song's lyrics turn the singer's body inside out, into a body politic, 'larger than life', with 'senses nobody else has', on 'a stage which is all hers' – she is 'hysteria', 'an empire'. This is musical trash which indeed trashes borders, a point rammed home by the singer's transsexual identity.[9]

It is not surprising that diasporic musics feature prominently; their otherness has been forced to the edge of the world and has returned to the centre, on the rebound. That the two most striking cases – African-American and Jewish – became, ironically, indispensable components of the *mainstream* American popular song lineage of the twentieth century suggests that Jacques Attali (1985) was right all along – music may not exactly predict coming change in political economy but it certainly seems to have the power to encapsulate at an early stage what is coming to be – just as the fact that this extraordinary phenomenon goes largely unremarked is a sure sign that, as quasi-national mediators, they vanished. The 'double consciousness' model of subjectivity which W.E.B. Du Bois (1999 [1903]) theorized for African-American culture, but which (*mutatis mutandis*) may be generalized across to other diasporic cultures as well, should thus be rethought in the context of 'empire': with the end of outside, the self that is always already doubled with an other claimed as a self (and vice versa) is becoming normal. But to put identities in question in this way, to side-step interpellations, is inevitably to create instability, and the shaking voices (and often bodies too) of many African-American and Jewish singers point up the fact that at the root of these traditions lie founding traumas that may well mark this symptomology as a form of cultural hysteria.[10] To what extent might this also apply to other music cultures discussed in this book?

The mention of hysteria may rouse Lacanian minded readers (not to mention Žižekians) from their slumbers. And there is certainly grist that can be milled here. I am struck by the structural similarity between the 'dialectical squares' and Lacan's schema for the functions of discourse.[11] It would be nonsensical simply to conflate them; they come out of different intellectual contexts and are aimed at somewhat different problems. Still, in both cases we are dealing with formulae that understand the construction of meaning as bound up in *movement* – movement that implicates both subjects and social forces. It is telling too that, even though Lacan's schema takes the form not so much of a square linking dialectical moments as a formula linking discursive positions, here again there is a distinction between an upper level where overt factors are represented and a lower level where more implicit or repressed factors are located (Figure 5).

For Lacan there are four fundamental modes of discourse, which he associates with the Master, the University, the Hysteric and the Analyst, respectively. These are created by the variable positions in the formula taken up by four key factors: the Master-Signifier (S_1), the System of Knowledge (S_2), the (always already divided) Subject ($) and lastly the issue of this division – the object of desire which covers the subject's lack and stands for excess, Plus-de-Jouir (a). The Discourse of the Master, for example, is shown in Figure 6.

Figure 5   Lacan's schema for the functions of discourse

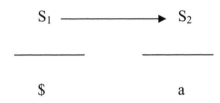

Figure 6   Lacan's Discourse of the Master

The position of agency is occupied by a Master-Signifier (in our context, it could be 'Nation' or it could be 'Capital'), which ties together for the subject – creates an identity from – the whole field of relevant knowledge (S_2). In the process, the entire system of the divided subject and his fantasies is suppressed – it is this that 'vanishes' – including even the divisions and supporting desires which structure those who take up the Master's position, who speak on his behalf. It is not difficult to see how this applies to the case of capitalist globalization, and how this Master learned his tricks from the pre-existing methods of nation-states (and Hegel – the Hegel of rational state theory – may be implicated in this).

How might we escape such totalizing structures? Unlike the Greimasian square, Lacan's schema includes the capacity for the four factors to move, clock-like, round the four positions in the formula.[12] The key lies in which factor occupies the position of Agent; thus to release what Masters make 'vanish' we need to supplant them in that position. Who is this 'we'? The Discourse of the Hysteric may point us in the direction of an answer. It should be pointed out that, although the clinical condition of hysterical neurosis has its specificity, nevertheless for Lacan (following Freud) there is also a sense in which, despite the fact that the hysterical subject is usually referred to in the feminine, all subjects are, to some extent, hysterics. Hysteria is normal. This Discourse places the divided Subject, in 'her' alienation, in all the negative conditions of her subjectivity (to recall Žižek's account of the dialectic), in the key position (Figure 7). The Hysteric, then, refuses official interpellations (master-signifiers), centring her desire (a) around a symptomatology which reveals her alienation as such. This subversion is addressed to an Other in the form of a demand for the provision of a new Master-Signifier (indeed, in the clinical condition, the desire is routed through an attempted identification with this Master), which in turn produces an alternative value-system (S_2). Thus, while the Hysteric's insistence that lack *is* Truth and that

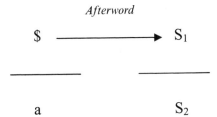

Figure 7   Lacan's Discourse of the Hysteric

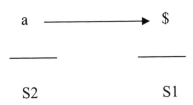

Figure 8   The Discourse of the Analyst

this situation is permanent marks her out as the only real realist, at the same time her discourse cannot move past the moment of contradiction: the negation of the negation, we might say, lies beyond her. What, then, would it mean, in the context of the struggle for musical identifications, if we were to set out to hystericize our politics?

For Lacan, the Discourse of the Hysteric is a step on the way to the Discourse of the Analyst, which is the only discourse where the possibility of *revolution* lies (Figure 8). Here the subject's fantasy (a) takes centre stage, coaxed into visibility; hence the subject, albeit never freed from networks of 'mastery', but reconciled to his own alienation, is enabled to construct new, more fluid, manifestly conflictual Master-Signifiers. Moreover, beyond the fantasy, once it has been 'traversed', lies the level of Drive – the pulsations of the fragmented body in its relation with the traumatic impossibility of the Real of *jouissance*. Žižek (2002: 272–3) has written of an *ethic of the drive*. If the imperative of a hysterical ethic is 'to keep the *desire* alive at any price' (2002: 271), the point of the analytic discourse, and of the level of drive it will tendentially reveal, is 'to mark repeatedly the trauma as such, in its very "impossibility", in its non-integrated horror … This, then, is the point where the Left must not "give way": it must preserve the traces of all historical traumas, dreams and catastrophes which the ruling ideology of the "End of History" would prefer to obliterate – it must become itself their living monument' (2002: 273).

Some of those traumas are marked in the musics explored in this book; they are 'monuments', too, to dreams and catastrophes lying historically 'behind' the globalization ideology, 'before' but also possibly 'beyond' its moment. If, as seems likely, the self-introjection of the world-system calls up an increased demand for a psychoanalytic understanding of politics, a path that seeks the intertwining of hysterical and analytical discourses looks the right strategy. How exactly this will work is difficult to say. Perhaps we will not know until we try it.

Notes

1   For readers not from the UK, the term 'Geordie' may be unfamiliar: it is a term (somewhat contested) applied to those who were raised in Tyneside in the north-east of England and refers both to the identity and to the dialect which retains elements of Old English.

2   See Robert Hudson's chapter in this volume.

3   The term 'actant', taken from Greimas, refers to a set of semiotic elements within a narrative which together add up to some kind of uniform agency: it can work in ways similar to an 'actor' but need not be a single person.

4   This is really Deleuze's 'body without organs' (Deleuze and Guattari, 1988: 149–66) transposed to the level of the political body.

5   Some of Nairn's other criticisms (though not all) are less justified, I think.

6   I am aware that this perspective could look uncomfortably close to Hardt and Negri's absolutism and hence to the 'end of history' illusion. What distinguishes it (I believe) is the point that not only difference, but also antagonism, is likely to increase rather than disappear; if contradictions can no longer be 'resolved' by projecting difference outside, then we are going to have to get much more used to dealing, on social as well as on personal levels, with its introjection.

7   Interestingly, in writing about the 2005 Edinburgh G8 summit, Nairn comes close to the basic Hardt–Negri position. He points out that in all its previous stages capitalism had defined itself by contrasts and struggle with what it was against – but now it seems to itself to stand alone: 'capitalism needs symbiosis. Or to put it another way, it needs to breathe an air it can never itself manufacture or supply … Following the denouement of 1989, these historical assets had largely disappeared: what historical materialism had castigated as "bourgeois society" was not merely victorious but alone – condemned to the preposterous life-raft of neo-liberal orthodoxy.' However, 'there is no such thing as capitalism "as such" outside think-tanks … Its air has to come from somewhere else, and this cannot be pre-packaged, bought and sold' (Nairn 2005b: 20). I agree with Nairn that what will follow once the air begins once again to flow, once the process reaches a critical level, is less predictable than Hardt and Negri seem to allow; it is precisely what is at issue for political work.

8   As is the case of raï in Parvati Nair's chapter.

9   Bohlman (2004: 21–3) discusses the song in the context of the Eurovision Song Contest and I discuss the song and the performance in more detail in Middleton (2006).

10   My own favoured pair of exemplars, dating from a moment just before the mediatory role of these traditions 'vanished', would be Al Jolson and Cab Calloway; but readers may easily supply their own alternatives.

11   My presentation of this is simplified in the extreme. For a good summary and discussion, see Bracher (1994).

12   To be fair, Jameson, in his 'Foreword' to the English translation of Greimas's *On Meaning*, drew attention to the transformational and narratological dimensions of his semantic theory, and the potential for dialectical interpretation these produce. This,

he suggests, is most strikingly illustrated in 'the attempt, by rotating the square and generating its implicit positions, to find one's way out of the conceptual or ideological closure' (Jameson, 1987: xvi–xvii).

Glossary of Musical Genres and Subgenres

African Rumba: Another name for **soukous**.

Afro-Cuban Rumba: See **rumba**.

Afropop: A term referring to both contemporary (usually urban, electronic) and traditional dance music from all over Africa. It probably originated in the USA and was the name given to a national public radio programme on African popular music.

Alternative rock: This rather loose term can reference any number of musical styles, but has tended to encompass those bands from the early 1980s onwards that attached themselves to the new wave and punk traditions and which tended to shun larger multinational record labels. Recent usages are usually synonymous with grunge and post-grunge, although in non-Anglophone contexts it is usually another term for indie rock.

Arabesk: The name given to a style of music which became popular in the 1940s in Turkey (but which has also subsequently been used to refer to any Western-style dance music which explicitly references musics from the Middle East). The Turkish arabesk style became popular in response to the state policy of banning Arab musics, thus giving this illicit music a certain counter-cultural force. The style is eclectic, drawing on Egyptian influences (notably the dance orchestra styles of the 1940s, 1950s and 1960s) and rural Turkish folk musics.

Bachata: Taking its name from working-class parties, this urban style evolved out of the Dominican *canciones de amargue* (songs of bitterness related to the Cuban **bolero**) to emerge as a distinct genre in the early 1970s. It can be distinguished from other Dominican styles by its emphasis on guitar and a restricted nasal vocal style. Lyrics may be highly erotic or comment frankly on working-class life. A more lyrical, sentimental, bachata – also known as technobachata – developed in the 1990s to great commercial success both in the Dominican Republic and abroad.

Banda: Contemporary banda exploded in the 1990s in Mexico and California with the rise in popularity of *la quebradita*, a dance popular in the *barrios* of Los Angeles. It is a development of the Banda Sinaloense, which emerged in the 1920s, and which was performed by agile brass and percussion ensembles or 'bandas'. The repertory includes **cumbia**, **merengue**, **norteña**, polkas, **ranchera** and **salsa**.

Banda Sinaloense (*tambora*): See **banda**.

Beats: A trend in dance music that commonly relates to trip-hop, which includes dominant female vocal samples against complex rhythms.

Bhangra: Originally a Punjabi rural dance music accompanied by drum and later melodic instruments such as the alghoza duct flute, *thumbi* (one-stringed fiddle) and zither. In Britain, in the 1970s, this genre was transformed into a mass-produced, more pop-oriented style, including instruments such as synthesizers and kit-drums, popular with Asian youth.

Big beat: 'White' dance music which borrows from any genre that seems most appropriate. Stylistic influences are drawn from **hip hop** and traditional **rock 'n' roll**. This is often figured as the more commercial end of dance music.

Blues: The origins of blues is a subject of much speculation, but most scholars agree that it began as an African-American form, and is probably an outgrowth of plantation 'worksongs'. The form has evolved and has many subcategories and other forms that have splintered off from it (**country blues**, for example). The musical feature which survives intact in most invocations of the blues is its twelve-bar structure and the harmonic structure ‖I---‖IV-I-‖V---‖.

Bolero: The Cuban bolero shares only its name with its Spanish homonym. It is a duple-metre song form which emerged in the mid to late nineteenth century in the Oriente province. A syncretic Afro-Cuban genre, it originally had a strict syncopated rhythmic base, the 'cinquillo' played on the clave (concussion sticks). As the bolero has developed, the hegemony of this patterning has been replaced by freer rhythms that follow the prosody of the lyrics. Love in its multiple variations, both affirmative and negative, is the predominant (although not the only) theme of the bolero. Over the course of the twentieth century the bolero has been transformed into a transnational phenomenon with a move away from simple guitar accompaniment to the use of orchestras and big bands.

Bossa nova: This new wave blend of samba and jazz was devised by Tom (Antonio Carlos) Jobim in Rio de Janeiro in the late 1950s and gained international popularity in the 1960s, becoming a staple in jazz repertory as a sophisticated, urban, lounge style. It is characterized by bittersweet lyrics which may be sung in Portuguese or English. Although commonly labelled as easy listening, bossa nova is often musically challenging with frequent use of difficult harmonies, including chords with added notes (so-called 'aletered' chords), 'stacked' chords (including added sevenths, ninths and thirteenths) and a consequent tonal instability, using swift modulations (often between major/minor) to distant tonalities (perhaps the best-known tune 'A garota da Ipanema' ['The Girl from Ipanema] is a fine example of this).

Bouzoúki: A popular urban folk music commonly played for tourists in Greece, it derives its name from the long-necked lute with four pairs of strings of the same name.

Calypso: A duple-metre song and dance form from the Southern and Eastern Caribbean, Calypso developed in Trinidad in the nineteenth century out of a variety of West African slave traditions, in particular the art of 'picong' or impromptu versifying emerges from the boasting tradition of the chantwell singer. It is usually played by a steel band (pans) and is characterized by sarcastic (often ribald) lyrics which address topical, social and political issues. Calypsonians compete annually for the title of Calypso monarch and, in keeping with the tradition of inversion of hierarchies during carnival, many of their monikers signify status.

Cantigas: A late medieval and early renaissance song form from Spain and Portugal. Brazilian singer/songwriter Nóbrega refers to some of his songs as 'cantigas do Descobrimento' ['cantigas of discovery] and the antiquated form 'cantiga' is clearly meant to have a historicist resonance.

Celtic music: A loose but persistent term covering a wide variety of mostly folk-derived musics from Ireland, Scotland, Wales, Northumbria in England, Brittany in France, and Galicia and Asturias in Spain.

Četnik songs: Songs associated with the Serbian Second World War Royalist Resistance Movement which were adapted by Serb nationalists during the Balkan Wars.

Chanson: In popular French and French Canadian music, this term refers to popular song of the 1930s and 1940s which had a revival in the late 1950s and 1960s. Characterized by melodramatic lyrics, and a rough and ready vocalization, the French chanson is a loose form that embraces a wide variety of musical styles.

Cheese: Humoristic and unpretentious dance music with catchy refrains.

Chinese new folk: See **New folk (China)**.

Classical: An informal term taken from 'Viennese classicism' (an art music style that developed in the late 1760s and which was characterized by its commitment to aesthetic notions such as balance, symmetry, clarity and order) but which usually refers to the whole Western art music tradition. It is invariably used as the 'other' of popular music, although this binarism has come under intense critical scrutiny in recent scholarship.

Congolese rumba: From the Democratic Republic of the Congo (formerly Zaire, and before that the Belgian Congo), and the Republic of the Congo (formerly the People's Republic of the Congo, and before that the French Middle Congo), this form developed in the 1960s from the Afro-Cuban genres of **rumba** and **son** which were sponsored by state radios. It is characterized by complex rhythms and a guitar-led texture. This fusion dance form spread throughout Western and Central Africa to become a popular pan-African genre. Other forms which are often included as substyles of Congolese rumba include **soukous** and **ndombolo**.

Corrido ballads: Originally guitar-based in the nineteenth century, the Golden Age of the corrido ballad was the 1920s when the accordion was incorporated and songs of the Mexican revolution were recorded, primarily in Texas, and became popular on both sides of the border. The term has come to be applied to Tex-Mex ballads.

Country, country and western: Currently, the older form 'country and western' is usually rendered as country. The former references so-called western swing, a type of country music that originated from fiddle and guitar bands in Texas in the late 1920s. Country music has undergone several phases of development, from its origins in folk music and both black and white religious music of the southern states of the USA, to its transformation into a commercial form with the so-called 'Nashville sound' through to recent developments in so-called New Country, a loose term that captures a wide range of musical styles from straight **rock**, folk rock and **folk** to **blues**, **jazz** and **world beat**.

Country blues: A subgenre of **country** and **blues**, this is also sometimes referred to as 'white blues' and is a hybrid. Hillbilly and country artists began playing with blues styles as early as the 1920s and this has remained a strong substratum of country.

Cumbia: A popular dance genre from Colombia's Atlantic coast which has spread throughout Latin America (and was particularly commercially successful in Mexico in the 1980s). It is a fusion of African polyrhythmic percussive elements with European melodic verse forms and, in its more traditional form, incorporates indigenous instruments such as the *gaita* (duct flute) and *maracas*. Cumbia has also developed into a big band form, incorporating diverse instruments such as keyboards, brass and accordion. When fused with **salsa**, it loses its characteristic off-beat.

Dancehall: This style arose in Jamaica in the 1980s with the rise of a number of DJ-ing stars who used digitized pre-set rhythm tracks (or riddims). It developed out of the practice of 'toasting' in the 1960s–1970s whereby **reggae** DJs added vocals ('toasts') to tracks. Evolving out of oral culture, dancehall lyrics in Jamaican *patwa* [patois] often focus on violence, drugs and sex, and have been criticized for their 'slackness', misogyny and homophobia. Dancehall has become the dominant reggae style producing other variations such as bam bam (where the guitar carries the rhythm rather than the bass) and **ragga** (using only digitized instruments).

Deep house: Characterized by deep, hovering organ fills, with an abundance of xylophone samples, driven by 120 bpm rhythm lines.

Disco: Probably an outgrowth of Motown and **soul**, disco is a style of dance music from the 1970s. Disco emerged in Afro-American, gay and Latino subcultures in New York and was characterized in particular by its boomy lower frequencies, orchestral textures and a strong regular beat.

Downtempo/Chill-out: Ambient in style with easy-listening tendencies. Meditative vocal lines and wave-like background sounds characterize the aesthetics of this style.

Drill 'n' bass: A harsh, jarring and tortuous industrial dance style put together in a way that is suggestive of controlled chaos.

Eklektisk (Eclectic): A mixture of any number of genres that together constitute a sense of eclecticism that challenges any sense of commercialism.

Fado: Usually refers to a song form from Lisbon, Portugal, but sometimes also refers to the canção de Coimbra – a distinct, but related, song tradition. Some have suggested that its origins lie in Portugal's encounter with the Americas and that the name is taken from a traditional Brazilian dance form also called fado. The current form is characterized by nostalgic lyrics sung in a highly charged dramatic manner accompanied on the guitarra or Portuguese guitar and the lower register viola baixo (a type of acoustic bass guitar).

Flamenco: The origins of flamenco are highly contested: some believe it to have been brought to Spain by gypsy immigrants (originally from North Africa or from North India); others believe it to be the music of displaced Arabs left in Spain after the seventeenth-century expulsions; and others believe it to be a hybrid of several musical lumpen-traditions subsisting on the counter-cultural margins of Spanish cultural life in the late eighteenth century. It is a form, usually sung, which deals invariably with the thematics of loss, pain, desire and jealousy. It ranges from the *cante jondo* or 'deep song' style characterized by melodramatic vocal melismas accompanied by virtuosic guitar, to the 'cante chico' or light song in which faster rhythms (in 12, 4 or 3) give flight to more melodic song. All forms can also be danced. So-called *nuevo flamenco* [new flamenco], often referred to as the 'third wave' (the 'second' referring to hybrid forms popular in the late 1960s and 1970s), demonstrates an open-ended attitude to both traditional flamenco practices and their hybridization with more global musical styles such as **rock, blues, jazz** and **folk**.

Folk music: The term *Volksmusik* was probably first coined by Johann Gottfried Herder (1744–1803) to denote 'simply' the music of the people. It has become a term that has so many competing meanings that unitary definitions are misleading. The term has done an inordinate amount of cultural work, referring variously to musics of the rural proletariat, music of 'the people' before industrialization, rural musics, musics which adhere to tradition (another term sometimes used is 'traditional music'), or musics not included in art or mass popular repertories. In the West, the term has been used somewhat simplistically to refer to musics which are indigenous but which have purportedly not been touched by urban cultures.

Funk: Refers to music with a very strong bass line, complex syncopated rhythms and a vocal style closely related to some forms of soul music. The origins of the music have been linked with the arm of the civil rights movement closely allied to Black Power movements (see James Brown's 1968 track 'Say It Loud, I'm Black and I'm Proud'). The period 1973–75 saw the intensification of funk as a bona fide style, mixing a strong backbeat with complex guitar figuration, thick and elaborated textures and some borrowings from avant-garde jazz.

Grupo: The grupo ensemble with its synthesized instruments and lead vocalist is one of Mexico's commercially most successful popular musics; grupos' main repertoire consists of easy-listening Mexican and international pop ballads.

Heavy metal: In the early 1970s, a form of rock music emerged in response to the over-distorted pyrotechnics of Jimi Hendrix that emphasized virtuosity but also a new intensity in the guitar sound and rhythmic drive. The style draws on blues, rock 'n' roll and some form of classical virtuosity (especially baroque and romantic).

Hip hop (hip hop): Refers both to the multi-ethnic urban subcultures of late 1970s East Coast USA and the predominantly black (and lately also white) musical form **rap**. In the late 1970s, **rap** used spoken declamation over a rhythmic background and samples (usually from **funk**) and drew on Jamaican MC techniques. Samples now include other rap artists' work, soul and a wide range of musical genres. Where hip hop is not based in the Anglophone territories, it also samples local traditional and popular musical styles. It has to be said, however, that hip hop has tended to remain an 'internationalizing' style.

House: An outgrowth of disco from the American Midwest in the late 1980s, this paired-down dance music relied on a clear 4/4 beat, synthesizers, samples and simple accumulative structures.

Irish pop-rock: The Irish pop-rock scene can be divided into two main tendencies: an international sound and crossovers which combine this with indigenous musics.

Jazz: The term embraces a number of differing meanings, referring both to its 'origins' and a number of radically differing performance practices. The term can reference Black American musics that developed in the early 1920s, American popular musics characterized by a creative and expressive combination of pre-composed and 'free' elements, and musics which make harmonic reference to other African-American forms such as **blues** and swing. Its usage is also much broader, referencing elements of popular American musical entertainment that characterized the so-called 'Jazz Age' in the 1920s, some improvised musics from the 1940s onwards and a certain attitude to rhythm, locatable in particular in the use of syncopation and supple melodic phrasing.

Juju: A popular Nigerian dance music combining traditional musical forms of the Yoruba peoples with foreign influences, notably Bollywood film musics and rock. Other influences include **country and western**, **blues** and **soul**. The music is characterized by driving rhythms, an up-tempo beat, a lead singer accompanied by front-end rhythmically complex guitars and a number of percussionists.

Jump up: A style that fuses rough jungle with **hip hop**. This style leans in the direction of **big beat**, as opposed to the more rhythmically complex and challenging textures of **drum 'n' bass**.

Kolo: A fast two-beat Serbian ring-dance, popular on social occasions such as weddings.

Latin pop: In the 1980s and 1990s, Latin pop was the most commercially successful Latin music in the USA, with a number of artists achieving crossover success in the late 1990s. As a category it embraces a variety of musical styles including **rock**, pop and dance music. It emerged from a background of different Latino genres which had incorporated US production techniques and modern instruments. In the clubs of New York and Miami, where there are important Latino communities, a dance music style known as Latin freestyle evolved which combined Latin rhythms with synthesizers and drum machines. Latin pop has been dominated by up-tempo dance-pop which blends pop melodies with Latin-inflected rhythms and sweeping ballads. When sung in English, these have provided crossover hits in the US and international pop charts.

Mambo: An up-tempo Latin dance genre originating in Cuba in the 1940s with its roots in danzón, **rumba** and **son**. Popularized by New York Latin big bands in the 1950s and characterized by swinging horn sections and polyrhythmic percussive accompaniment including *timbales*, maracas and clave, it later gave rise to other dances such as the cha cha cha.

Mangue beat: Originally termed mangue bit (from 'mangue' meaning mangrove and computer bytes/bits), this diverse movement emerged in the early 1990s in the north-eastern Brazilian city of Recife. It mixes traditional **folk** genres of the Pernambuco region such as **maracatu** with international influences from **rap**, **rock**, pop, **funk** and electronica. It is characterized by the use of local slang as reflected in its manifesto of 'Crabs with Brains'.

Maracatu: A carnival procession form from the region of Pernambuco in the north-east of Brazil. The *maracatu nação* or *maracatu de baque virado* developed in the eighteenth century from the Brazilian adaptation of the 'congada' or coronation festivities for the Congolese King and Queen, while the *maracatu de orquesta* or *maracatu de baque solto* emerged in the second half of the nineteenth century. The maracatu blends African and indigenous traditions and is characterized by its call and response format, improvisational verses, use of an *apito* (wooden tritone whistle) by the band leader and variety of percussive instruments including drums, snares, shakers, rattles and *guonguê* (double bells).

Marcha-de-bloco (Frevo-de-bloco): Fast, binary tempo carnival procession music from Recife in the north-east of Brazil.

Mbalax: A fast-paced Senegalese popular music style which was developed by Wolof musicians in the 1970s. It takes its name from the Wolof term used by griots to describe the distinctive rhythms of the *mbung mbung* drum commonly heard at boxing matches. It is characterized by its driving rhythms, a highly elaborate vocalizing style, overdubbed electric guitars and complex layered rhythmic texture.

Meddaha: Traditional wedding songs sung by groups of women in and around the city of Oran in Algeria.

Mento: A Jamaican rural roots or folk dance music which developed in the nineteenth century. It is characterized by a shuffling strum (later adopted by *reggae*) and strong accents on the last beat of the four-beat bar. Sung in Jamaican *patwa* [patois], it is similar to *calypso* with its topical, satirical lyrics. Structurally it resembles Afro-Cuban *rumba* with a mix of solo improvisation and group participation. A wide variety of string, wind and percussive instruments are played, but it typically features guitar, banjo, fiddle and rhumba box (thumb piano).

Merengue: A couples dance of the Dominican Republic which developed in the mid to late nineteenth century as a Creole variant of the European-derived contredanse. Merengue was rejected by the local elites due to its African influences. Its rural form or *merengue típico*, which is still performed today particularly in the Cibao region, commonly features the *tambora* (double-headed drum), the *güiro* (metal scraper), the button accordion and the alto saxophone. Originally guitars or *cuatros* and *marimbas* (thumb pianos) were also used. Under the dictator Rafael Trujillo (1930–60), merengue in its big band format was adopted as the national musical form. Modern, urban merengue has evolved to incorporate various instruments such as keyboards, guitar, bass and tight brass sections emphasizing the role of the saxophone. Groups on the whole are smaller and the tempo faster. Characterized by a frenetic rhythm and steady half-note thumping pulse, the basic two-step pattern of merengue led to it superseding **salsa** as the pervasive pan-Latin-Caribbean dance in the 1980s. Popular amongst the diasporic Dominican community in the USA, merengue has continued to evolve, incorporating elements from genres as diverse as **salsa**, **soukous**, **reggae**, **rap** and techno.

Miami bass: Consists of very rapid breakbeats and large, booming bass lines, with dashes of electro and textural colourings. The aesthetic is predominantly heterosexual fixated.

Minimalist techno: Economic, hard, speedy and funky in style, minimalist techno is characterized by a considerable increase in tempo on its 1980s predecessor Detroit techno.

MPB: Catch-all term for Brazilian popular music, first used in the 1930s but more commonly used to refer to the key figures of the 1960s. The military coup of 1964 and subsequent dictatorship provided the creative impulse for socially-politically involved musicians who were heavily censored and in some case persecuted. In the north-east of Brazil the short-lived Tropicalismo movement blended regional genres, rock influences (such as the use of electric guitars) and dense lyrics.

Música tropical: Refers mainly to musics from the Hispanic Caribbean such as **salsa**, **merengue** and **cumbia**.

Narodnalizvorna muzika: Serbian and Croatian term for **folk music**.

Ndombolo: Recent variant of soukous.

Netherlands trance: One of the most popular dance trends to emerge at the end of the 1990s, characterized by a movie soundtrack-type ambience, described by Netherlanders as 'movie trance'. In contrast to conventional trance, this style is lighter in feel and more melodic.

New Age: Taken from the New Age movement of the late 1970s, this is not really a musical style but a set of attitudes to music-making and listening that together add up to a relatively coherent world-view. The musics of alternative healing communities from the early 1980s in the USA tended to reference Eastern musical forms, simple open and resonant textures, and meditative forms that used repetition as a way of focusing on the inner life.

New folk (China): Chinese 'new folk' consists mainly of solo recordings of contemporary compositions, and enjoys a certain expressive freedom afforded by the octave-based modal structure (usually either heptatonic or pentatonic) which allows for interesting subtleties of tonal colour. The unique rhythms – characterized by extensive use of asymmetry and syncopation – associated with the traditional folk singing style and traditional stringed instruments such as the *dutar* (or two-stringed lute) mark this musical tradition out as radically different from the musics performed by state troupes. Moreover, its song lyrics address prevalent social and political issues, borrowing or adapting lines by both well-known and less well-known poets and writers.

Norteña: Also known as Tex-Mex in the USA, norteña developed out of the **corrido ballads** and European-derived salon dances to become popular throughout Mexico. The lyrics commonly feature antiheroes who stand up to the system.

Novokompanovana narodna muzika: Literally newly composed national (or **folk**) music, this term refers to a mass-produced urban style drawing on traditional musical forms but also urban Bosnian music. It is often compared to **country and western** in the USA.

Nu skool: Features gigantic bass lines, with unusual breakbeats and squeamish samples taken from kung-fu and sci-fi films.

Poco (Pocomania): Music associated with the Afro-Protestant religions (of the same name) which emerged in Jamaica in the nineteenth century. It is characterized by persistent hypnotic percussion, rhythmic breathing known as 'sounding' or 'groaning' and trumping (circling around a symbolic object until possessed).

Poptrance: A style where juxtapositionings of dark, broody synth riffs and out-dated rhythm patterns are set against foreboding female vocal lines.

Psychedelic trance: Also known as Goa-trance, this style draws on a wealth of influences connected to trance. It is derived from the legendary full-moon parties held in Goa.

Ragga (Raggamuffin): A subgenre of **dancehall** emerging in the mid-1980s in Jamaica and the UK with the introduction of synthesizers. It is characterized by its eclectic mix of **hip hop**, **reggae**, R&B and **rock**. Lyrics are often witty while raggamuffin DJs commonly perform in an aggressive or bombastic style.

Raï: A musical tradition that flourished from the 1970s in Algeria and Morocco, and, from the mid-1980s, in North African immigrant communities in other parts of Europe, especially France and Spain. It usually (especially since the mid-1980s) combines a hoarse vocalizing style with a mixture of 'Western' and North African instruments and is characterized by its stylistic plurality.

Ranchera: Developed in the early twentieth century, this urban musical form, often accompanied by a mariachi band, is in duple time and deals with texts from the 1910 Revolution. It is associated with a 'roots' or 'folk' mentality and blends several regional styles.

Rap: This is a predominantly African-American form although it is multi-ethnic in origin and has spread to all corners of the globe to become associated with minority communities' experience. It usually consists of a declamatory rhymed and speedy citation accompanied by sampled sounds from African-American and white American popular musics. Where rap has taken hold in non-Anglophone communities, samples are invariably taken from more mixed repertories.

Reggae: A term that is wide-ranging in its usage but which properly refers to a contemporary Jamaican popular music style with its roots in **mento**. Reggae (roots reggae) as a distinct form can be dated to 1968 with its reliance on a two-chord pattern in the rhythm guitar, slowed down rock steady beat of the electric bass, emphasis placed on the second beat, and singers intoning a mixture of political, pathos-laden and witty lyrics designed to reference 'the everyday' (the term is said by some to come from 'regular' meaning the poor majority and many reggae musicians are linked to the Rastafari religion, which seeks social justice). In the 1970s reggae exploded onto the international music scene to become a global phenomenon. Subsequently new forms have evolved both in Jamaica and in its diaspora, such as rockers/militant style, dub and **dancehall**.

Rock: A term that covers a wide range of musical styles, but which can be located specifically in a 'white', technically 'committed' musical practice which emerged in the mid-1960s. The term is often contrasted with 'pop' which has often been used as the 'lower' more 'commercial' other of 'serious' rock music. Its various subgenres include **heavy metal**, thrash, glam rock, grunge, punk, soft rock, **alternative rock** and many more.

Rock 'n' roll: Although often used as a catch-all, this term refers specifically to a short-lived style of popular music from the 1950s which merged blues, tin pan alley and other forms with inflections from gospel, boogie-woogie and hillbilly forms. It is characterized by its light and open electric guitar sound, a simple driving drum beat and clear vocal line which employed whoops and yodels from earlier American song forms.

Rumba (Afro-Cuban): The rumba dance form which emerged in Cuba in the late nineteenth century has its origins in the dances of the West African Kongo cult. It is a vocal and percussive form characterized by its two-part structure (solo vocal followed by choral call and response). The rhythms of the clave (concussion sticks) which fall into two-bar cycles provide the foundation to the extensively syncopated, interlocking cross rhythms of a variety of percussive instruments. Its three extant forms are the guaguancó, yambú and columbia. The first two are couples dances in which the male dancer tries to get close to the evasive woman. The more popular guaguancó is faster while the yambú is usually danced by older people and accompanied by *cajones* (wooden boxes) rather than congas. The columbia is a highly acrobatic solo male dance.

Rumba (Congolese): see **Congolese rumba**

Rumba (Sengalese): see **Sengalese rumba**

Salsa: A wide-ranging and highly contested term for a pan-Latin dance music, salsa was developed in New York City and Puerto Rico in the 1960s and 1970s. It is a highly hybrid form but has clear Cuban antecedents, particularly **son** with its two-part formal structure, clave or two-bar timeline and anticipated bass pattern in which the downbeat is omitted. Although salsa is dismissed by some as 'just Cuban music' by another name, it can be differentiated by its driving rhythms, strident brass (particularly trombone) and diverse musical influences ranging from US **jazz**, **rock** and **disco** to Puerto Rican bomba, plena and Dominican **merengue**. Emerging from the harsh surrounding of New York's Latino neighbourhoods, many lyrics made reference to social themes. During the 1970s salsa was adopted as a symbol of Puerto Rican national identity but also spread to other parts of Latin America, particularly Colombia, Panama and Venezuela. In the late 1980s and 1990s, a new style evolved which fused salsa rhythms with sentimental lyrics – salsa romántica. Salsa has emerged as one of the most significant transnational musical genres, popular throughout the Americas, Europe and as far afield as Japan. In Cuba in the 1980s musicians fused **son** with innovative Afro-Cuban **jazz**, **hip hop**, **rap** and **reggae** to produce timba, a contemporary form commonly likened to salsa.

Samba: This term is used to refer to a diverse range of Afro-Brazilian forms including caipira folk samba, samba de lenço, samba-roda, samba-de-roda, samba-de-matuto, partido-alto, pernada-carioca, samba de morro or batucada, samba de breque, samba de enredo, samba-canção, samba-choro, samba-fox, samba-pagode and samba-reggae. Samba has its origins in West African circle dances and is characterized by syncopated rhythms and a vocal call and response format. Urban samba was standardized in the 1920s and the carnival institution of samba schools was developed in Rio de Janeiro in the 1930s. More recently, in the 1980s two significant subgenres of samba emerged: the working-class pagode movement and Bahian samba-reggae which vindicates Afro-Brazilian aesthetics.

Sean nós: A Gaelic term used to describe a traditional and complex unaccompanied style of singing from the West of Ireland, which is characterized by a nasal style of delivery. The songs of this tradition are invariably very long and the lyrics derive from the bardic tradition. The performance style is associated with subtle vocal articulations.

Senegalese rumba: In the 1930s, Afro-Cuban dance rhythms were very popular in Senegal, particularly in Dakar. By the 1960s, several Senegalese bands were playing music with distinct Latin influences. In the 1970s, Latin musics were integrated into a new form in which Wolof and Mandinka lyrics mixed with Spanish or Portuguese Creole, and the *tama* (talking drum) was incorporated to make Senegalese rumba.

Sevdah (or sevda, sevdahlenka, sevdalenka, sevdalinka, sevdahlinka): An urban folk song form from Bosnia-Hercegovina, usually a love song, which employs Turkish musical folk articulations (modes with a flattened sixth and raised seventh degree, for example) combined with various ensembles, usually containing an accordion, but also guitar, sometimes percussion and synthesizers. The lyrics are invariably very dark, referencing longing and despair.

Sha'bī song: Algerian sha'bī ('people's') songs are long and narrative in format. Most commonly associated with the working classes of the city of Algiers, they can be characterized by the use of colloquial language. The form contrasts solo vocalization with noisy chorus interjections. Instrumentation varies but usually includes fretted instruments, violins, the darbukka goblet drum and, in more modern ensembles, synthesizers.

Slåttemusikken: Refers to Norwegian folk music. Characterized by a strong vocal tradition and highly distinctive fiddle traditions, especially of the Hardanger fiddle (with four sympathetic vibrating strings under the bowed strings) in the south-west and west, but also the flatfele or European flat fiddle, contemporary Norwegian folk music is still grounded in older musical idioms. The solo male dance, the halling, is an improvised form in which the dancer displays his athletic prowess.

Soca: A dance genre which developed out of the Trinidadian **calypso** tradition in the late 1970s. Its name is derived from Lord Shorty's 'Soul Calypso Music' (So-Ca) from 1973. Its international musical focus is reflected in the wide range of influences incorporated into the sound mix. These include **disco**, **funk**, **merengue**, **salsa**, mid-tempo ska, **soul**, **zouk** and traditional **calypso**. In contrast to calypso, the focus is less on social and political comment and more on dance (reflected in the use of drum machines) and a party culture (referred to as 'jam and wine'). Soca has spread to the islands of Barbados, Grenada and St Vincent. It has been fused with a variety of other genres to give rise to styles such as parang soca, ragga soca, rapso and chutney soca (acknowledging the influence of Trinidad's East Indian community).

Son: Not to be confused with its Mexican homonym, the Cuban son is a highly syncretic fusion of African and European influences. From its origins in the late nineteenth century in Oriente, son evolved to become an important symbol of Cuban national identity with numerous sub-classifications such as changüí, ñongo, regina and sucu-sucu. Structurally similar to **rumba**, it is in duple metre and has a two-part structure. The initial song or canto resembles European-derived musics in its moderate tempo, harmonic progressions and melody, whereas the faster, improvisatory call and response or montuno section reflects West African forms. Lyrics, while using Hispanic poetic forms such as coplas, cuartetas and décimas, are rooted in Afro-Cuban or mulatto culture. Musically, son can be characterized by a high degree of syncopation, the prominence of the clave pattern and the anticipated bass pattern later adopted by **salsa**. Acoustic son is performed on a variety of instruments including the Cuban tres (triple set of double strings), guitar, bass, bongo, maracas, clave, *güiro/guayo* (scraper), *botija* (jug bass) and *marímbula* (thumb piano). Over the course of the twentieth century son has developed increasingly sophisticated harmonies and rhythms. Charanga ensembles incorporated flute and violins, while modern dance bands often substitute keyboards for the guitar and tres, use an electric bass and add conga drums and timbales as well as a tight horn section.

Soukous: Perhaps one of the most popular world musics, this Central African dance music originated in the Democratic Republic of the Congo (formerly Zaire, and before that the Belgian Congo), and the Republic of the Congo (formerly the People's Republic of the Congo and, before that, the French Middle Congo) and was first popularized in the 1960s. It is characterized by very full guitar-led textures and an up-beat tempo. It differs from the **Congolese rumba**, from which it developed, in that it is faster and its textures are thicker and more intricate. It uses the inter-ethnic trading language of Lingala. **Ndombolo** is a recent variant of soukous.

Soul: Usually used to designate the new gospel-influenced black American musics from the 1960s onwards. Connected to record labels like Stax, Motown and Atlantic, the golden age of soul is considered to be from around 1964 to 1967 (the death of Otis Redding). The music is characterized by subtle scoring, complex verse-chorus structures and strongly foregrounded vocals (especially rich in use of harmonizing backing vocals).

Svatbarska muzika: Literally 'wedding' music, this musical style, associated in particular with Eastern European gypsies, and probably originating from Bulgaria, has been cited as one of the influences on **turbo folk**. The style is a mix of traditional rural **folk** tunes and dance tunes and modern arrangements which emphasize its 'oriental' character but which nonetheless also integrate American **jazz** and **rock** influences and older salon styles from the 1920s and 1930s. It has become popular all over Eastern Europe.

Tech-house: A blend of techno and house styles with an abundance of percussion sounds and very heavy bass. The tempo is notably faster than normal house and characterized by harder beats.

Technobanda: A form of **banda**. In contrast to the traditional acoustic banda with its clarinets, trumpets, trombones, tuba, horns, tambora and tarola (double-headed bass drum and snare drum, respectively), technobandas are made up of electric bass, keyboard synthesizer, saxophones and trumpets, and feature a vocalist.

Turbo folk: This Serbian music is a fusion of Western **rock**, oriental Turkish rhythms and **sevdah**, the latter a Bosnian urban form probably founded some time at the turn of the nineteenth and twentieth centuries. It is an amalgam of these forms, mixed also with Bulgarian turbo folk. What has marked this style of music out from others has not been its musical features so much as its ideological commitment to nationalist struggle in the name of a greater Serbia.

World beat: This term can be distinguished from the broader term **world music** (although they are now often juxtaposed indiscriminately) in that it is a form forged largely in the West by borrowing from non-Western traditions and generating a particularly 'fused' or hybrid idiom. Its origins are probably to be found in the early WOMAD festivals and the work of artists like Peter Gabriel, David Byrne, Sting and so on. The style (such as it is) is very eclectic.

World music: This problematic and complex term has numerous different meanings but the one that dominates in the West is as a music (note the singularization of the extraordinary diversity of musical traditions here) that is not initially made in the West but which is subsequently categorized (colonized, perhaps) as marketable within the West. There are no stylistic or idiomatic features which could be said to adhere to it.

Zouk: A dance music popular throughout the Creole-speaking Caribbean, particularly Guadeloupe and Martinique but also Dominica, Haiti, St Lucia and French Guiana. The term 'zouk' is derived from the Martinican Creole slang for a party which came to refer to sound systems in the 1960s. In the 1980s it emerged as the tag for a new style of music associated with Antillean groups in Paris, particularly the group Kassav. The lyrics are usually in Kweyol (Creole) and zouk blends a dazzling variety of traditional, popular and mass-mediated genres from the Caribbean and beyond, including the West African derived gwo ka of Guadeloupe, Martinican and Guadeloupan biguine, Antillean cadence, Haitian kadans-rampa and kompa direk, Dominican cadence-lypso, Trinidadian **calypso** and **soca**, US big band **jazz**, **soul** and **funk**, and Latin American **merengue** and **salsa**. It typically features rhythm and brass sections, synthesizers, guitar and bass but also hi-tech drum machines and digital samplers.

Bibliography

Acuña, Rodolfo F. (1996), *Anything But Mexican: Chicanos in Contemporary Los Angeles*, London: Verso.

Adorno, Theodor (1973), *The Jargon of Authenticity*, London: Routledge and Kegan Paul.

Adorno, Theodor (1976), *Introduction to the Sociology of Music*, trans. E.B. Ashton, New York: Continuum.

Allworth, Edward and Pahta, Gulamettin (1988), 'A Gentle, New Allegory by an Older Uyghur Author', *Doğu Türkistan'in Sesi*, 5 (7), 19–20.

Ämät, Abliz (2001), *Uyghur Xälq Maqal-Tämsilliri Izahliq Lughiti* [Annotated Dictionary of Uyghur Folk Sayings], Qäšqär: Qäšqär Uyghur Näšriyati.

Amnesty International (1997), *People's Republic of China. Xinjiang: Trials after Recent Ethnic Unrest*, AI Index: ASA 17/018/1997, 21 March, http://web.amnesty.org/library/index/ENGASA170181997 (accessed 15 May 1997).

Amnesty International (1998), *China: 1997 – No Cause for Complacency*, AI Index: ASA 17/007/1998, 3 March, http://web.amnesty.org/library/index/ENGASA170071998 (accessed 2 April 1998).

Amnesty International (1999a), *People's Republic of China: Xinjiang Uighur Autonomous Region – Appeal for Uighurs Arbitrarily Detained*, AI Index: ASA 17/002/1999, 1 January, http://web.amnesty.org/library/index/ENGASA170021999 (accessed 27 February 1999).

Amnesty International (1999b) *China: Gross Violations of Human Rights in the Xinjiang Uighur Autonomous Region*, AI Index: ASA 17/018/1999, 1 April, http://web.amnesty.org/library/index/ENGASA170181999 (accessed 6 June 1999).

Amnesty International (2002), *China's Anti-Terrorism Legislation and Repression in the Xinjiang Uighur Autonomous Region*, AI Index: ASA 17/010/2002, 22 March, http://web.amnesty.org/library/index/ENGASA170102002 (accessed 13 May 2002).

Anderson, Benedict (1991 [1983]), *Imagined Communities: Reflections on the Origin and Spread of Nationalism*, London and New York: Verso, revised and extended edition.

Anthias, Floya (1999), 'Theorizing Identity, Difference and Social Division', in O'Brien, Martin, Penna, Sue and Hay, Colin (eds) *Theorizing Modernity: Reflexivity, Environment and Identity in Giddens' Social Theory*, Harlow: Longman, pp. 156–79.

Appadurai, Arjun (1990), 'Disjuncture and Difference in the Global Culture Economy', in Featherstone, Mike (ed.), *Global Culture: Nationalism, Globalization and Modernity*, London, Newbury Park, CA and New Delhi: Sage, pp. 295–310.

Appadurai, Arjun (1991), 'Global Ethnoscapes: Notes and Queries for a Transnational Anthropology', in Fox, Richard (ed.), *Recapturing Anthropology: Working in the Present*, Santa Fe, NM: School of American Research Press, pp. 191–210.

Appadurai, Arjun (2000), *Modernity at Large: Cultural Dimensions of Globalization*, Minneapolis: University of Minnesota Press.

Appiah, Kwame Anthony (1992), 'The Postcolonial and the Postmodern', in *In My Father's House: Africa in the Philosophy of Culture*, London: Methuen, pp. 221–54.

Armstrong, Piers (2001), 'Songs of Olodum: Ethnicity, Activism, and Art in a Globalized Carnival Community', in Perrone, Charles and Dunn, Christopher (eds), *Brazilian Popular Music and Globalization*, Gainsville: University of Florida Press, pp. 177–91.

Askew, Kelly Michelle (1997), 'Performing the Nation: Swahili Musical Performance and the Production of Tanzanian National Culture', unpublished PhD dissertation, Harvard University.

Attali, Jacques (1985), *Noise: The Political Economy of Music*, trans. Brian Massumi, Manchester: University of Manchester Press.

Augestad, Kate (1997), '"Å, Sissel, Sissel, når eg ser deg slik" – En sangartist som nasjonalsymbol', in Time, Sveinung (ed.), *Om kulturell identitet*, Bergen: Høgskolen i Bergen, pp. 129–50.

Baily, John (1994) 'The Role of Music in the Creation of an Afghan National Identity, 1923–73', in Stokes, Martin (ed.), *Ethnicity, Identity and Music: The Musical Construction of Place*, Oxford and Providence, RI: Berg, pp. 45–60.

Bakhtin, Mikhail (1984) *Rabelais and His World*, trans. Hélène Iswolsky, Bloomington: Indiana University Press.

Bakhtin, Mikhail (1994 [1965]), 'Introduction *Rabelais and His World*', in Morris, Pam (ed.), *The Bakhtin Reader*, London: Arnold, pp. 195–206.

Banerji, Sabita and Baumann, Gerd (1990), 'Bhangra 1948–8: Fusion and Professionalism in a Genre of South Asian Dance Music', in Oliver, Paul (ed.), *Black Music in Britain: Essays on the Afro-Asian Contribution to Popular Music*, Buckingham: Open University Press, pp. 137–52.

Barañao, Ascensión, Martí, Josep, Abril, Gonzalo, Cruces, Francisco and Carvalho, José Jorge (2003), 'World Music, ¿El folklore de la globalización?', *Trans: Revista Transcultural de Música: Transcultural Music Review*, 7, December, http://www.sibetrans.com/trans/trans7/redonda.htm (accessed 29 January 2004).

Baranovitch, Nimrod (2001), 'Between Alterity and Identity: New Voices of Minority People in China', *Modern China*, 27 (3), 359–401.

Barber-Kersovan, Alenka (2001), 'Popular Music in ex-Yugoslavia: Between Global Participation and Provincial Seclusion', in Gebesmair, Andreas and Smudits, Alfred (eds), *Global Repertoires: Popular Music Within and Beyond the Transnational Music Industry*, Aldershot: Ashgate, pp. 73–87.

Barfield, Thomas. J. (1989), *The Perilous Frontier: Nomadic Empires and China*, London: Basil Blackwell.

Barth, Fredrik (1969), 'Introduction', in Barth, Fredrik (ed.), *Ethnic Groups and Boundaries: The Social Organisation of Cultural Difference*, Oslo: Universitetsforlaget, pp. 9–38.

Barthes, Roland (1997), *Image-Music-Text*, London: Routledge.

Bazin, Hugues (1995), *Culture Hip-hop*, Paris: Desclée de Brouwer.

BBC Monitoring (1995), *Summary of World Broadcasts (Asia Pacific)*, FE/2240 G/4, 1 March.

Beardsell, Peter (2000), *Europe and Latin America: Returning the Gaze*, Manchester: Manchester University Press.

Bebey, Francis (1975 [1969]), *African Music: A People's Art*, trans. Josephine Bennett, London: Harrap.

Beck, Ulrich (1992), *Risk Society*, London, Thousand Oaks, CA and New Delhi: Sage.

Bellér-Hann, Ildikó (1991), 'Script Changes in Xinjiang', in Akiner, Shirin (ed.), *Cultural Change and Continuity in Central Asia*, London: Kegan Paul International, pp. 71–83.

Bellér-Hann, Ildikó (2002), 'Temperamental Neighbours: Uighur-Han Relations in Xinjiang, Northwest China', in Schlee, Günther (ed.), *Imagined Differences: Hatred and the Construction of Identity*, Hamburg: Lit Verlag, pp. 57–81.

Bender, Wolfgang (1991), *Sweet Mother: Modern African Music*, trans. Wolfgang Freis, Chicago and London: University of Chicago Press.

Benedetto, André (1976), *Les Drapiers Jacobins*, in *Théâtre 1*, Paris: Editions PJ Oswald.

Benedetto, André (1980), *Carnaval-Express*, Rognes: Editions Provence.

Bennett, Andy (2000), *Popular Music and Youth Culture: Music, Identity and Place*, London: Macmillan.

Benson, Linda. (1990), *The Ili Rebellion: The Moslem Challenge to Chinese Authority in Xinjiang, 1944–1949*, Armonk, NY: M.E. Sharpe.

Berkaak, Odd Are (1996), 'Om "norsk nerk" og "virtuelle selv": Noen refleksjoner omkring kulturarv og formidlingsideologier', *Norsklæraren*, 4, 5–14.

Bhabha, Homi K. (ed.) (1990), *Nation and Narration*, London and New York: Routledge.

Bhabha, Homi K. (1994), *The Location of Culture*, London and New York: Routledge.

Bidder, Sean (1999), *House: The Rough Guide*, London: Penguin Books.

Black, Robert (1994), 'The Ethnic Cleansing Balladeers get their Marching Orders', *The Independent*, 25 March (consulted on the web, page no longer active).

Bohlman, Philip V. (1993), 'Musicology as a Political Act', *The Journal of Musicology*, 11 (4), Autumn, 411–36.

Bohlman, Philip V. (2002), *World Music: A Very Short Introduction*, Oxford: Oxford University Press.

Bohlman, Philip V. (2004), *The Music of European Nationalism: Cultural Identity and Modern History*, Santa Barbara, CA: ABC-Clio.

Born, Georgina and Hesmondhalgh, David (eds) (2000), *Western Music and its Others: Difference, Representation and Appropriation in Music*, Berkeley and London: University of California Press.

Bosi, Alfredo (1994), *Dialética da colonização*, São Paulo: Editora Schwarz.

Bourdieu, Pierre (1992), *Language and Symbolic Power*, Cambridge: Polity.

Bovingdon, Gardner (2002), 'The Not-so-silent Majority: Uyghur Resistance to Han Rule in Xinjiang', *Modern China*, 28 (1), 39–78.

Bovingdon, Gardner (2003), '"We are People from Taklimakan": Popular Representations of Uyghur Identity in Orally Transmitted Histories', paper presented at the 55th Annual Meeting of the Association for Asian Studies, New York Hilton, 27–30 March.

Bracher, Mark (1994), 'On the Psychological and Social Functions of Language: Lacan's Theory of the Four Discourses', in Bracher, Mark, Alcorn Jr, Marshall W., Corthell, Ronald J. and Massardier-Kenney, Françoise (eds), *Lacanian Theory of Discourse: Subject, Structure, and Society*, New York: New York University Press, pp. 107–28.

Brennan, Timothy (1997), *At Home in the World: Cosmopolitanism Now*, Cambridge, MA and London: Harvard University Press.

Brook, Peter (1987), *The Shifting Point: Forty Years of Theatrical Exploration*, London: Methuen.

Burton, Kim (1999), 'Serbian and Montenegro: "Balkan Beats"', in Broughton, Simon, Ellingham, Mark and Trillo, Richard (eds), *World Music: The Rough Guide*, London: The Rough Guides, pp. 273–6.

Calio, Jean (1998), *Le Rap: une réponse des banlieues?*, Lyon: Aléas.

Calvacanti, Arturo (2000), *Raízes Musicais Brasileiras: IV* (sound recording), Radio Nederland Wereldomroep, http://www.rnw.nl/parceria/html//es030611raizes_musicais. html (accessed 5 August 2003).

Cardoso, Maurício (1999), 'O Maior Show da Terra: o Rodeio Vira um Negócio Bilionário', *Veja* (19 May), pp. 130–33.

Cartwright, Garth (2000/1), 'World Music is ...', in *Tower Guide to ... World Music*, London: Tower Music Guides, pp. 4–6.

Castan, Félix (1984), *Manifeste multiculturel et anti-régionaliste*, Montauban: Editions Cocagne.

Chant, Sylvia (1999), 'Population, Migration, Employment and Gender', in Robert, Gwynne and Kay, Cristóbal (eds), *Latin America Transformed: Globalization and Modernity*, London: Arnold, pp. 226–69.

Clark, William A.V. (1996), 'Residential Patterns: Avoidance, Assimilation, and Succession', in Waldinger, Roger and Bozorgmehr, Mehdi (eds), *Ethnic Los Angeles*, New York: Russell Sage Foundation, pp. 109–38.

Clifford, James (1988), *The Predicament of Culture*, Cambridge, MA: Harvard University Press.

Cloonan, Martin (1999), 'Pop and the Nation-state: Towards a Theorisation', *Popular Music*, 18 (2), 193–207.

Cloonan, Martin and Garofalo, Reebee (2003), *Policing Pop*, Philadelphia: Temple University Press.

Cohen, Sara (1991), *Rock Culture in Liverpool: Popular Music in the Making*, Oxford: Oxford University Press.

Cohen, Sara (1994), 'Mapping the Sound: Identity, Place and the Liverpool Sound', in Stokes, Martin (ed.), *Ethnicity, Identity and Music: The Musical Construction of Place*, Oxford and Providence, RI: Berg, pp. 117–34.

Cohen, Sara (1998), 'Sounding Out the City: Music and the Sensuous Production of Place', in Leyshon, Andrew, Matless, David and Revill, George (eds), *The Place of Music*, New York and London: Guilford Publications, pp. 155–76.

Cohen, Sara (1999) 'Scenes', in Horner, Bruce and Swiss, Thomas (eds), *Key Terms in Popular Music and Culture*, Oxford and Malden, MA: Blackwell, pp. 239–50.

Collins, John and Richards, Paul (1989), 'Popular Music in West Africa', in Frith, Simon (ed.), *World Music, Politics and Social Change*, Manchester and New York: Manchester University Press, pp. 12–46.

Čolović, Ivan (1994), *Bordel Ratnika: Folklor, Politika i Rat*, Belgrade: Biblioteka XX Vek.

Connell, John and Gibson, Chris (2003), *Sound Tracks: Popular Music, Identity and Place*, London and New York: Routledge.

Connor, Walker (1994), 'A Nation is a Nation, is a State, is an Ethnic Group, is a ...', in Hutchinson, John and Smith, Anthony (eds), *Nationalism*, Oxford: Oxford University Press, pp. 36–46.

Cook, Guy (1992), *The Discourse of Advertising*, London: Routledge.

Cooke, Peter and Doornbos, Martin (1982), 'Rwenzururu Protest Songs', *Africa*, 52 (1), 37–60.

Craig, Timothy and King, Richard (eds) (2002), *Global Goes Local: Popular Culture in Asia*, Vancouver and Toronto: UBC Press.

Crain, Mary (1999), 'New North African Immigration to Spain', *Middle East Report*, 211, Summer, pp. 23–5.

Crook, Larry (2001), 'Turned-Around Beat: "Maracatu de Baque Virado" and Chico Science', in Perrone, Charles and Dunn, Christopher (eds), *Brazilian Popular Music and Globalization*, Gainsville: University of Florida Press, pp. 233–44.

Crystal, David, (1999) 'Death Sentence', *The Guardian, G2*, 25 October, 2–5.

Dagbladet, 'Klubbkaos', 7 May 1999.

Deleuze, Gilles and Guattari, Félix (1988), *A Thousand Plateaus: Capitalism and Schizophrenia*, trans. Brian Massumi, London: Athlone Press.

De Vos, George (1975), 'Ethnic Pluralism: Conflict and Accommodation', in De Vos, George and Romanucci-Ross, Lola (eds), *Ethnic Identity: Cultural Continuities and Change*, Palo Alto, CA: Mayfield, pp. 6–39.

Diamond, Beverley (1994), 'Issues of Hegemony and Identity in Canadian Music', in Diamond, Beverley and Witmer, Robert (eds), *Canadian Music: Issues of Hegemony and Identity*, Toronto: Canadian Scholars' Press, pp. 1–22.

Diop, Abdoulaye-Bara (1981), *La Société wolof: tradition et changement, les systèmes d'inégalité et de domination*, Paris: Karthala.

Douglas, Mary (1985), *Risk Acceptability According to the Social Sciences*, New York: Russell Sage Foundation.

Douglas, Mary (1992), *Risk and Blame: Essays in Cultural Theory*, London: Routledge.

Du Bois, W.E.B. (1999 [1903]), *The Souls of Black Folk*, ed. Henry Louis Gates Jr and Terri Hume Oliver, New York: Norton.

Duffett, Mark (2000), 'Going Down like a Song: National Identity, Global Commerce and the Great Canadian Party', *Popular Music*, 19 (1), 1–11.

Dunn, Christopher (2001), *Brutality Garden: Tropicália and the Emergence of a Brazilian Counterculture*, Chapel Hill: University of North Carolina Press.

Dunn, Leslie C. and Jones, Nancy A. (1994), 'Introduction', in Dunn, Leslie C. and Jones, Nancy A. (eds), *Embodied Voices: Representing Female Vocality in Western Culture*, Cambridge: Cambridge University Press, pp. 1–16.

Dyer, Geoff (2000), 'New Middle Class in Brazil get their Kicks from Rodeo', *Financial Times* weekend, 26 August.

Eriksen, Thomas H.E. (1993), 'Being Norwegian in a Shrinking World: Reflections on Norwegian Identity', in Kiel, Anne Cohen (ed.), *Continuity and Change: Aspects of Modern Norway*, Oslo: Scandinavian University Press, pp. 5–39. Available online at http://folk.uio.no/geirthe/Norwegian.html.

Erlmann, Veit (1993), 'The Politics and Aesthetics of Transnational Musics', *World of Music*, 35 (2), 3–15.

Erlmann, Veit (1999), *Music, Modernity and the Global Imagination: South Africa and the West*, New York and Oxford: Oxford University Press.

Ewens, Graeme (1991), *Africa O-Ye! A Celebration of African Music*, Enfield: Guinness.

Fairley, Jan (2001), 'The "Local" and the "Global" in Popular Music', in Frith, Simon, Straw, Will and Street, John (eds), *The Cambridge Companion to Pop and Rock*, Cambridge: Cambridge University Press, pp. 272–89.

Featherstone, Mike (1990a), 'Global Culture(s): An Introduction', in Featherstone, Mike (ed.), *Global Culture: Nationalism, Globalization and Modernity*, London, Newbury Park, CA and New Delhi: Sage, pp. 1–14.

Featherstone, Mike (ed.) (1990b), *Global Culture: Nationalism, Globalization and Modernity*, London, Newbury Park, CA and New Delhi: Sage.

Feld, Steven (1994), 'From Schizophonia to Schismogenesis: On the Discourses and Commodification Practices of "World Music" and "World Beat"', in Keil, Charles and Feld, Steven, *Music Grooves*, Chicago and London: University of Chicago Press, pp. 257–89.

Feld, Steven (2000), 'A Sweet Lullaby for World Music', *Public Culture*, 12 (1), Winter, 145–71.

Feld, Steven and Basso, Keith H. (eds) (1996), *Senses of Place*, Santa Fe, NM: School of American Research Press.

Ferreira de Castro, Paulo (1997), 'Nacionalismo musical ou os equivocos da portugalidade'/ 'Musical Nationalism, or, the Ambiguities of Portugueseness', trans. Ivan Moody, in El-Shawan Castelo-Branco, Salwa (ed.), *Portugal e o mundo: O encontro de culturas na música / Portugal and the World: The Encounter of Cultures in Music*, Lisbon: Dom Quixote, pp. 155–62; pp. 153–70.

Finnegan, Ruth (1989), *The Hidden Musicians: Music-Making in an English Town*, Cambridge: Cambridge University Press.

Fischer, Michael M.J. (1986), 'Ethnicity and the Post-Modern Arts of Memory', in Clifford, James and Marcus, George E. (eds), *Writing Culture: The Poetics and Politics of Ethnography*, Berkeley: University of California Press, pp. 194–233.

Folkestad, Göran (2002), 'National Identity and Music', in McDonald, Raymond, Hargreaves, David and Miell, Dorothy (eds), *Musical Identities*, Oxford: Oxford University Press, pp. 151–62.

Forbes, Andrew D.W. (1986), *Warlords and Muslims in Chinese Central Asia: A Political History of Republican Sinkiang 1911–1949*, Cambridge: Cambridge University Press.

Forney, Matthew (2002), 'Man of Constant Sorrow: One Uighur Makes Music for the Masses', feature, 'Xinjiang: One Nation – Divided', *Time Asia*, 159 (11), 25 March. Available online at TIMEAsia.com http://www.time.com/time/asia/features/xinjiang/culture.html (accessed April 2002).

Fraser, Nicholas (2000), 'In Poll after Poll, a Majority of French Voters admitted to holding Racist Ideas: The Front National has made Hatred Legitimate', *The Guardian, Weekend*, 26 August, 5.

Freud, Sigmund (1976 [1905]), *Jokes and their Relation to the Unconscious*, trans. J. Strachey, Harmondsworth: Penguin.

Friedman, Jonathan (1994), *Cultural Identity and Global Process*, London: Sage.

Frith, Simon (ed.) (1989), *World Music, Politics and Social Change*, Manchester and New York: Manchester University Press.

Frith, Simon (1991), 'A Critical Response', in Robinson, Deanna Campbell, Buck, Elizabeth B. and Cuthbert, Marlene (eds), *Music at the Margins: Popular Music and Global Cultural Diversity*, London: Sage, pp. 284–7.

Frith, Simon (1992), 'The Cultural Study of Popular Music', in Grossberg, Lawrence, Nelson, Cary and Treichler, Paula A. (eds), *Cultural Studies*, London and New York: Routledge, pp. 174–86.

Frith, Simon (1996), 'Music and Identity', in Hall, Stuart and Du Gay, Paul (eds), *Questions of Cultural Identity*, London: Sage, pp. 108–27.

García Canclini, Néstor (1990), *Culturas híbridas: estrategias para entrar y salir de la modernidad*, Mexico City: Grijalbo.

García Canclini, Néstor (1999), *La globalización imaginada*, Buenos Aires: Ediciones Paidós.

García Lorca, Federico (1989 [1936]), *Primeras canciones, Seis poemas galegos, Poemas sueltos, Colección de canciones populares antiguas*, Madrid: Akal.

Garofalo, Reebee (1993), 'Whose World, What Beat: The Transnational Music Industry, Identity, and Cultural Imperialism', *World of Music*, 35 (2), 16–32.

Gebesmair, Andreas and Smudits, Alfred (eds) (2001), *Global Repertoires: Popular Music Within and Beyond the Transnational Music Industry*, Aldershot: Ashgate.

Geertz, Clifford (1996), 'Afterword', in Feld, Steven and Basso, Keith H. (eds), *Senses of Place*, Santa Fe, NM: School of American Research Press, pp. 159–262.

Gellner, Ernest (1983), *Nations and Nationalism*, Oxford: Blackwell.

Gellner, Ernest (1995), *Conditions of Liberty: Civil Society and Its Rivals*, Harmondsworth: Penguin.

Geng, Shimin (1984), 'On the Fusion of Nationalities in the Tarim Basin and the Formation of the Modern Uighur Nationality', *Central Asian Survey*, 3 (4), 1–14.

Giddens, Anthony (1991), *Modernity and Self-Identity*, Cambridge: Polity.

Giddens, Anthony (1998), *The Third Way*, Cambridge: Polity.

Gilroy, Paul (1993), *The Black Atlantic: Modernity and Double Consciousness*, London and New York: Verso.

Gladney, Dru C. (1990), 'The Ethnogenesis of the Uighur', *Central Asian Survey*, 9 (1), 1–28.

Gladney, Dru C. (1994), 'Representing Nationality in China: Refiguring Majority/Minority Identities', *Journal of Asian Studies*, 53 (l), 92–123.

Gladney, Dru C. (1996) 'Relational Alterity: Constructing Dungan (Hui), Uygur, and Kazakh Identities Across China, Central Asia, and Turkey', *History and Anthropology*, 9 (4): 445–77.

Glick Schiller, Nina, Basch, Linda and Blanc-Szanton, Cristina (1992), 'Transnationalism: A New Analytic Framework for Understanding Migration', in Glick Schiller, Nina, Basch, Linda and Blanc-Szanton, Cristina (eds), *Transnational Perspective on Migration: Race, Class, Ethnicity, and Nationalism Reconsidered*, New York: The New York Academy of Science, pp. 1–44.

Goffman, Erving (1971), *The Presentation of Self in Everyday Life*, Harmondsworth: Penguin.

Goffman, Erving (1981), *Forms of Talk*, Blackwell: Oxford.

Goffman, Erving (1986), *Frame Analysis: An Essay on the Organization of Experience*, Boston: Northeastern University Press.

Goodwin, Andrew and Gore, Joe (1990), 'World Beat and the Cultural Imperialism Debate', *Socialist Review*, 20 (3), 63–80.

Graham, Colin (1999), '"… maybe that's just Blarney": Irish Culture and the Persistence of Authenticity', in Graham, Colin and Kirkland, Richard (eds), *Ireland and Cultural Theory: The Mechanics of Authenticity*, Basingstoke and London: Macmillan, pp. 7–28.

Graham, Colin and Kirkland, Richard (eds) (1999), *Ireland and Cultural Theory: The Mechanics of Authenticity*, Basingstoke and London: Macmillan.

Green, Lucy (1988), *Music on Deaf Ears: Musical Meaning, Ideology and Education*, Manchester University Press.

Green, Lucy (1997), *Music, Gender, Education*, Cambridge: Cambridge University Press.

Green, Lucy (2001), *How Popular Musicians Learn: A Way Ahead for Music Education*, Aldershot and Burlington, VT: Ashgate.

Greimas, Algirdas Julien (1987), 'The Interaction of Semiotic Constraints', in *On Meaning: Selected Writings in Semiotic Theory*, trans. Paul J. Perron and Frank H. Collins, Minneapolis: University of Minnesota Press, pp. 48–62.

Grenier, Line and Guilbault, Jocelyne (1990), '"Authority" Revisited: The "Other" in Anthropology and Popular Music Studies', *Ethnomusicology*, 34 (3), 381–97.

Greve, Martin (1997), *Alla turca: Berliner Musik aus der Türkei*, Berlin: Ausländer-beauftragte des Senats.

Guilbault, Jocelyne (1993), 'On Redefining the "Local" Through World Music', *World of Music*, 35 (2), 33–47.

Guilbault, Jocelyne (1997), 'Interpreting World Music: A Challenge in Theory and Practice', *Popular Music*, 16 (1), 31–44.

Guilbault, Jocelyne (2001), 'World Music', in Frith, Simon, Straw, Will and Street, John (eds), *The Cambridge Companion to Pop and Rock*, Cambridge: Cambridge University Press, pp. 176–92.

Gupta, Akhil and Ferguson, James (1997), 'Culture, Power, Place: Ethnography at the End of an Era', in Gupta, Akhil and Ferguson, James (eds), *Culture, Power, Place: Explorations in Critical Anthropology*, Durham, NC: Duke University Press, pp. 1–29.

Habermas, Jürgen (1984), *The Theory of Communicative Action: I*, London: Heinemann.

Habermas, Jürgen (1989), *The Theory of Communicative Action: II*, Cambridge: Polity.

Habermas, Jürgen (1996), *Between Facts and Norms*, Cambridge: Polity.

Habermas, Jürgen (1998), *On the Pragmatics of Communication*, Cambridge, MA: MIT Press.

Hall, Stuart (1990), 'Cultural Identity and Diaspora', in Rutherford, Jonathan (ed.), *Identity: Community, Culture, Difference*, London: Lawrence and Wishart, pp. 222–37.

Hall, Stuart (1996), 'Introduction: Who Needs "Identity"?', in Hall, Stuart and Du Gay, Paul (eds), *Questions of Cultural Identity*, London: Sage, pp. 1–17.

Hall, Stuart and Du Gay, Paul (eds) (1996), *Questions of Cultural Identity*, London: Sage.

Hamm, Charles (1989), 'Afterword', in Frith, Simon (ed.), *World Music, Politics and Social Change*, Manchester and New York: Manchester University Press, pp. 211–16.

Hanchard, Michael (1999), 'Introduction', in Hanchard, Michael (ed.), *Racial Politics in Contemporary Brazil*, Durham, NC: Duke University Press, pp. 1–29.

Haneda, Akira (1978), 'The Problems of Turkicization and Islamization of East Turkestan', *Acta Asiatica*, 34, 1–21.

Hannerz, Ulf (1990), 'Cosmopolitans and Locals in World Culture', in Featherstone, Mike (ed.), *Global Culture: Nationalism, Globalization and Modernity*, London, Newbury Park, CA and New Delhi: Sage, pp. 237–51.

Harding, Jeremy (2000), *The Uninvited: Refugees at the Rich Man's Gate*, London: Profile Books.

Hardt, Michael and Negri, Antonio (2000), *Empire*, Cambridge, MA: Harvard University Press.

Hardt, Michael and Negri, Antonio (2004), *Multitude*, London: Hamish Hamilton.

Harris, Rachel (2002), 'Cassettes, Bazaars, and Saving the Nation: The Uyghur Music Industry in Xinjiang, China', in Craig, Timothy and King, Richard (eds), *Global Goes Local: Popular Culture in Asia*, Vancouver and Toronto: UBC Press, pp. 265–82.

Harris, Rachel (2004), *Singing the Village: Memories, Music and Ritual amongst the Sibe of Xinjiang*, Oxford: Oxford University Press, British Academy Postdoctoral Fellow Monograph.

Harvey, David (1990), *The Condition of Postmodernity: An Enquiry into the Origins of Cultural Change*, Cambridge, MA: Blackwell.

Hasenbalg, Carlos and do Valle Silva, Nelson (1999), 'Notes on Racial and Political Inequality in Brazil', in Hanchard, Michael (ed.), *Racial Politics in Contemporary Brazil*, Durham, NC: Duke University Press, pp. 154–78.

Hawkins, Stan (1999), 'Press, Play, Record', paper presented at International Association for the Study of Popular Music conference, Sydney University, 9–13 July.

Hawkins, Stan (2001), 'Joy in Repetition: Structures, Idiolects, and Concepts of Repetition in Club Music', *Studia Musicologica Norvegica*, 27, 53–78.

Hawkins, Stan (2002), *Settling the Pop Score: Pop Texts and Identity Politics*, Aldershot: Ashgate.

Hawkins, Stan (2003), 'Feel the Beat Come Down: House Music as Rhetoric', in Moore, Allan (ed.), *Analyzing Popular Music*, Cambridge: Cambridge University Press, pp. 80–102.

Hayes-Bautista, David E. and Rodríguez, Gregory (1994), 'L.A.'s Culture Comes Full Circle', *Los Angeles Times*, 5 May.

Hegel, Friedrich (1980 [1807]), *Phänomenologie des Geistes*, vol. 9 of *Gesammelte Werke*, ed. Wolfgang Bonsiepen and Reinhard Heede, Hamburg: Meiner.

Hesmondhalgh, David (2000), 'International Times: Fusions, Exoticism and Anti-racism in Electronic Dance Music', in Born, Georgina and Hesmondhalgh, David (eds), *Western Music and its Others: Difference, Representation and Appropriation in Music*, Berkeley and London: University of California Press, pp. 280–304.

Hesmondhalgh, David (2002), *The Cultural Industries*, London: Sage.

Hesmondhalgh, David and Negus, Keith (eds) (2002), *Popular Music Studies*, London: Arnold.

Holloway, Karla (1994), 'The Lyrical Dimensions of Spirituality: Music, Voice and Language in the Novels of Toni Morrison', in Dunn, Leslie C. and Jones, Nancy A. (eds), *Embodied Voices: Representing Female Vocality in Western Culture*, Cambridge, Cambridge University Press, pp. 197–211.

Holton, Milne and Mihailovich, Vasa D. (1998), *Serbian Poetry from the Beginnings to the Present*, New Haven, CT: Yale Center for International and Area Studies.

Holton, Robert J. (1998), *Globalization and the Nation State*, Basingstoke: Macmillan.

Homan, Shane (2000), 'Losing the Local: Sydney and the Oz Rock Tradition', *Popular Music*, 19 (1), 31–49.

Hoppe, Thomas (1992) 'Die Chinesische Position in Ost-Turkestan/Xinjiang', *China Aktuell*, June, 360.

Horner, Bruce and Swiss, Thomas (1999), *Key Terms in Popular Music and Culture*, Malden, MA: Blackwell.

Hudson, Mark (1999 [1998]), *The Music in My Head*, London: Vintage.

Hudson, Mark (2000a), 'The Leopoldville Sound: Africa's Human Effervescence Expressed in the Congolese Rumba', *Times Literary Supplement*, 5078, 28 July, 4.

Hudson, Robert (2000b), 'Songs of Love and Hate: The Role of the Intelligentsia, Music and Poetry in Forging Serbian Ethnic National Identity', in Andrew, Joe, Crook, Malcolm and Waller, Michael (eds), *Why Europe? Problems of Culture and Identity*, Basingstoke: Macmillan, pp. 167–81.

Hudson, Robert (2003), 'Songs of Seduction: Popular Music and Serbian Nationalism', *Patterns of Prejudice*, 37 (2), June, 157–76.

Hutnyk, John (2000), *Critique of Exotica*, London: Pluto Press.

Human Rights Watch (2001), *China: Human Rights Concerns in Xinjiang*, New York: Human Rights Watch.

Hutchinson, John and Smith, Anthony (eds) (1994), *Nationalism*, Oxford: Oxford University Press.

Irele, Abiola (1993), 'Is African Music Possible? In an Age after Modernism, What Role is Left for Local Difference?', *Transition*, 61, 56–71.

Ivić, Pavle (ed.) (1995), *The History of Serbian Culture*, Edgeware: Porthill.

Izzo, Jean-Claude (1995), *Total Kheops*, Paris: Gallimard Série Noire.

Jameson, Fredric (1972), *The Prison-House of Language: A Critical Account of Structuralism*, Princeton, NJ: Princeton University Press.

Jameson, Fredric (1987), 'Foreword', in Greimas, Algirdas Julien (ed.), *On Meaning: Selected Writings in Semiotic Theory*, trans. Paul J. Perron and Frank H. Collins, Minneapolis: University of Minnesota Press, pp. vi–xxiii.

Jameson, Fredric (1988 [1973]), 'The Vanishing Mediator; or, Max Weber as Storyteller', in *The Ideologies of Theory*, 2 vols, Minneapolis: University of Minnesota Press, vol. 2, pp. 3–34.

JanMohamed, Abdul R. and Lloyd, David (1990), 'Introduction: Towards a Theory of Minority Discourse: What is to be Done?', in JanMohamed, Abdul R. and Lloyd, David (eds), *The Nature and Context of Minority Discourse*, Oxford and New York: Oxford University Press, pp. 1–16.

Johansen, Anders (1995), *Den Store Misforståelsen*, Oslo: Spartacus Forlag.

Johnson, Sherry (2000), 'Authenticity: Who Needs It?', *British Journal of Music Education*, 17 (3), 277–86.

Judah, Tim (1997), *The Serbs: History, Myth and the Destruction of Yugoslavia*, New Haven and London: Yale University Press.

Kassabian, Anahid (1999), 'Popular', in Horner, Bruce and Swiss, Thomas (eds), *Key Terms in Popular Music and Culture*, Malden, MA: Blackwell, pp. 113–23.

Kassabian, Anahid (2004), 'Would You Like Some World Music With Your Latte? Starbucks, Putumayo, and Distributed Tourism', *Twentieth-century Music*, 1 (2), 209–23.

Keil, Charles and Feld, Steven (1994), *Music Grooves*, Chicago and London: University of Chicago Press.

Kellner, Thierry (2002), 'China: The Uighur Situation from Independence for the Central Asian Republics to the Post 11 September Era', Writenet Paper, United Nations High Commissioner for Refugees (UNHCR) Emergency and Security Services.

Kennedy, Paul and Danks, Catherine J. (2001), *Globalization and National Identities: Crisis or Opportunity?*, Basingstoke: Palgrave.

Kim Ho-dong (1986), 'The Muslim Rebellion of the Kashgar Emirate in Chinese Central Asia 1864–1877', unpublished PhD dissertation, Harvard University.

Kovćežić, Vuk (1971), *Boj na Kosovu: Narodne Pesme, Sveska Četvrta Narodne Biblioteka*, Belgrade: Beogradski Izdavačko-Grafićki Zavod.

Krims, Adam (2000), *Rap Music and the Poetics of Identity*, Cambridge: Cambridge University Press.

Kvifte, Tellef (2001), 'Hunting for the Gold at the End of the Rainbow: Identity and Global Romanticism: On the Roots of Ethnic Music', *Popular Musicology Online*, http://www.cyberstudia.com/popular-musicology-online/papers-5/kvifte.html (accessed 1 August 2001).

Labi, Philippe, Daum, Marc and Crazy, J.-M. (1990), 'Jack Lang: Je crois à la culture rap', *VSD*, 1 November, 40–41.

Lacan, Jacques (1997), *The Language of the Self: The Function of Language in Psychoanalysis*, trans. Anthony Wilden, Baltimore, MD: Johns Hopkins University Press.

Laing, Dave (1986), 'The Music Industry and the "Cultural Imperialism" Thesis', *Media, Culture and Society*, 8 (3), 331–41.

Lakićević, Dragan (1999), *Srpske Narodne Epske Pesme*, Belgrade: Bookland.

Larrain, Jorge (1999), 'Modernity and Identity: Cultural Change in Latin America', in Gwynne, Robert and Kay, Cristóbal (eds), *Latin America Transformed: Globalization and Modernity*, London: Arnold, pp. 182–202.

Lazarus, Neil (1999), *Nationalism and Cultural Practice in the Postcolonial World*, Cambridge: Cambridge University Press.

Letts, Richard (2000), 'Some Effects of Globalisation on Music', *Resonance*, 29, 4–8.

Leyshon, Andrew, Matless, David and Revill, George (eds) (1998), *The Place of Music*, New York and London: Guilford Publications.

Lipsitz, George (1990), *Time Passages: Collective Memory and American Popular Culture*. Minneapolis: University of Minnesota Press.

Lipsitz, George (1994), *Dangerous Crossroads: Popular Music, Postmodernism and the Poetics of Place*, London and New York: Verso.

Lomax, Alan (1968, repr. 1978), *Folk Song Style and Culture*, New Brunswick, NJ: Transaction Books.

Lou, Vicente (2000), 'Antonio Nóbrega: o Corpo e a Alma Brasileira', *Leros*, 107, 24–5.

Lupton, Deborah (1999), *Risk*, London: Routledge.

McCrone, David (1998), *The Sociology of Nationalism*, London and New York: Routledge.

McGowan, Chris and Pessanha, Ricardo (1998), *The Brazilian Sound: Samba, Bossa Nova and the Popular Music of Brazil*, Philadelphia: Temple University Press.

Mackerras, Colin (1985), 'Uygur Performing Arts in Contemporary China', *China Quarterly*, 101, 58–77.

McLaughlin, Noel and McLoone, Martin (2000), 'Hybridity and National Musics: The Case of Irish Rock Music', *Popular Music*, 19 (2), 181–99.

McLoone, Martin (ed.) (1991), *Culture, Identity and Broadcasting in Ireland: Local Issues, Global Perspectives*, Belfast: Institute of Irish Studies, Queen's University.

Magaldi, Cristina (1999), 'Adopting Imports: New Images and Alliances in Brazilian Popular Music', *Popular Music*, 18 (3), 309–29.

Malm, Krister (2001), 'Globalization-Localization, Homogenization-Diversification and Other Discordant Trends: A Challenge to Music Policy Makers', in Gebesmair, Andreas and Smudits, Alfred (eds), *Global Repertoires: Popular Music Within and Beyond the Transnational Music Industry*, Aldershot: Ashgate, pp. 89–95.

Malm, Krister and Wallis, Roger (1992), *Media Policy and Music Activity*, London and New York: Routledge.

Manuel, Peter (1988), *Popular Musics of the Non-Western World: An Introductory Survey*, New York and Oxford: Oxford University Press.

Manuel, Peter (1993), *Cassette Culture: Music and Technology in North India*, Chicago and London: University of Chicago Press.

Manuel, Peter (1995a), 'Music as Symbol, Music as Simulacrum: Postmodern, Pre-Modern, and Modern Aesthetics in Subcultural Popular Music', *Popular Music*, 14 (2), 227–39.

Manuel, Peter (1995b) *Caribbean Currents: Caribbean Music from Rumba to Reggae*, with Bilby, Kenneth and Largey, Michael, Philadelphia: Temple University Press.

Manuel, Peter (1998), 'Chutney and Indo-Trinidadian Cultural Identity', *Popular Music*, 17 (1), 21–43.

Maróthy, János (1974), *Music and the Bourgeois, Music and the Proletarian*, Budapest: Akadémiai Kiadó.

Martín-Barbero, Jesús (1998), *De los medios a las mediaciones: comunicación, cultura y hegemonía*, Santa Fe de Bogotá: Convenio Andrés Bello.

Martínez, Rubén (1994), 'The Dance of Nuevo L.A.', *Los Angeles Times Magazine*, 30 January.

Matović, Ana (1995), 'Uticaj srpskog pozorista na ocuvanje i prenosenje narodnih melodija', *Srpska Akademija Nauka i Umetnosti, Muzikoloski Institut*, Belgrade: Serbian Academy of Arts and Sciences Papers, pp. 155–65.

Maxwell, Kenneth (1999), 'The Two Brazils', *Wilson Quarterly*, Winter, 1999/2000, 50–60.

Middleton, Richard (1990), *Studying Popular Music*, Milton Keynes and Philadelphia: Open University Press.

Middleton, Richard (2000), 'Introduction: Locating the Popular Music Text', in Middleton, Richard (ed.), *Reading Pop*, Oxford: Oxford University Press, pp. 1–19.

Middleton, Richard (2006), *Voicing the Popular: On the Subjects of Popular Music*, New York: Routledge.

Miller, David (1995), *On Nationality*, Oxford: Clarendon Press.

Milošević, Mira (2000), *Los tristes y los héroes: Historias de nacionalistas serbios*, Madrid: Espasa Calpe.

Mitchell, Timothy (1994), *Flamenco Deep Song*, New Haven, CT: Yale University Press.

Mitchell, Tony (1996), *Popular Music and Local Identity: Rock, Pop and Rap in Europe and Oceania*, London and New York: Cassell.

Mitchell, Tony (ed.) (2001), *Global Noise: Rap and Hip-hop Outside the USA*, Middletown, CT: Wesleyan University Press.

Monroe, Alexei (2000), 'Balkan Hardcore', http://www.Central/EuropeReview.com/, vol. 2, no. 24 (accessed 19 June 2000).

Moore, Allan (2002), 'Authenticity as Authentication', *Popular Music*, 21 (2), 209–33.

Morgan, Peter (1997), *A Barrel of Stones: In Search of Serbia*, Aberystwyth: Planet.

Münch, Richard (1999), 'McDonaldized Culture: The End of Communication', in Smart, Barry (ed.), *Resisting McDonaldization*, London: Sage, pp. 135–47.

Murphy, David (2000), *Sembene: Imagining Alternatives in Film and Fiction*, Oxford: James Currey; Trenton, NJ: Africa World Press.

Murphy, John (2001), 'Self-Discovery in Brazilian Popular Music: Mestre Ambrósio', in Perrone, Charles and Dunn, Christopher (eds), *Brazilian Popular Music and Globalization*, Gainsville: University of Florida Press, pp. 245–57.

Murphy, Michael (2001), 'Introduction', in Murphy, Michael and White, Harry (eds), *Musical Constructions of Nationalism; Essays on the History and Ideology of European Musical Culture 1800–1945*, Cork: Cork University Press, pp. 1–15.

Naby, Eden (1986), 'Uighur Elites in Xinjiang', *Central Asian Survey*, 5 (3/4), 241–54.

Nairn, Tom (2005a), 'Make for the Boondocks', *London Review of Books*, 5 May, 11–14.

Nairn, Tom (2005b), 'Democratic Warming', *London Review of Books*, 4 August, 19–20.

Nederveen Pieterse, Jan (1995), 'Globalization as Hybridization', in Featherstone, Mike, Lash, Scott and Robertson, Roland (eds), *Global Modernities*, London: Sage, pp. 45–68.

Negus, Keith (1996), *Popular Music in Theory: An Introduction*, London: Polity Press.

Nóbrega, Antônio (1997), 'Brincante e Segundas Estórias', in *Antônio Nóbrega*, São Paulo: Philips Brasilis, 6 (Programme for the stage version of *Madeira que Cupim não Rói*.)

Ó Cinnéide, Barra (2002), *Riverdance: The Phenomenon*, Dublin: Blackhall Publishing.

O'Connor, Nuala (1991), *Bringing It All Back Home: The Influence of Irish Music*, London: BBC Books.

Oliver, Paul (2001), 'Savannah Syncopators', in Oliver, Paul, Russell, Tony, Dixon, Robert M., Godrich, W. John and Rye, Howard, *Yonder Come the Blues: The Evolution of a Genre*, Cambridge: Cambridge University Press, pp. 11–142.

Ortiz, Renato (1994), *Mundalização e cultura*, São Paolo: Brasiliense.

Østerberg, Dag (1998), *Arkitektur og Sosiologi i Oslo: en sosio-materiell fortolkning*, Oslo: Pax Forlag A/S.

Otero Garabís, Juan (2000), *Nación y ritmo: 'descargas' desde el Caribe*, San Juan: Ediciones Callejón.

Oumano, Elena and Lopetegui, Enrique (1993) 'The Hottest Sound in L.A. is ... *Banda*?!', *Los Angeles Times* (Calendar), 1 May.

Pacini Hernández, Deborah (1993), 'A View from the South: Spanish Caribbean Perspectives on World Beat', *World of Music*, 35 (2), 48–69.

Pejović, Roksana (1995), 'Musical Composition and Performance from the Eighteenth Century to the Present', in Ivić, Pavle (ed.), *The History of Serbian Culture*, Edgeware: Porthill, pp. 243–54.

Perris, Arnold (1985), *Music as Propaganda: Art to Persuade, Art to Control*, Westport, CT: Greenwood Press.

Perrone, Charles and Dunn, Christopher (2001), '"Chiclete com Banana": Internationalization in Brazilian Popular Music', in Perrone, Charles and Dunn, Christopher (eds), *Brazilian Popular Music and Globalization*, Gainsville: University of Florida Press, pp. 1–38.

Pessoa, Fernando (1950), *Obras Completas V: Mensagem*, Lisboa: Ática.

Pierre-Adolphe, Philippe and Bocquet, José-Louis (1997), *Rapologie*, Paris: Editions 1001 Nuits.

Poignant, Bernard (1998), *Langues et cultures régionales*, Paris: La documentation française.

Porter, James (1993), 'Convergence, Divergence, and Dialectic in Folksong Paradigms', *The Journal of American Folklore*, 106 (1), 61–98.

Preston, Peter W. (1997), *Political/Cultural Identity: Citizens and Nations in a Global Era*, London: Sage.

Pritchard, Eleanor (1999), 'Turbofolk in Serbia: Some Preliminary Notes', *Slovo*, vol. 11, London: School of Slavonic and East European Studies, pp. 141–50.

Radano, Ronald Michael and Bohlman, Philip V. (eds) (2000), *Music and the Racial Imagination*, Chicago: University of Chicago Press.

Reed, John (1994 [1916]), *War in Eastern Europe: Travels through the Balkans in 1915*, London: Orion.

Regás, Rosa (1998), *Barcelona, un día*, Madrid: Alfaguara.

Regev, Motti (1996), 'Musica Mizrakhit, Israeli Rock and National Culture in Israel', *Popular Music*, 15 (3), 275–84.

Regev, Motti (1997), 'Rock Aesthetics and Musics of the World', *Theory, Culture and Society*, 14 (3), 125–42.

Ricros, Andre (1993), 'Estrategias en la Comunidad Europea sobre el estudio y la recuperación del patrimonio musical tradicional y popular', *La promoción de los patrimonios musicales populares y tradicionales en Europa*, Madrid: Centro de Documentación Musical, Instituto Nacional de las Artes Escénicas y de la Música, pp. 31–41.

Roberts, Martin (1992), '"World Music" and the Global Cultural Economy', *Diaspora*, 2 (2), 229–42.

Roberts, Sean R. (1998), 'Negotiating Locality, Islam, and National Culture in a Changing Borderlands: The Revival of the Mäshräp Ritual among Young Uighur Men in the Ili Valley', *Central Asian Survey*, 17 (4), 673–99.

Robertson, Roland (1990), 'Mapping the Global Conditions: Globalization as the Central Concept', in Featherstone, Mike (ed.), *Global Culture: Nationalism, Globalization and Modernity*, London, Newbury Park, CA and New Delhi: Sage, pp. 15–30.

Robertson, Roland (1992), *Globalization: Social Theory and Global Culture*, London, Newbury Park, CA and New Delhi: Sage.

Robertson, Roland (1995), 'Glocalization: Time–Space and Homogeneity–Heterogeneity', in Featherstone, Mike, Lash, Scott and Robertson, Roland (eds), *Global Modernities*, London: Sage, pp. 25–44.

Román-Velázquez, Patria (1999), *The Making of Latin London*, Aldershot: Ashgate.

Rosaldo, Renato (1993), *Culture and Truth: The Remaking of Social Analysis*, Boston: Beacon Press.

Rose, Tricia (1994), *Black Noise: Rap Music and Black Culture in Contemporary America*, Hanover, NH: University Press of New England.

Rudelson, Justin Jon (1997), *Oasis Identities: Uighur Nationalism Along China's Silk Road*, New York: Columbia University Press.

Ruiz Olabuénaga, J.I., Ruiz Vieytez, E.J. and Vicente Torrado, T.L. (1995), *Los inmigrantes irregulares en España*, Bilbao: Universidad de Deusto Press.

Ruud, Even (1997), 'Musikk – identitetens lydspor', in Time, Sveinung (ed.), *Om kulturell identitet*, Bergen: Høgskolen I Bergen, pp. 29–40.

Sadie, Stanley (ed.) (2001) 'Nationalism', in *The New Grove Dictionary of Music and Musicians*, 2nd edn, vol. 12, London: Macmillan, pp. 689–706.

Saguchi, Toru (1978), 'Kashgaria', *Acta Asiatica*, 34, 61–78.

Sampaio, Ivanildo (1998), 'Extensao Cultural', *Jornal do Commércio*, Recife, 20 April, http://www2.uol.com.br/JC_1998/2004/editoria.htm (accessed 16 October 2003).

Sankhare, Oumar (1998), *Youssou N'Dour: Le Poète*, Senegal: Les Nouvelles Editions Africaines du Sénégal.

Schade-Poulsen, Marc (1999), *Men and Popular Music in Algeria*, Austin: University of Texas Press.

Schlee, Günther (ed.) (2002), *Imagined Differences: Hatred and the Construction of Identity*, Hamburg: Lit Verlag.

Schlesinger, Philip (1991), 'Collective Identities in a Changing Europe', in McLoone, Martin (ed.), *Culture, Identity and Broadcasting in Ireland: Local Issues, Global Perspectives*, Belfast: Institute of Irish Studies, Queen's University, pp. 41–52.

Schreiner, Claus (1993), *Música Brasileira: A History of Popular Music and the People of Brazil*, New York: Marion Boyars.

Schwarz, Henry G. (1984), *The Minorities of Northern China: A Survey*, Washington: Western Washington University Press.

Schwarz, Roberto (1992), *Misplaced Ideas: Essays on Brazilian Culture*, London: Verso.

Shabazz, David L. (1999), *Public Enemy Number One: A Research Study of Rap Music, Culture and Black Nationalism in America*, Clinton, SC: Awesome Records.

Shank, Barry (1994), *Dissonant Identities: The Rock 'n' Roll Scene in Austin, Texas*, Hanover, NH: University Press of New England.

Sharma, Sanjay, Hutnyk, John and Sharma, Ashwani (eds) (1996), *Dis-Orienting Rhythms: The Politics of the New Asian Dance Music*, London: Zed Books.

Shepherd, John (1999), 'Text', in Horner, Bruce and Swiss, Thomas (eds), *Key Terms in Popular Music and Culture*, Malden, MA.: Blackwell, pp. 156–77.

Shepherd, John and Wicke, Peter (1997), *Music and Cultural Theory*, Cambridge: Polity Press.

Shohat, Ella (1992), 'Notes on the "Post-Colonial"', *Social Text*, 31–2, 99–113.

Shuker, Roy (1994), *Understanding Popular Music*, London and New York: Routledge.

Shuker, Roy and Pickering, Michael (1994), 'Kiwi Rock: Popular Music and Cultural Identity in New Zealand', *Popular Music*, 13 (3), 261–78.

Shusterman, Richard (1992), *L'art à l'état vif. La pensée pragmatique et l'esthétique populaire*, Paris: Minuit.

Simonett, Helena (1997), 'Loud and Proud: The Social History and Cultural Power of Mexican Banda Music', PhD dissertation, University of California, Los Angeles, Ann Arbor: UMI Dissertation Services.

Simonett, Helena (1999), 'Strike Up the Tambora: A Social History of Sinaloan Band Music,' *Latin American Music Review*, 20 (1), 59–104.

Simonett, Helena (2001), *Banda: Mexican Musical Life across Borders*, Middletown, CT.: Wesleyan University Press.

Skårberg, Odd (2003), 'Da Elvis kom til Norge: Stilbevegelser, verdier og historiekonstruksjon I rocken fra 1955 til 1960', unpublished PhD dissertation, Department of Music and Theatre Studies, University of Oslo.

Slobin, Mark (1993), *Subcultural Sounds: Micromusics of the West*, Hanover, NH: Wesleyan University Press.

Slobin, Mark (ed.) (1996), *Returning Culture: Musical Changes in Central and Eastern Europe*, Durham, NC: Duke University Press.

Smith, Anthony D. (1991), *National Identity*, Harmondsworth: Penguin.

Smith, Joanne N. (1997), 'China's Muslims Sharpen their Knives Against Peking', *The Independent*, 5 March.

Smith, Joanne N. (1999), 'Changing Uyghur Identities in Xinjiang in the 1990s', unpublished PhD thesis, University of Leeds.

Smith, Joanne N. (2000), 'Four Generations of Uyghurs: The Shift towards Ethno-political Ideologies among Xinjiang's Youth', *Inner Asia*, 2 (2), 195–224.

Smith, Joanne N. (2002), 'Making Culture Matter: Symbolic, Spatial, and Social Boundaries Between Uyghurs and Han Chinese', *Asian Ethnicity*, 3 (2), 153–74.

Solie, Ruth (ed.) (1993), *Musicology and Difference: Gender and Sexuality in Music Scholarship*, London: University of California Press.

Srbljanović, Biljana (2000), 'TV Entertainment meets the Twilight Zone', http://www. Archiv.mildenhilfe.ch/projekte/SER/MediaFocus/iwpfrfy.09.htm (accessed 4 March 2003).

Stapleton, Chris and May, Chris (1987), *African All-Stars: The Pop Music of a Continent*, London and New York: Quartet Books.

Steingress, Gerhard (1997), 'Romantische Wahlverwandtschaften und nationale Gluckseligkeiten: Ein Versuch uber musikalische Beruhrungen von spanischer Zarzuela, Wiener Operette und andalusischem Cante flamenco', in *Das Land des Glucks: Österreich und seine Operetten*, Klagenfurt: Hermagoras, pp. 180–206.

Stokes, Martin (1992), *The Arabesk Debate: Music and Musicians in Modern Turkey*, Oxford: Clarendon Press.

Stokes, Martin (ed.) (1994), *Ethnicity, Identity and Music: The Musical Construction of Place*, Oxford and Providence, RI: Berg.

Stokes, Martin (2003), 'Globalization and the Politics of World Music', in Clayton, Martin, Herbert, Trevor and Middleton, Richard (eds), *The Cultural Study of Music*, New York and London: Routledge, pp. 297–308.

Storey, John (1996), *Cultural Studies and the Study of Popular Culture: Theories and Methods*, Edinburgh: Edinburgh University Press.

Straw, William (1991), 'Systems of Articulation, Logics of Change: Communities and Scenes in Popular Music' *Cultural Studies*, 5 (3), October, 368–88.

Street, John (1993), 'Local Differences? Popular Music and the Local State', *Popular Music*, 12 (1), 43–56.

Street, John (1995), '(Dis)located? Rhetoric, Politics, Meaning and the Locality', in Straw, Will et al. (eds), *Popular Music, Style and Identity*, Montréal: The Centre for Research on Canadian Cultural Industries and Institutions, pp. 255–63.

Sugarman, Jane C. (1999), 'Imagining the Homeland: Poetry, Songs, and the Discourses of Albanian Nationalism', *Ethnomusicology*, 43 (3), 419–58.

Swanwick, Keith (1999), *Teaching Music Musically*, London: Routledge.

Szeftel, Morris (1994), 'Ethnicity and Democratization in South Africa', paper presented to African Studies Seminar, Department of Politics, University of Leeds, 7 December.

Taylor, Timothy D. (1997), *Global Pop: World Music, World Markets*, London and New York: Routledge.

Thomas, Robert (1999), *Serbia under Milošević in the 1990s*, London: Hurst.

Todorova, Maria (1997), *Imagining the Balkans*, New York and London: Oxford University Press.

Tolaba, Lídia, (2000), 'PS: Que Festa é Esta?', *Revista E 83*, http://www.sescsp.org.br/sesc/revistas/e/index.htm (accessed 4 August 2001).

Tolbert, Elizabeth (1994), 'The Voice of Lament: Female Vocality and Performative Efficacy in the Finnish-Karelian *itkuvirski*', in Dunn, Leslie C. and Jones, Nancy A. (eds), *Embodied Voices: Representing Female Vocality in Western Culture*, Cambridge, Cambridge University Press, pp. 179–96.

Tomlinson, John (1991), *Cultural Imperialism: A Critical Introduction*, London: Pinter Publishers.

Toops, Stanley (1992), 'Recent Uygur Leaders in Xinjiang', *Central Asian Survey*, 11 (2), 77–99.

Tsernianski, Miloš (1994), *Migrations*, London: Harvill.

Tsing, Yuan (1961), 'Yaqub Beg (1820–1877) and the Moslem Rebellion in Chinese Turkestan', *Central Asian Journal*, 6 (2), 134–67.

Tuohy, Sue (2001), 'The Sonic Dimensions of Nationalism in Modern China: Musical Representation and Transformation', *Ethnomusicology*, 45 (1), 107–31.

Vernon, Paul (1998), *A History of the Portuguese Fado*, Aldershot: Ashgate.

Vianna, Hermano (1999), *The Mystery of Samba: Popular Music and National Identity in Brazil*, Chapel Hill: University of North Carolina Press.

Wade, Peter (1998), 'Music, Blackness and National Identity: Three Moments in Colombian History', *Popular Music*, 17 (1), 1–19.

Wade, Peter (2000), *Music, Race and Nation: Música tropical in Colombia*, Chicago and London: University of Chicago Press

Waldinger, Roger and Bozorgmehr, Mehdi (eds) (1996), *Ethnic Los Angeles*, New York: Russell Sage Foundation.

Wallis, Roger and Malm, Krister (1984), *Big Sounds from Small Peoples: The Music Industries in Small Countries*, London: Constable.

Waterman, Christopher Alan (1990), *Juju: A Social History and Ethnography of an African Popular Music*, Chicago and London: University of Chicago Press.

Waxer, Lise (ed.) (2002), *Situating Salsa: Global Markets and Local Meaning in Latin Popular Music*, New York and London: Routledge.

Wiggins, Trevor (1996), 'Globalisation: L'Afrique occidentale dans le monde ou le monde en Afrique occidentale' [Globalization: Western Africa in the World or the World in Western Africa], *Cahiers de musiques traditionnelles*, 9, 189–200.

Williams, Raymond (1981), *Culture*, Glasgow: Fontana.

Winant, Howard (1999), 'Racial Democracy and Racial Identity: Comparing the United States and Brazil', in Hanchard, Michael (ed.), *Racial Politics in Contemporary Brazil*, Durham, NC: Duke University Press, pp. 98–115.

Wrong, Michela (2000), *In the Footsteps of Mr Kurtz: Living on the Brink of Disaster in the Congo*, London: Fourth Estate.

Young, Richard (ed.) (2002), *Music, Popular Culture, Identities*, Amsterdam: Rodopi.

Yuval-Davis, Nira (1997), *Gender and Nation*, London: Sage.

Žižek, Slavoj (1989), *The Sublime Object of Ideology*, London: Verso.

Žižek, Slavoj (1991), *Looking Awry: An Introduction to Jacques Lacan through Popular Culture*, Cambridge, MA: MIT Press.

Žižek, Slavoj (1992), *Enjoy Your Symptom: Jacques Lacan in Hollywood and Out*, London: Routledge.

Žižek, Slavoj (2002), *For They Know Not What They Do: Enjoyment as a Political Factor*, 2nd edn, London: Verso.

Žižek, Slavoj (2004), *Iraq: The Borrowed Kettle*, New York: Verso.

Index